RECLAIMING JUSTICE

Reclaiming Justice

THE INTERNATIONAL TRIBUNAL FOR THE FORMER YUGOSLAVIA AND LOCAL COURTS

Sanja Kutnjak Ivković
John Hagan

OXFORD
UNIVERSITY PRESS

OXFORD
UNIVERSITY PRESS

Oxford University Press, Inc., publishes works that further Oxford University's objective of excellence in research, scholarship, and education.

Oxford New York
Auckland Cape Town Dar es Salaam Hong Kong Karachi Kuala Lumpur Madrid Melbourne
Mexico City Nairobi New Delhi Shanghai Taipei Toronto

With offices in
Argentina Austria Brazil Chile Czech Republic France Greece Guatemala Hungary Italy
Japan Poland Portugal Singapore South Korea Switzerland Thailand Turkey Ukraine
Vietnam

Published by Oxford University Press, Inc.
198 Madison Avenue, New York, New York 10016

Library of Congress Cataloging-in-Publication Data

Kutnjak Ivković, Sanja, 1965-
Reclaiming justice : the International Tribunal for the former Yugoslavia and local courts / Sanja Kutnjak Ivković, John Hagan.
p. cm.
Includes bibliographical references and index.
ISBN 978-0-19-534032-7 (hardback)
1. International Tribunal for the Prosecution of Persons Responsible for Serious Violations of International Humanitarian Law Committed in the Territory of the Former Yugoslavia since 1991. 2. Yugoslav War Crime Trials, Hague, Netherlands, 1994- 3. Yugoslav War, 1991-1995--Atrocities. 4. War crimes--Former Yugoslav republics.
I. Hagan, John, 1946- II. Title.
KZ1203.A12K88 2011
341.6'9 dc22

2010046328

Note to Readers

This publication is designed to provide accurate and authoritative information in regard to the subject matter covered. It is based upon sources believed to be accurate and reliable and is intended to be current as of the time it was written. It is sold with the understanding that the publisher is not engaged in rendering legal, accounting, or other professional services. If legal advice or other expert assistance is required, the services of a competent professional person should be sought. Also, to confirm that the information has not been affected or changed by recent developments, traditional legal research techniques should be used, including checking primary sources where appropriate.

(Based on the Declaration of Principles jointly adopted by a Committee of the American Bar Association and a Committee of Publishers and Associations.)

To our families

Contents

Acknowledgments

THIS BOOK TELLS A COMPLEX STORY of how people from the former Yugoslavia view justice in the aftermath of the recent war. Many have been victimized directly—as victims of murder, assault, torture, rape—or indirectly—as displaced persons and refugees who witnessed the suffering and victimization of their loved ones. Their stories are heart-wrenching and poignant.

We often wondered what the right measure of justice would be for individuals who are convicted of war crimes and crimes against humanity, be it for the crimes committed in the former Yugoslavia, Rwanda, Sudan, or Germany. The hundreds of people who participated in our surveys expressed their ideas and views of the justice dispensed by the International Tribunal for the Former Yugoslavia and by the local courts. This book would not have been possible without their willingness to share their thoughts and perceptions with us. We want to express our most sincere gratitude to all of them.

1

STUDYING THE ICTY

WAR COMES WITH A HEFTY PRICE in death and human suffering. The war in the former Yugoslavia was no exception. In a period of four years (1991–1995), the war in Croatia and Bosnia and Herzegovina resulted in more than three million refugees, 200,000–250,000 persons killed, 50,000 victims of torture, 20,000 cases of rape, and a large-scale destruction of public and private property (UNGA, 1994).

In an unprecedented effort, the international community decided to establish an ad hoc tribunal to address these severe violations of human rights. In 1993, while the war was still going on in Bosnia and Herzegovina, the International Criminal Tribunal for the former Yugoslavia (ICTY) was established with the main purposes of punishing the offenders guilty of serious violations of international humanitarian law, deterring potential future offenders, establishing peace and security in the region, and obtaining justice for the victims. Bringing justice and accountability to the former Yugoslavia became key tasks of the ICTY as they "represent an investment in the peace and future of south-eastern Europe" (ICTY, 2005). To date, over 3,500 witnesses have testified before the ICTY and have thus contributed toward the creation of the historical record (ICTY, 2010).

By 2005, the ICTY grew into an organization with more than 1,000 employees from 79 countries and with an annual budget of $276 million (ICTY, 2005). At the time, it had 47 defendants in custody, 24 on a provisional leave, and 43 defendants convicted and sentenced (ICTY, 2005). For the first time in legal history, in 1999, an indictment was filed by the ICTY against an acting head of state, Slobodan Milošević, for crimes allegedly committed while he was in office (ICTY, 2005). Through its judgments, the ICTY is setting precedents and expanding the boundaries of international criminal and humanitarian law. Together with its sister tribunal, the ICTR, the ICTY is the predecessor to the newly established *permanent* International Criminal Court.

THE EARLY PERIOD: THE INDEPENDENT COMMISSION OF EXPERTS

The story of the ICTY starts with the UN Commission of Experts, established in 1992. Sheriff Bassiouni, the head of the Commission of Experts, seized the opportunity to change ethnic cleansing from a rationalizing euphemism into an incriminating metaphor when he prepared the final report on violations of international humanitarian law in the former Yugoslavia (UNGA, 1994). Ethnic cleansing is generally understood as the systematic removal of a group or groups from an area by killing, expulsion, and/or imprisonment. A crucial concern is the policy-driven nature of the cleansing of ethnic groups. Andrew Bell-Fialkoff (1993:110) writes that "... ethnic cleansing can be understood as the expulsion of an 'undesirable' population from a given territory due to religious or ethnic discrimination, political, strategic, or ideological considerations, or a combination of these." Although the UN General Assembly has identified ethnic cleansing as a violation of international humanitarian law (1992: Resolution 47/121) and has explicitly declared that "... the abhorrent policy of 'ethnic cleansing'... is a form of genocide...," the concept of ethnic cleansing is better understood as not only overlapping with, but also extending beyond, genocide.

The most incriminating part of the Commission report consisted of 131 pages of single-spaced documentation and analysis of events in Prijedor. The report included extensive background materials and nearly 400 interviews of victims and witnesses of these events. Names were often redacted from the report for purposes of confidentiality, but full statements were separately collected into four large and confidential volumes that were later transferred to the International Criminal Tribunal and used to guide investigations and prosecutions.

The Commission's report on Prijedor argued that the facts on the ground constituted the elements of the crime of genocide. Because the Prijedor report's authors, Hanne Sophie Greve and Morten Bergsmo, believed the events were genocide, and because the term 'ethnic cleansing' was only then beginning to enter public discourse, they did not use this term in the Prijedor report itself. However, when Bassiouni (UNGA, 1994) prepared the final report of the Commission, he included a series of introductory paragraphs which explained that, in the context of the former Yugoslavia, the term ethnic cleansing was widely understood as referring to the use of force and intimidation to render an area ethnically homogeneous by removing persons of other groups.

Bassiouni further explained that the policy of ethnic cleansing was linked to political doctrines involving "Greater Serbia" and claims that date as far back as the 1389 battle of Kosovo. His explanation thus began to turn the rationalizing euphemism of ethnic cleansing, widely known and endorsed among Serbian military and political leaders, into an incriminating metaphor that social scientists would recognize today as a collective framing device (Benford and Snow, 2000). In this context, ethnic cleansing was a way of framing an arc-like geography of aggression that began by linking Serbia proper with Serb-inhabited areas of Croatia and Bosnia and Herzegovina, leading to the semi-circular sweep of Kosovo, sometimes called Operation Horseshoe (see Ignatieff, 2000). Although the Prijedor report could not fully tell this still-unfolding story, Bassiouni emphasized in the final report of the Commission that the pattern documented in Prijedor closely matched similar information received in other regions, including Banja Luka, Brčko, Zvornik, and Foča.

When the Prijedor team completed their report of the ethnic cleansing of this region, they had no doubt about its legal meaning: "It is unquestionable that the events in Opština Prijedor since April 30, 1992 qualify as crimes against humanity. Furthermore, it is likely to be confirmed in court under due process of law that these events constitute genocide" (UNGA 1994). Yet, it was the metaphorical framing of the events in Prijedor as ethnic cleansing that most persuasively summarized what happened in this locality. The result of the Commission's efforts was to spur an international response to massive and ongoing atrocities in the former Yugoslavia.

THE ESTABLISHMENT AND GROWTH OF THE ICTY: THE BATTLE FOR SURVIVAL

Human rights and international criminal law groups worked with Cherif Bassiouni to launch successfully the ICTY as a United Nations institution. Richard Goldstone, a South African constitutional court judge, was appointed its first chief prosecutor. Goldstone was not an expert in domestic or international criminal law and he approached the challenge of establishing the ICTY with some hesitancy about immediately pursuing major war crime suspects in the former Yugoslavia. The Tribunal was further limited by its lack of investigation and arrest powers. For these reasons, as well as limited financial resources, neither Bassiouni nor Goldstone at the outset could have had a clearly workable plan to achieve arrests of the persons they might indict for war crimes and/or crimes against humanity and bring to the ICTY for trial. Nonetheless, Goldstone was able to launch an important investigation of the massacre at Srebrenica. In the process, and with the assistance of American authorities, the ICTY investigators and prosecutors were able to establish their power to legally enter and begin mass grave exhumations in areas under Serb control in Bosnia. This led in turn to the development of a recognized power to search and seize military evidence in this and surrounding areas about the Srebrenica massacre.

Still, the largest obstacle to the early survival of the Tribunal was the inability of its first chief prosecutor, Richard Goldstone, to convert ICTY indictments into arrests and, therefore, the inability to begin trials of high level military or political figures. An early trial of a low-level figure, Duško Tadić, was disappointing to human rights groups. Goldstone was able to sufficiently vilify Bosnian Serb leader Radovan Karadžić in court hearings so that he was removed from office, establishing some force to the ICTY's institutional position, but Goldstone was not able to bring Karadžić nor any other major indicted figure to trial and, during this period, the ICTY therefore began to take on the appearance of a largely "virtual tribunal."

Louise Arbour, the Tribunal's second chief prosecutor, was able to draw on her experience as a criminal lawyer in Canada to better establish the legal force of the ICTY. Arbour recognized that her UN mandate could be viewed as granting a criminal law power to use the domestic criminal practice of sealed or secret indictments to facilitate surprise arrests of individuals from the former Yugoslavia indicted for war crimes and/or crimes against humanity by international authorities such as NATO military forces. The challenge in doing this was to transfer the traditional criminal law prerogative of secret indictments from the domestic to the international context. The idea of secrecy seemed to contradict expectations of deference and transparency emphasized by norms of international diplomacy. Arbour's point was that the traditional tools of criminal law could not defer to the dictates of diplomacy. She began using sealed indictments as a means of reassuring U.S., British, and other NATO force commanders that they could count on elements of surprise and vulnerability, making arrests easier, less prone to violence, and, therefore, freer of local political disruption. The indictment of Slobodan Milošević was ultimately sealed for several days before its public announcement.

Arbour also encouraged international political and financial authorities, starting with the Council of Europe, to make monetary aid contingent on transfers of indicted individuals, thus encouraging Croatia to send individuals indicted for war crimes and/or crimes against humanity to The Hague. Arbour often assumed, rather than requested, the authority to initiate and pursue her policies and practices, and with her success in doing so, she established a new force for the ICTY and, by implication, for international criminal law.

Arbour's ICTY indictment of Milošević played a role in his electoral defeat in Serbia, but when Carla Del Ponte followed Arbour into the chief prosecutor's role, Milošević was in Belgrade, out of the reach of the Tribunal. Carla Del Ponte worked to elaborate Arbour's economic strategy. She did this by drawing on her Swiss financial background to convince the United States to join with the World Bank and the European Union in using international aid as an inducement with the new Federal Republic of Yugoslavia. International financial assistance was made contingent on the transfer of Milošević and broader Serbian cooperation in providing documentary evidence and fellow indictees to the ICTY. Del Ponte also expanded the naming power of the Tribunal's criminal law mandate by upping the charges against Milošević from crimes against humanity in Kosovo to include genocide in Bosnia and Herzegovina. Arbour had worried that the genocide charge would result in a protracted trial and a less certain outcome. Indeed, Milošević died in his jail cell following a more than four year and still unfinished trial.

Still, it could now be said that the ICTY was finally moving along both the coercive dimension of a forcible arrest power and the more cooperative dimension of financial inducement. The element of economic inducement has persisted and grown through the European Union's contingent offer of membership to the nations of the former Yugoslavia on the basis of cooperation with the ICTY. The Serbian government has resisted most strongly, but, by 2005, had helped transfer 10 indicted suspects, mostly Bosnian Serbs, to the Tribunal. The Serbian government linked these transfers directly to negotiations with the EU on a preliminary agreement as the first step toward membership. The EU's spokesperson nonetheless emphasized that full membership was conditional on the arrest of all individuals indicted for war crimes and/or crimes against humanity, including the two most wanted suspects, Radovan Karadžić and Ratko Mladić. Even discussion of this precondition as a possibility represented a departure from earlier indications by the Serbian government that arrests would enrage public opinion, destabilize the government, and encourage Serbia's nationalist opposition. In 2008, the transfer of Radovan Karadžić to the ICTY for trial became the latest signal of growing cooperation by Serbia, with Ratko Mladić still at large.

During most of the history of the ICTY, the primary focus was on building the institutional resources and capacities of the ICTY. While during these years the ICTY grew into a powerful international institution, as Arzt (2006, p. 230) argues, "[ICTY] personnel were focused on the tasks of institution building and did not pay much attention to the continual fanning of the flames of ethnic hatred by regional leaders and media, who were simultaneously spewing paranoid rhetoric against the tribunal itself." In 1999, the ICTY established the Outreach Programme to counter the accusations of its lack of impartiality and independence. As Gabrielle Kirk McDonald, a former presiding judge at the ICTY, described (McDonald, 2004), these outreach efforts involved quite a variety of activities, from audio and video broadcasts of trials in the local languages and frequent press releases, to television interviews, roundtables, and conferences with local officials, NGOs, and victim groups. McDonald (2004, p. 22) argued that "[t]he people for whom the Tribunal was established must have access to the judgments and must be educated about its procedures and processes. They must 'buy into' the Tribunal if it is to help achieve a lasting peace and lay the groundwork for reconciliation." How successful the ICTY has been in communicating with its constituency is an empirical question which we explore in the subsequent chapters.

THE PERCEPTIONS OF THE ICTY IN THE FORMER YUGOSLAVIA

During the last decade, numerous journal articles and books have been written about the ICTY (see, e.g., Askin, 1997; Clark and Sann, 1996; Goldstone, 2000; Hagan, 2003; Kerr, 2004; McDonald, 2000; Schabas, 2006; Scharf, 1997). They have tended to focus on its operation, either from a legalistic perspective (Askin, 1997; Clark and Sann, 1996;

Goldstone, 2000; Kerr, 2004; McDonald, 2000; Schabas, 2006; Scharf, 1997) or a social-science perspective (Hagan and Levi, 2004; Stover, 2005; Stover and Weinstein, 2004). However, none has fully answered crucial questions about international justice in a systematic and comprehensive manner: what do the ICTY's constituencies in general and the victims in particular think about the ICTY and what shapes their opinions? If the ICTY is to bring justice to the victims and thus achieve one of its key tasks, the victims have to perceive it as a credible international institution and its proceedings and decisions as just.

Unlike Stover's respondents (Stover, 2005)—victims who testified before the ICTY—the overwhelming majority of the victims in the former Yugoslavia, regardless of their ethnicity, will never be summoned to testify before the ICTY and experience its operation first-hand. Rather, without direct experience, they will rely on the TV, radio, and newspaper accounts of the ICTY and its work to form their judgments of the ICTY. Their opinions about the ICTY and the fairness of its decisions and procedures will thus be shaped by the dominant political views in the country about the ICTY, the way the media in their country portray the ICTY, and other knowledge of the ICTY obtained second-hand. Prior research also has shown that the credibility of the ICTY in the eyes of its constituencies is affected by how well the ICTY judges indicated they knew basic facts about the former Yugoslavia (e.g., geography, history, culture; Klarin, 2004, p. 552), how sensitive they were to its complexity (Stover, 2005, p. 132), how they treated defendants and victims (see, e.g., Stover, 2005), and the ICTY's decisions (see, e.g., Stover, 2005, p. 106).

Whereas prior empirical research on the public perceptions of the ICTY is quite limited (e.g., Arzt, 2006; Human Rights Center, 2000; Stover, 2005; Stover and Weinstein, 2004), it nevertheless suggests that the ICTY does not enjoy substantial support from its constituencies in the former Yugoslavia. However, the degree to which the ICTY is trusted varies greatly across the former Yugoslav republics and autonomous provinces. According to the 2002 International Institute for Democracy and Electoral Assistance survey of public opinion, only one-quarter or even fewer respondents from Montenegro (24 percent), Macedonia (22 percent), Croatia (21 percent), Serbia (8 percent), and Republika Srpska (4 percent) indicated even moderate levels of trust in the ICTY. The situation seems to be somewhat better in the Bosnian Federation, where just about one-half of the respondents (51 percent) expressed trust in the ICTY. Unlike any other part of the former Yugoslavia, the population in Kosovo seems to support the ICTY overwhelmingly: 83 percent of the respondents in Kosovo showed at least a moderate level of trust in the ICTY.

In a study of the perception of justice and social reconstruction, Biro and colleagues (2004) reported a variety of attitudes toward the ICTY. Bosniaks (Muslims) from Prijedor (Republika Srpska) and Mostar (Bosnian Federation) expressed a substantially higher degree of support for the ICTY than did either the Croats from Vukovar (Croatia) or Mostar (Bosnian Federation) or the Serbs from Prijedor (Republika Srpska) or Vukovar (Croatia). Based on the comments from the respondents, Biro and colleagues (2004, p. 193) concluded that the "Croats and Serbs were deeply convinced that the

ICTY was biased against them. . . . One of the most common comments (especially among Bosniaks) was that the ICTY sentences are too soft."

Part of the explanation, as Biro and colleagues argued (2004, p. 194), may lie in the fact that almost one-half of the respondents—Croats in Mostar and Serbs in Prijedor (in both cases the dominant majority)—did not accept the fact that their group participated in the commission of war crimes and crimes against humanity. On the other hand, about three-quarters of the Bosniaks in Mostar, Bosniaks in Prijedor, and Serbs in Vukovar (in all cases the minority) were willing to accept the possibility that the members of their ethnic group participated in the commission of war crimes and crimes against humanity. In seems that when the ethnic group is in the majority in each city (rather than in the minority), the group identity is stronger and works as a mechanism that "does not permit the possibility that a part of 'us' can be war criminals, nor does it permit the possibility that a part of 'them' can be worthy of our respect or empathy" (Biro et al., 2004, p. 195).

The group identity—be it through the victimhood of the war or the victimhood of the international interference—that is created and influenced by the political views in the country, further prevents the realization that the members of the same group can be both victims *and* aggressors (see, e.g., Stover, 2005, p. 143). For the population from Bosnia and Herzegovina and Croatia, who largely see themselves as victims and see their own political and military leaders exclusively as defenders of their homeland, having any defendants of their own ethnicity tried by the ICTY may signal that the ICTY does not understand the reasons and the roles performed during the war and, thus, that the ICTY is biased against their ethnic group. Therefore, it is not surprising that Bosniaks are more supportive of the ICTY because their own image of their ethnic group—as the principal victims of the war—matches how the international community sees them, while Croats and Serbs feel singled out and harbor more negative feelings toward the ICTY (see Biro et al., 2004, p. 200). Indeed, the results of the survey indicate the presence of this victimhood notion; the respondents expressed negative views of the ICTY primarily because they "were convinced that the court was biased against their national group" (Biro et al., 2004, p. 200; Stover, 2005, p. 144). Local judges and prosecutors were also influenced by the views of collective victimhood of their ethnic group; the 1999 Berkeley survey of judges and prosecutors in Bosnia indicated that the ICTY is viewed as "a political institution," one that is "biased and incapable of providing fair trials" (Stover, 2005, p. 38). The Bosnian judges and prosecutors expressed their reservations with respect to the ICTY's location, judicial appointments, hybrid nature of the ICTY's procedures, political nature of the ICTY, and the lack of communication between the ICTY and local legal professionals (Berkeley, 2000, p. 41). The same sentiments were echoed by the residents from Mostar, Prijedor (Bosnia and Herzegovina), and Vukovar (Croatia) who participated in the study by Čorkalo and colleagues (2004, p. 147); they challenged ICTY's impartiality and argued that the ICTY is a political court.

Public opinion polls conducted in Croatia and Serbia at the same time revealed very similar attitudes. About 60 percent of the Croatian respondents in a 2000 survey

(Jutarnji list, 2000, p. 13) believed that the ICTY is unfair, and about one-half (52 percent) believed that "The Hague wants to criminalize the Homeland War." The July 2003 opinion poll of the Serbian population revealed that it overwhelmingly distrusts the ICTY. The reason for this high level of distrust lies in widespread perceptions of the ICTY as politically motivated and biased against the defeated, that is, the Serbs; over 70 percent of the respondents believed that the ICTY will act partially with respect to Serb defendants (Arzt, 2006, pp. 233–234). However, part of the problem may lie in the fact that the Serbian respondents may not know what the ICTY actually does and, fueled by the media propaganda featuring the ICTY as anti-Serb, assume that there are no defendants of non-Serb ethnicity (McMahon and Miller, 2009, p. 19). In fact, 2004 and 2005 polls conducted by the Belgrade Centre for Human Rights suggest that three-quarters of the respondents did not know what the ICTY does (Transitional Justice Report, 2006, p. 29). What is more, some "moderate Serbs" participating in the survey were not aware that a number of non-Serbs were indicted and tried.

Local judges and prosecutors in the Berkeley study went as far as to refuse to "accept the record of the war" that the ICTY was building because they emphasized the discrepancies between "the truth" as they knew it and "the truth" as the ICTY's records indicated (Fletcher and Weinstein, 2002). Empirical evidence demonstrates that the ICTY's record of events sometimes has little effect on how people in the region view the events (see, e.g., Stover, 2005, p. 144).

Stover (2005) provided an in-depth study of victims' experiences as witnesses testifying before the ICTY. Stover interviewed 87 victims (p. xi): he examined their motivation to testify, the witnesses' pre-trial preparation, the actual experience of testifying, as well as their post-trial experience. At the end, three out of four respondents evaluated their overall experience as positive (Stover, 2005, p. 103) and said that they would probably testify again. The victims argued that all suspects should be tried. They emphasized several reasons why the suspects should be tried, from the opportunity for the truth to be heard and for the victims to tell their stories, to the goal of general deterrence and the expected educational function of the rules of international law (Stover, 2005, pp. 110–111). Most of the respondents preferred that the trials be held before the ICTY instead of the local courts because of political influence over, and corruption in, the local courts (Stover, 2005, p. 114). Whereas Stover's analysis allows for a valuable understanding of the experience of being a witness in The Hague, most of those who lived in the former Yugoslavia, and thus were a constituency, including the victims directly affected by the war, will never be summoned as witnesses to The Hague, and their views of the ICTY will be based on other, indirectly obtained information.

This book extends the limited prior literature by providing a comprehensive view of how people from Bosnia and Herzegovina, Croatia, Kosovo, and Serbia view and evaluate the ICTY. We look into the general opinions of the ICTY, its legality and judicial independence, as well as specific issues of substantive and procedural justice and collective and individual responsibility. We also provide an in-depth analysis of perceptions about the

ICTY, the subsequent work of its linked local courts, and decisions reached by these local courts. The book also examines the relation between the views of the ICTY and ethnicity, a particularly relevant concern because the war was fought largely along ethnic lines.

THE DATA

This book is based on analyses of a unique data set collected through seven surveys administered to the citizens of Sarajevo (Bosnia and Herzegovina), Zagreb (Croatia), Vukovar (Croatia), Belgrade (Serbia), and Priština (Kosovo) between 1997 and 2005. The surveys include most of the former Yugoslav republics and provide a systematic exploration of the respondents' views and opinions of the ICTY and its work.

The earliest survey was conducted in spring of 1997. At the time, the number of displaced persons and refugees was large and the usual telephone or household sources of information that would allow us to establish unbiased sampling frames were not available. Instead, refugees from Bosnia and Herzegovina and displaced persons from Croatia were approached while they waited to receive financial support from the Croatian Office for Displaced Persons and Refugees. At that time, the war was over in both Croatia and Bosnia and Herzegovina, the ICTY was established and functioning, Karadžić and Mladić had been indicted for genocide, crimes against humanity, and war crimes, and the first trials at the ICTY had commenced. Potential respondents had not only begun to think about the ICTY in the abstract, but also to follow a few actual trials.

Two further surveys were conducted in early summer of 2000 and in December of 2003, to assess the perception of the ICTY and its decisions in Sarajevo. The surveys were timed strategically to follow significant events. The 2000 survey occurred soon after the arrest and transfer of Major General Stanislav Galić (the commander of the Romanija Corps that maintained the siege of Sarajevo from 1992 to 1994) to the ICTY, and Galić was sentenced to 20 years' imprisonment just before the 2003 survey (the Appeals Chamber rendered its judgement in 2006, sentencing Galić to life imprisonment). Neither telephone nor household sources of information were sufficiently developed to establish unbiased sampling frames. In these limiting circumstances, the respondents were sampled from the streets, coffee shops, and department stores of the central business district of Sarajevo. Potential respondents were asked whether they would like to participate in a study of the ICTY.

The four most recent sweeps of the study—the 2004 Belgrade survey, the 2004 Priština survey, the 2004 Vukovar survey, and the 2005 Belgrade survey—all include multi-stage random probability household samples of the adult population (18 years and older). Each survey was conducted by the Serbian or Croatian affiliate of Gallup International using a structured survey instrument we designed to measure attitudes toward the ICTY. Table 1.1 shows the sample characteristics. The samples vary from 263 in the 1997 Zagreb sample to 507 in the 2005 Belgrade sample.

Each sample's ethnic composition was compared with the ethnic composition of the population living in the respective geographic area at the time. Given its importance before, during, and after the war, ethnicity remained one of the key variables that the international organizations and municipalities observed and listed on their websites. We relied either on the official census data or on the estimates provided by the international organizations (sources are listed in Table 1.2) for the baselines in our comparisons.

Our four random samples (e.g., 2004 Priština, 2004 Vukovar, 2004 Belgrade, 2005 Belgrade), collected by the Gallup International affiliate in each country, match the demographic characteristics of the population very closely (see Table 1.2). Specifically, 93 percent of the ethnically declared population of Belgrade Municipality was Serb, as were 91 percent and 94 percent of the respondents in our Belgrade 2004 and Belgrade 2005 samples, respectively (Table 1.2). Similarly, 95 percent of the ethnically declared Priština population was Kosovar Albanian, as was 99 percent in our sample (see Table 1.2). Finally, about 60 percent of both the sample and population in the City of Vukovar were declared Croat (60 percent and 57 percent, respectively), while 33 percent of both the sample and population were declared Serb (see Table 1.2).

The 1997 Zagreb sample was a convenience sample of refugees from Bosnia and Herzegovina and displaced persons from Croatia. A comparison of the ethnic distribution of this sample with the ethnic composition of the population of Croatia and the ethnic composition of the population of the City of Zagreb (as determined by the 2001 Census; see Table 1.2) suggests that the 1997 Zagreb sample matches both populations closely, with more than 90 percent being Croat (90 percent of the sample, 92 percent of the ethnically declared population of Croatia, and 95 percent of the ethnically declared population of Zagreb were Croats), with fewer than 5 percent of our sample and the populations of Croatia and Zagreb being Serb or Bosniak/Muslim (see Table 1.2).

Our two Sarajevo samples reflect the population changes in the city over time. The data provided by the International Crisis Group (1998) indicate that the Muslim population

TABLE 1.1

Sample Characteristics

Location/country	Year of the survey	Sample size	Percent
Zagreb, Croatia	1997	263	8.6%
Sarajevo, Bosnia and Herzegovina	2000	299	9.8%
Sarajevo, Bosnia and Herzegovina	2003	473	15.5%
Belgrade, Serbia	2004	500	16.4%
Priština, Kosovo	2004	500	16.4%
Vukovar, Croatia	2004	501	16.5%
Belgrade, Serbia	2005	507	16.7%
Total		3,043	100.0%

TABLE 1.2

Sample and Population Ethnicity Composition

Sample/Population	Croats	Bosniaks/ Muslims	Serbs	Others	Total
1997 Zagreb sample	90%	4%	2%	3%	249 (100%)
2001 City of Zagreb Census[a]	95%	1%	3%	1%	
2001 Croatia Census[a]	92%	1%	5%	2%	
2000 Sarajevo sample	14%	79%	5%	2%	289 (100%)
Sarajevo Canton 12/97[b]	5%	87%	5%	3%	
2003 Sarajevo sample	19%	66%	11%	4%	471 (100%)
Sarajevo Canton 2002[c]	7%	80%	11%	2%	
2004 Priština sample	0%	1%	0%	99%	493 (100%)
Priština 2005[d]	0%	2%	3%	95%	
2004 Vukovar sample	60%	1%	33%	6%	498 (100%)
City of Vukovar 2001[e]	57%	0%	33%	10%	
2004 Belgrade sample	1%	2%	91%	6%	492 (100%)
2005 Belgrade sample	1%	1%	94%	4%	501 (100%)
Belgrade Municipality 2002[f]	1%	0%	93%	6%	

[a] Source: Croatia, 2006 (ethnically declared only).
[b] Source: International Crisis Group, 1998, p. 5.
[c] Source: Canton Sarajevo, 2004.
[d] Source: OSCE, 2008.
[e] Source: Grad Vukovar, 2010.
[f] Source: Belgrade, 2010 (ethnically declared only).

of the city peaked in the late 1990s; since the late 1990s, the representation of Muslims has declined (see Canton Sarajevo, 2004). The non-Muslim population slowly began to return to the city in 1997 (5 percent of all internally displaced persons and refugees were Croat, 2 percent were Serb) and, therefore, the ratio of non-Muslim population in the city started to increase in 1998. At the end of 2002, the Muslims constituted three-quarters of the population in the city (80 percent in the Canton Sarajevo and 77 percent in the City of Sarajevo; see Canton Sarajevo, 2004). Our 2000 and 2003 samples are predominantly Muslim, with Croats somewhat overrepresented and Serbs proportionate to their population. While not intentional, the increased sampling of minorities is fortuitous for subsequent analyses of potential differences among groups.

THE RESPONDENTS

The seven samples collected across the former Yugoslavia vary in their characteristics. The ethnicity of the majority of the respondents in each sample matches closely with the dominant ethnicity in that region/state. Thus, the Croats constitute the majority in the 1997 Zagreb sample and 2004 Vukovar sample, Bosniaks constitute the majority in the two Sarajevo samples, Serbs constitute the overwhelming majority in the two Belgrade samples, and, finally, Albanians ("Others") constitute the majority of the respondents in the 2004 Priština sample (Table 1.3). The two Belgrade samples and the Priština sample are more homogeneous than the two Sarajevo samples and the Vukovar sample, reflecting the more homogeneous nature of these societies.

About one-half of our respondents are women (see Table 1.4) and most of the respondents are high-school graduates (see Table 1.4). The respondents' education varied somewhat across the samples. The respondents in the two Sarajevo samples tended to be somewhat more educated (a higher percentage of high-school graduates and, to a certain degree, college graduates) than the respondents in the other two samples. The 1997 Zagreb sample has fewer high-school graduates, with more extended tails of the distribution, both less educated and college-educated respondents, while the 2004 Priština, 2004 Vukovar, and 2005 Belgrade sample tends to have a somewhat larger number of less educated respondents.

Although we could not measure how seriously the war had affected each of our respondents, we could measure perceptions of their war-related victimization (see Table 1.5). We inquired whether they viewed themselves as victims of war crimes or crimes against humanity. Whereas about 70 percent of the respondents in the earlier samples (1997 Zagreb, 2000 Sarajevo, 2003 Sarajevo) viewed themselves as victims of war crimes or crimes against humanity, the same is true of only about one-half of the respondents in the 2004 Priština and 2004 Vukovar samples and about one-quarter or fewer in the two Belgrade samples.[1] The respondents in the three earlier samples (1997 Zagreb, 2000 Sarajevo, and 2003 Sarajevo) were also much more likely to say that they had witnessed a war crime or a crime against humanity. When asked whether members of their family had been victimized, more than three-quarters of the respondents in Zagreb and Sarajevo replied affirmatively (see Table 1.5). At the same time, compared to the percentage of the respondents reporting their own victimization, the percentage of the respondents in the 2004 Priština and 2004 Vukovar samples reporting that their family members had been victimized is larger, with more than one-half reporting that their family members had been victimized, while the corresponding percentage in the two

[1] In the 2005 Belgrade survey, 299 respondents said that the question about their victimization is not applicable in their case. If we were to include their answers in the calculation and classify them under "not a victim," the percentage of the respondents who said that they had been victimized would drop from 28.8 percent to only 11.7 percent. The same 299 respondents also opted that the question about witnessing a war crime or crime against humanity action is not applicable in their case. If we were to include their answers in the analysis, the corresponding percentage of the respondents who said that they witnessed a war crime or a crime against humanity would drop from 19.6 percent to 8.1 percent.

TABLE 1.3

Respondents' Ethnicity by Sample

Sample	Croats	Bosniaks/ Muslims	Serbs	Others	Total
1997 Zagreb	90.2%	4.0%	2.0%	3.2%	249 (100%)
2000 Sarajevo	13.8%	79.6%	4.5%	2.1%	289 (100%)
2003 Sarajevo	18.9%	65.4%	11.5%	4.2%	471 (100%)
2004 Belgrade	1.2%	1.8%	90.7%	6.3%	492 (100%)
2004 Priština	0.0%	1.0%	0.0%	99.0%	493 (100%)
2004 Vukovar	60.2%	0.6%	32.7%	6.4%	498 (100%)
2005 Belgrade	1.0%	0.6%	93.6%	4.8%	501 (100%)
Total	666 (22.3%)	568 (19.0%)	1150 (38.4%)	609 (20.3%)	2,993
Chi-square	5,628.4***				
Cramer's V	.792***				

Belgrade samples remained low. Finally, we also asked about the victimization of neighbors or acquaintances. Almost all respondents from the two Sarajevo samples, about three-quarters of those in the 1997 Zagreb, 2004 Priština, and 2004 Vukovar samples, and only about one-third of the respondents in the Belgrade sample answered affirmatively.

TABLE 1.4

Respondents' Gender and Education by Sample

Sample	Percent Women	Below High School	High School	College
1997 Zagreb	51.9%	23.8%	52.7%	23.4%
2000 Sarajevo	47.0%	1.7%	74.1%	24.1%
2003 Sarajevo	44.2%	3.4%	80.3%	16.3%
2004 Belgrade	49.8%	17.9%	67.6%	14.5%
2004 Priština	53.6%	28.2%	55.6%	16.2%
2004 Vukovar	54.3%	35.1%	53.7%	11.2%
2005 Belgrade	51.9%	26.4%	60.0%	13.6%
Chi-square	14.5*	273.1***		
Cramer's V	.069*	.212***		

* $p < .05$; ** $p < .01$; *** $p < .001$

TABLE 1.5

Respondents' Reported Victimization Experience by Sample[a]

Sample	Victim	Witness	Family victimized	Neighbors victimized
1997 Zagreb	73.6%	68.6%	75.7%	80.9%
2000 Sarajevo	69.6%	65.2%	84.6%	95.2%
2003 Sarajevo	82.2%	73.8%	89.4%	94.7%
2004 Belgrade	17.6%	18.9%	28.6%	41.9%
2004 Priština	49.2%	17.3%	52.5%	72.1%
2004 Vukovar	54.6%	29.6%	64.7%	81.1%
2005 Belgrade	28.8%	19.6%	18.3%	33.4%
Total	1,434 (100.0%)	1,083 (100.0%)	1,678 (100.0%)	2,043 (100.0%)
Chi-square	535.5***	647.2***	806.7***	748.3***
Cramer's V	.446***	.488***	.518***	.501***

[a] Percent of respondents saying "yes."
* $p < .05$; ** $p < .01$; *** $p < .001$

ATTITUDES TOWARD PUNISHMENT FOR WAR CRIMES AND ITS PURPOSES

International criminal law usually is advanced with the intent of denouncing and deterring current and future human rights crimes. Indeed, the ICTY's Trial Chamber has often emphasized deterrence—both special and general—as the most important factor taken into account in determining the length of the sentence. Yet, the victims of these crimes may be more concerned, especially retrospectively, with punishing the offenders. In particular, the citizens of recently victorious nation-states characteristically seek retribution as much as, or more than, deterrence. Justice Robert Jackson, the appointed U.S. prosecutor at Nuremberg, is well known for having foresworn premature retribution by the Allies. "That four great nations," Jackson proudly declared (Bass 2001) "flushed with victory and stung with injury, stay the hand of vengeance and voluntarily submit their captive enemies to the judgment of the law is one of the most significant tributes that Power has ever paid to Reason." Yet this did not prevent others from declaring Nuremberg a barely constrained and thinly disguised form of "victims' vengeance" and "victor's justice" for the United States, Great Britain, the Soviet Union, and France.

In the former Yugoslavia, there are no declared "victors." Instead, the war in Bosnia and Herzegovina was ended by the Dayton Peace Agreement of 1995. This may make the International Tribunal a substitute for military conflict, with court outcomes symbolically calibrating who are considered the "victors" and "vanquished" through the sentencing of defendants representing former warring parties (see also Chambliss and

Seidman 1982:236). This may also make the respective parties especially sensitive in their perceptions of the justness of these court outcomes.

All of the respondents in our seven samples, from Croatia in the Northwest to Kosovo in the Southeast, have heard about the ICTY (Table 1.7). The overwhelming majority of the respondents in all samples, with the exception of the earliest Zagreb 1997 sample, said that TV, the newspapers, and radio were their key sources of information about the ICTY (Table 1.7).[2] This indicates that the local governments, which had the tendency to control the media (to varying degrees) and interpret the events for the readers/viewers, had many opportunities to shape the respondents' views of, and thinking about, the ICTY.

We next explore respondents' general attitudes toward punishment of those who committed war crimes and crimes against humanity. Our respondents were uniform in their view that people who committed war crimes and crimes against humanity should be punished (see Table 1.6). What differed is the strength of their conviction. The respondents in the three pre-2004 convenience samples (Zagreb 1997, Sarajevo 2000, Sarajevo 2003) seemed to be much more determined that the offenders should be punished than the respondents in the later random samples were (Vukovar 2004, Priština 2004, Belgrade 2004, Belgrade 2005; Table 1.6). One possible explanation is that, compared to the 2004/2005 samples, the pre-2004 samples, being convenience samples, included a larger proportion of victims who may have been more predisposed to seek the punishment of the offenders than non-victims were. However, the same analysis including only the respondents who declared themselves as victims does not change the results substantially.

The respondents were offered four rationales for punishing the offenders: specific deterrence ("deterrence of these punished offenders from committing new war crimes"), general deterrence ("deterrence of future perpetrators of war crimes in our country and in the world"), retribution ("punishment of the offenders for the offenses they have already committed"), and other purposes. Some groups of respondents (Sarajevo 2000, Sarajevo 2003, Vukovar 2004) tended to select one purpose—retribution—as their dominant concern. Other groups (Zagreb 1997, Priština, 2004, Belgrade, 2004, Belgrade 2005) supported two purposes of punishment: general deterrence and retribution. A common result across all groups was that retribution was viewed as one of the most dominant purposes of punishment for war crimes and crimes against humanity. Once again, results

[2] A potential reason why the respondents in the earliest, 1997 Zagreb sample were much less likely to say that they relied on the media may be related to the nature of the samples. Unlike the other samples, which were typically random samples of general population, the Zagreb sample was collected at the Croatian Offices of Refugees and Displaced Persons when refugees and displaced persons were receiving their monthly financial support. At the time they were surveyed in 1997, refugees and displaced persons resided either in temporary housing or with relatives. Thus, because of their status, they probably had more limited access and/or resources to obtain access to the media reports on a regular basis and relied more on the information obtained through the network of friends and relatives than the other groups of respondents did. Moreover, the vast majority of them did not hold steady employment and thus had ample time for social interaction with other displaced persons and refugees, an integral part of which undoubtedly were daily discussions related to the war.

TABLE 1.6

Attitudes toward War Crimes and Crimes Against Humanity and Their Punishment

	1997 Zagreb (N=255)	2000 Sarajevo (N=295)	2003 Sarajevo (N=472)	2004 Vukovar (N=498)	2004 Priština (N=493)	2004 Belgrade (N=497)	2005 Belgrade (N=501)	*Chi-Square*	Phi
Offenders should be punished[a]									
Definitely yes	89.0%	82.1%	93.4%	67.4%	64.6%	54.9%	68.1%	293.2***	.315
Yes	10.6%	17.9%	6.6%	30.3%	35.4%	40.8%	31.3%		
No + Definitely no	0.4%	0.0%	0.0%	2.3%	0.0%	4.2%	0.6%		
Punishment purpose[b]									
Special deterrence	12.9%	3.4%	2.9%	9.2%	28.8%	5.5%	6.6%	374.3***	.370
General deterrence	44.4%	30.9%	23.0%	27.0%	35.2%	43.3%	52.1%		
Retribution	42.7%	65.6%	74.1%	63.8%	36.1%	51.2%	41.4%		
Punishment purpose *(victims only)*	*(N = 178)*	*(N = 181)*	*(N = 337)*	*(N = 246)*	*(N = 228)*	*(N = 79)*	*(N = 54)*		
Special deterrence	12.4%	3.3%	3.0%	9.8%	28.9%	6.3%	0.0%	205.5***	.397
General deterrence	48.9%	32.0%	22.0%	25.2%	37.3%	38.0%	50.0%		
Retribution	38.8%	64.6%	75.1%	65.0%	33.8%	55.7%	50.0%		

Appropriate punishment[c]									
Death penalty	43.1%	33.9%	41.2%	10.4%	34.9%	13.4%	25.3%	443.6***	.415
Life imprisonment	52.3%	62.8%	44.4%	57.3%	58.0%	42.7%	38.0%		
Imprisonment or fine	4.6%	3.2%	14.4%	32.3%	7.1%	43.8%	36.7%		
Appropriate punishment (*victims only*)	(*N* = *176*)	(*N* = *195*)	(*N* = *361*)	(*N* = *194*)	(*N* = *221*)	(*N* = *71*)	(*N* = *48*)		
Death penalty	44.3%	35.4%	43.8%	12.9%	34.8%	21.1%	33.3%	192.1***	.390
Life imprisonment	52.8%	63.6%	42.1%	59.3%	59.3%	40.8%	31.3%		
Imprisonment or fine	2.8%	1.0%	14.1%	27.8%	5.9%	38.0%	35.4%		

*** $p < .001$

[a] The question was worded as follows: "Do you think that persons who raped, robbed, tortured, and killed during the war in Croatia and Bosnia and Herzegovina should be punished?" The answers ranged on a four-point scale from "definitely yes" to "definitely no."

[b] The question was worded as follows: "According to your opinion, what is the purpose of punishing the war criminals?" The answers were: "a) deterrence of these punished offenders from committing new war crimes [i.e., special deterrence]; b) deterrence of future perpetrators of war crimes in our country and in the world [i.e., general deterrence]; c) punishment of the offenders for the offenses they have already committed [i.e., retribution]; d) ___________."

[c] The question was worded as follows: "According to your opinion, what is the purpose of punishing the war criminals?" The answers were: "a) the death penalty; b) life imprisonment; c) imprisonment for 21–50 years; d) imprisonment for 15–20 years; e) imprisonment for up to 15 years; f) monetary fine; g) ___________."

TABLE 1.7

Source of Information about the ICTY and Punishment for War Crimes and Crimes Against Humanity

	1997 Zagreb (N=255)	2000 Sarajevo (N=295)	2003 Sarajevo (N=472)	2004 Vukovar (N=498)	2004 Priština (N=493)	2004 Belgrade (N=497)	2005 Belgrade (N=501)	*Chi-Square*	Phi
Heard about the ICTY[a]									
Yes	100%	100%	100%	100%	100%	100%	100%		
Source of information[b]									
TV, newspapers, radio	51.8%	97.6%	96.5%	97.8%	97.6%	86.2%	89.0%	593.8***	.455
Friends, relatives	42.4%	0.7%	2.4%	0.7%	1.0%	11.1%	7.8%		
Red Cross/human. org.	4.5%	0.7%	0.4%	0.7%	0.2%	0.6%	0.9%		
Other source	1.2%	1.0%	0.7%	0.9%	1.2%	2.0%	2.2%		

*** $p < .001$

[a] The question was worded as follows: "Have you heard of the International Tribunal for the former Yugoslavia in The Hague which is trying persons accused of the crimes committed during the war in the territory of Croatia and Bosnia and Herzegovina?" The answers were "yes" and "no."

[b] The question was worded as follows: "How did you learn about the existence of the International Tribunal in The Hague (please mark the most important source)?" The answers were: "a) TV, newspapers, radio (which ones?) ____________; b) friends, relatives; c) The Red Cross and other international organizations; d) __________; e) I have never heard of the International Tribunal."

from a separate analysis involving only those respondents who viewed themselves as victims were substantively the same.

Finally, the respondents expressed their views about the appropriate sanctions for war crimes and crimes against humanity. Without referencing specific cases, we asked them in general what they thought the appropriate sanctions for war crimes and crimes against humanity should be.[3] With the exception of the Vukovar and the Belgrade 2004 samples, at least 25 percent of the respondents picked the death penalty as the appropriate punishment (Table 1.6). For this group, regardless of the actual punishment that the ICTY would mete out in each case, it is reasonable to expect that they will be unhappy with the ICTY's decisions because the ICTY—a UN institution—is not authorized to impose the death penalty and thus, in their eyes, provide justice. For the majority of the respondents surveyed in Zagreb, Sarajevo (2000), Vukovar, and Priština, the most appropriate punishment for the offenders who committed war crimes and crimes against humanity was life imprisonment (Table 1.6). Life imprisonment was also a prevalent choice in other samples, being either the most frequently selected or one of the two most frequently selected punishment options. Compared to the respondents in the Zagreb, Sarajevo (2000), and Priština samples, the respondents in the Vukovar and two Belgrade samples leaned toward less severe punishment choices.

The homogeneity of opinions varied across samples, with the Zagreb, Sarajevo (2000), Vukovar, and Priština samples being the most homogeneous. Whereas there is a clear majority in these samples (selecting life imprisonment), in the other Sarajevo sample (2003) and the two Belgrade samples the respondents expressed a more heterogeneous set of views, with no majority choice and strong minority voices choosing two or even three types of punishments, from the death penalty to some imprisonment. One possible reason for such differences may lie in the fact that the respondents in the post-2000 surveys had more choices (we added a category—"imprisonment of 21–50 years"—after Tihomir Blaškić had been sentenced to 45 years). However, it does not appear that the addition of a new answer had a similar effect across all five samples: the effect seems to have been weaker among the respondents in the second Sarajevo sample (2003) and the Priština sample, with the respondents still more likely to select the death penalty and life imprisonment, than was the case among the Vukovar and the two Belgrade samples.

The two Belgrade samples—which, next to the Vukovar sample, showed the most lenient attitudes in terms of appropriate punishments—were also the two samples with the smallest percentage of the respondents declaring themselves as victims (15.9 percent and 10.1 percent, respectively, compared to 40 percent or more in the other samples).

[3] The respondents could have picked among the death penalty, life imprisonment, imprisonment of a specified length (up to 15 years, 15–20 years, and 21–50 years), fine, and other sanctions. Because the respondents in pre-2004 surveys did not have the option of 21–50 years of imprisonment, we constructed a scale involving "the death penalty," "life imprisonment," and "imprisonment or fine" (we merged all categories of pre-determined length of imprisonment and fine into one category).

An analysis of the subsets of the sample who declared themselves victims suggests that victimization may reduce this punishment severity gap; the differences shrunk to only a few percent across all samples, with the largest percent of the victims from the Belgrade 2005 sample selecting the death penalty (Table 1.6).

ORGANIZATION OF THE REMAINDER OF THE BOOK

The next chapter examines the overall level of support for the ICTY across the five research sites (Belgrade, Priština, Sarajevo, Vukovar, and Zagreb) and includes an in-depth exploration of its variation. It also provides a detailed analysis of the factors related to the level of support for the ICTY.

The third chapter explores the relation between support for the ICTY and ethnicity. Because ethnicity is a key variable in understanding the war, it is crucial to determine whether and how it affects the perceptions of the ICTY. We go beyond ethnicity as such and analyze the role of "cognitive landscapes" in the formation of the support for the ICTY across the former Yugoslavia.

The fourth chapter carries the analysis of the ICTY's legitimacy further by focusing on the respondents' perceptions of collective and individual responsibility. It explores how the use of "structural pre-conditionality" in the European Union intervention and the dissemination of a smoking-gun videotape shaped public support for the ICTY and prosecutions of war crimes and crimes against humanity.

The fifth chapter disentangles the degree to which the respondents' views of the ICTY's legitimacy are related to their perceptions of procedural and substantive justice. Although the respondents in our study, like most victims in the former Yugoslavia, did not have an opportunity to participate in the ICTY trials directly, they nevertheless belong to the ICTY's constituency. We explore what they think about the procedures used, and decisions meted out, by the ICTY.

In the concluding chapter, we argue that the extent and severity of atrocities and the ICTY's limited time and resources ultimately appear to *require* the involvement of the local criminal justice systems to address the widespread and systematic scale of violence that have occurred during the war in the former Yugoslavia. Experts criticized the local judicial systems for their lack of independence, incompetence, and corruption. Yet, our respondents show increasing confidence in their local courts. It seems that there is a predictable sequence to international efforts to restore a sense of domestic criminal justice, and that, ultimately, settings and persons who have experienced major crimes against their people will wish to reclaim an indigenous role in the restoration of locally experienced justice.

Failure to arrest and remove those leaders from the troubled post-Dayton political stage resulted in exactly what the Tribunal had warned the international players against: the inter-ethnic division resulting from the war was consolidated; political and economic tensions reached new heights; social, cultural and educational institutions were tainted; and ultra nationalist and racist elements affirmed their supremacy

(KLARIN, 2004, P. 551).

2

THE ICTY, ITS CONSTITUENCIES, AND ITS POLITICS

The Battle for Hearts and Minds

OVER TIME, THE battle for the ICTY's survival has been fought successfully (see Chapter 1) and the ICTY has grown dramatically—in terms of its resources, both human and financial, as well as in terms of the number of defendants indicted, arrested, and tried. The ICTY has survived and, in many ways, flourished.

The ICTY also has been winning the battle for respect with leading Western governments and international organizations. Yet, another type of battle still continues, one that Klarin (2004, p. 35) calls "the battle for hearts and minds" or, in narrower terms, the battle for the legitimacy of the ICTY in the eyes of the peoples in the former Yugoslavia. This outcome is far from certain. According to its 1999 internal report, this is the battle the ICTY neglected to address head on because it failed to design a comprehensive information policy, an oversight that allowed nationalist tendencies to spread their wings and influence how their constituencies view the ICTY (see, e.g., Stover, 2005, p. 38).

This chapter explores the overall level of support for the ICTY among its constituencies. Based on the results of surveys conducted at five research sites spread across the former Yugoslavia (Belgrade, Priština, Sarajevo, Vukovar, and Zagreb), we analyze respondents' views about the appropriate decision-makers for the war crimes cases and explore the reasoning behind their choices. We provide an in-depth analysis of respondents' thoughts about the ICTY, its fairness, and the factors associated with their evaluations of the ICTY's fairness.

POLITICS AND PUBLIC SUPPORT FOR THE ICTY

The literature on public support for the courts has long seen citizens' support for the U.S. Supreme Court as a finding to be explained and compared with responses to other national and transnational courts (Casey, 1974). This support is understood to confer legitimacy and to be calculated rationally in the sense that it can be diminished by decisions that conflict with the majority of public opinion (Caldeira, 1986), especially in transitional settings in which new courts lack a cushion of historical embeddedness and are susceptible to legitimacy shortfalls (Gibson and Caldeira, 1995; Gibson and Caldeira, 1998). Of course, in addition to the difference of historical longevity, in the international context, there is also the pull of national sovereignty.

The level of trust in the ICTY among its constituencies in Bosnia and Herzegovina (BiH), Croatia (HR), and Serbia is not high (International Institute for Democracy and Electoral Assistance, 2002). With the exception of Kosovo (83 percent of the respondents showed at least a moderate level of trust) and, to a certain degree, the Bosnian Federation (51 percent), respondents from the former Yugoslavia expressed low levels of trust: only one-quarter or fewer respondents from Montenegro (24 percent), Macedonia (22 percent), Croatia (21 percent), Serbia (8 percent), and Republika Srpska (RS) (4 percent) showed at least a moderate level of trust in the ICTY.

Public opinion about the ICTY in each country appears to be shaped by dominant political views in the country, the country's relationship with the ICTY, the way the ICTY is handling defendants and attorneys, as well as translators, journalists, and legal experts from the former Yugoslavia (see, e.g., Klarin, 2004, p. 552), the outcomes of ICTY trials (see, Stover, 2005), and the way the ICTY is perceived to be handling the "us" and "them" issue. Serbian respondents' perception that the ICTY views their own group as aggressors may be right: out of about 50 defendants whose cases were processed and completed by the ICTY by 2005, 67 percent were Serbs (see Table 2.1).[1] Key challenges to legitimacy among the ICTY's constituencies involve the ways in which the wars in Bosnia and Herzegovina and Croatia ended, the way the West treated the political and military war leaders (endorsing them one moment and condemning them the next), and the dominance of nationalistic tendencies in the political arenas across all three countries.

At the beginning of the war in Croatia in late 1990, the fighting involved Croatian police forces (Croatia, still a republic within the former Yugoslavia, did not have the legal right to establish a military) and the rebel Serbs who opposed the potential secession of Croatia from the Yugoslav federation. Over time, it became clear that the military force

---

[1] Another question—one that we do not discuss here—is how closely the proportion of the defendants belonging to each of the three ethnic groups in the ICTY's cases corresponds to the ethnicity of the perpetrators of war crimes and crimes against humanity committed in the territory of the former Yugoslavia.

TABLE 2.1

Defendants' Ethnicity in the ICTY's Cases Completed by 2005

	Croat	Serb	Bosniak (Muslim)	Total
Before 2000	2	3	4	9 (17.3%)
2000–2002	9	16	0	25 (48.1%)
2003–2004	2	16	0	18 (34.6%)
Total	13 (25.0%)	35 (67.3%)	4 (7.6%)	52 (100.0%)

of the former Yugoslavia, JNA ("Yugoslav People's Army"), wholeheartedly helped the rebel Serbs in Croatia achieve their goals.[2] After a series of ceasefires in 1991 and 1992, the war in Croatia eventually ended in 1995 with two military operations ("Operation Flash" and "Operation Storm") conducted by the Croatian military and a subsequent peaceful reintegration of Western Slavonia.

Meanwhile, on March 6, 1992, Bosnia and Herzegovina declared independence from the former Yugoslavia and the war erupted shortly thereafter.[3] While the war was raging in Bosnia and Herzegovina, the world community wavered between negotiating peace and imposing justice, two potentially contradictory goals. After the July 1995 killing of about 8,000 Muslim men and boys near Srebrenica, which both the ICTY (*Prosecutor v. Krstić*, 2004) and the International Court of Justice (*Bosnia and Herzegovina v. Serbia and Montenegro*, 2007) characterized as genocide, the wavering intensified. On the one hand, in July 1995, the ICTY prosecutor issued indictments against Radovan Karadžić, the political leader of Bosnian Serbs, and Ratko Mladić, the military leader of Bosnian Serbs (*Prosecutor v. Karadžić and Mladić*, 1995). On the other hand, in the summer of 1995 (in the aftermath of "Operation Storm" in Croatia and the military offensive against Republika Srpska in Bosnia and Herzegovina, paralleled with the NATO military's "Operation Deliberate Force"), the international community—mainly the members of the Contact Group (the United States, United Kingdom, France, Germany, Italy,

---

[2] The ICTY viewed the first few months of the war, until Croatia's moratorium on its independence (declared on June 25, 1991, but negotiated by the international community to be frozen for 3 months) had expired on October 8, 1991, as a civil war and the period starting on October 8, 1991 as an international war, with the involvement of the Yugoslav troops in the war.

[3] The war in Bosnia and Herzegovina, which took place between March 1992 and November 1995, was described in the ICTY's decisions as an international war, involving the Federal Republic of Yugoslavia (subsequently Serbia) and Croatia. The 2007 decision by the International Court of Justice—determining that Serbia was involved in the war, but finding that Serbia was only indirectly responsible for genocide in Bosnia—confirms this view (*Bosnia and Herzegovina v. Serbia and Montenegro*, 2007). The Court's judgment declares that Serbia is responsible for failing to prevent genocide in Srebrenica and for failing to catch and punish its perpetrators. Furthermore, the Court states that "the Respondent [Serbia] did have significant means of influencing the Bosnian Serb military and political authorities which it could, and therefore should, have employed in an attempt to prevent the atrocities" (*Bosnia and Herzegovina v. Serbia and Montenegro*, 2007, paragraph 462).

and Russia)—pushed for peace negotiations and arranged for the leaders of all three groups involved in the war in Bosnia and Herzegovina to attend the peace negotiations in Dayton, Ohio.

The Serbian side at the Dayton peace negotiations was represented by Slobodan Milošević, then Serbian president, with Momčilo Krajišnik, then speaker of the Republika Srpska Assembly, Milan Milutinović, then Serbian foreign minister, and Jovica Stanišić, then chief of the Serbian secret police. Officially, Milošević was in charge of representing the interests of the Bosnian Serbs because the July 1995 indictment by the ICTY prosecutor made Radovan Karadžić—then president of Republika Srpska and a political leader of the Bosnian Serbs—*persona non grata* at the peace negotiations. The Croatian side was represented by then Croatian president, Franjo Tudjman, and the Bosnian side was represented by then Bosnian president, Alija Izetbegović, with then Bosnian foreign minister Muhamed "Mo" Sacirbey.

The Dayton Agreement, reached on November 21, 1995, officially ended the conflict in Bosnia and Herzegovina. At the time, all three presidents were viewed as peacemakers. In the aftermath of the negotiations, all three governments publicly argued to their constituencies the advantages of the Dayton Agreement. Upon the announcement of the successful end of the peace negotiations, Radoje Kontić, then Yugoslav prime minister, praised Milošević's role in the process and the importance of the Dayton peace accord (Tanjug, 1995):

> The peace agreement which has been reached in Dayton represents a final victory for reason and statesman-like wisdom over the forces of gloom and the destruction of human reason. . . . Accepting the Dayton agreement as a whole, the federal government judges it as being of vital importance for peace, stability and the normalization of relations, not only in the area of the former Yugoslavia but also beyond, in the Balkans and Europe.

Similarly, Franjo Tudjman, then Croatian president, issued a statement about the Dayton Agreement and its importance (Croatian Radio, 1995):

> All in all—peace. Peace above all. This means that we can go back to our homes, back to building and reconstruction, and not only to the economic, but also cultural and scientific development. The Dayton round of talks, talks which lasted more than any peace talks in recent history, are of inestimable value for Croatia and the whole world. With its presence and its role—Croatia's role was decisive—Croatia really achieved results which will have an immediate impact this year and in the years to come.

Haris Silajdžić, then Bosnian prime minister, was also positive, but was more critical of the agreement (Radio Bosnia-Herzegovina, 1995):

> [T]he Dayton agreement is more than just a map. Fifteen documents of some 150 pages have been signed and they are all aimed at preserving Bosnia, at ensuring its reintegration. The internal border as outlined in all these documents is not absolute. The Dayton agreement is unjust because it is based on a situation created by aggression and violence. However, it offers peace and the opportunity to use economic recovery and the democratization of relations and other peaceful means to remove the injustices created by war. That is what makes this agreement acceptable. The internal community is showing a resolve to preserve the integrity of Bosnia-Herzegovina and to establish a stable peace in the region. That is why this internal demarcation line should not be considered definitive. It should not be seen as a Chinese wall, since, in that case, there would be no peace.

Silajdžić seemed to have it right when he warned that this division into entities should not be allowed to become "the Great Wall of China." Yet, the reality was that the Dayton Agreement contained two almost inherently conflicting parts, on the one hand dividing the country into entities based on territory captured during the war and, on the other hand, striving to create a unified nation and bring long-lasting peace (see, e.g., Cousens and Doyle, 1995; Sommer, 1997). As subsequent events have shown, this ethnic division was to remain a serious obstacle to meaningful reunification of the country.

Over the last fifteen years, continued ethnic division has dominated many aspects of life in the region: the ordinary local courts in all three countries have been criticized for being politically biased and unwilling to initiate legal procedures in cases involving war crimes charges against "their own" (Human Rights Watch, 2004); the police have been accused of stonewalling investigations (Human Rights Watch, 2004), providing politically motivated policing (International Crisis Group, 2002), and allowing warlords active participation in political life (see, e.g., International Crisis Group, 2000; Klarin, 2004). In 1999, the International Crisis Group wrote: "Today, Bosnia and Herzegovina has three de facto mono-ethnic entities, three separate armies, three separate police forces, and a national government that exists mostly on paper and operates at the mercy of the entities." The struggle is not over; in October 2008, Paddy Ashdown, a former High Representative and EU special representative in Bosnia and Herzegovina, and Richard Holbrooke, the chief architect of the 1995 Dayton Peace Agreement, warned that nationalism is on the rise in Bosnia and Herzegovina (as witnessed by the results of the most recent local elections), that much of the progress has been reversed, and that the institutions of the federal government have been seriously weakened. In sum, "We are sleepwalking into another Balkan crisis" (Ashdown and Holbrooke, 2008; see also, Bilefsky, 2008). Despite 13 years of international presence and $14 billion in aid, a recent report suggested that Bosnians are unable to manage self-government and that the country's future is at risk ("Concerns Grow over Instability in Bosnia," 2008).

The political leaders in all three countries—Bosnia and Herzegovina, Croatia, and Serbia—have the power to shape public opinion about the war and the ICTY and have the power either to inflame or diminish ethnic tensions. The political leadership in Republika Srpska habitually opposes any attempts of the central Bosnian government toward unification of the country.[4] Milorad Dodik, the prime minister of Republika Srpska, exemplifies this tendency. He was embraced by some in the international community because of his opposition to the nationalist Serb Democratic Party (Ashdown and Holbrooke, 2008). Yet, as Ashdown and Holbrooke (2008) argue, his intentions seem to be nationalistic and his deeds harmful to the long-term progress of the country as a whole:

> Bosnian Serb Prime Minister Milorad Dodik, once the darling of the international community (and especially Washington) for his opposition to the nationalist Serb Democratic Party, has adopted that party's agenda without being tainted by their genocidal baggage. His long-term policy seems clear: to place his Serb entity, Republika Srpska, in a position to secede if the opportunity arises. Exploiting the weaknesses in the country's constitutional structure, the international community's weariness and EU inability to stick to its conditionality, he has, in two years, reversed much of the real progress in Bosnia over the past 13, crucially weakened the institutions of the Bosnian state, and all but stopped the country's evolution into a functioning (and EU-compatible) state.

The ICTY's activities (e.g., investigations, indictments, arrest warrants, and requests for documents) themselves also may be viewed as undermining and even threatening national identities (see, e.g., Klarin, 2004, p. 553). Indicting and potentially arresting top political and military leaders, as the ICTY did with Serbs Milošević, Karadžić, and Mladić, or Croats Blaškić, Gotovina, Čermak, and Markač, certainly sent a strong message to constituencies in these countries, possibly contributing to the wave of opposition to the ICTY and the evolving view that those who cooperate with the ICTY are "against" the regimes. Yet, the ICTY was in the position of having neither its own enforcement agency to execute the arrest warrants nor open access to evidence, and it had to rely on the Implementation Force (IFOR) and local governments either to do its work or to allow ICTY investigators access to evidence. Although the original agreement at Dayton was that the NATO-led troops would not hunt war crimes and crimes against humanity suspects (Bass, 2000; McMahon and Miller, 2009, p. 12), two years later, in 1997, and "only because of a change of heart by the U.S. and Great Britain" (McMahon and Miller, 2009, p. 12), the Stabilisation

[4] The example of the local police clearly illustrates this point. Before 2008, there were numerous attempts to reform and restructure the organization of the police agencies, headed by 12 different ministries of the interior and criticized by NGOs for being political and "serv[ing] and protect[ing] 'one's own kind,' whether they be co-nationals, colleagues or political masters" (International Crisis Group, 2002). It took more than a decade to reach the point at which the Bosnian Parliament was in a position to *vote* on the law reforming the police and to actually reach the *majority* decision (Zornija, 2008).

Force (SFOR) started making arrests. By spring 2009, SFOR had made 27 arrests (McMahon and Miller, 2009, p. 12).

Klarin (2004, p. 548) describes the ICTY circumstances quite vividly: "Making the Tribunal dependent on the 'cooperation' of the then regimes in the countries of the former Yugoslavia could be likened to instructing the 'Untouchables' to cooperate with Mr. Al Capone and his henchmen in their mission to fight the bootleggers." In the end, it is not surprising that numerous reports to the UN by the ICTY prosecutor depicted the governments involved, primarily those in Croatia and Serbia, as dragging their feet and even openly refusing to cooperate with the ICTY in the arrest and transfer of the ICTY's indictees. The most recalcitrant among all of the governmental authorities involved is Republika Srpska; as of 2004, it had not turned over a single suspect (ICTY Report, 2004, p. 2). The more the ICTY prosecutors pressured the countries and threatened them with UN sanctions, the more insistently the governments labeled the ICTY's actions as intrusive and unjust, with a potentially adverse effect on the legitimacy of the ICTY in the eyes of its constituencies.

The ICTY prosecutors frequently accused the Croatian government of non-cooperation, despite numerous attempts by the Croatian government to show its cooperation with the ICTY (see, e.g., BBC, 1999). Upon receiving one such negative report by the prosecutor, Zvonimir Šeparović, then Croatian Minister of Justice in the Tudjman government, said: "We fear that the ICTY is still a means of political pressure against Croatia," citing examples of "the tribunal's unbalanced policy of prosecution, its failure to prosecute major criminals and crimes committed against Croats, as well as its insistence on evidence which goes beyond all limits" (BBC, 1999). He further remarked that "Croatia has cooperated and will continue to cooperate with The Hague tribunal, but 'its cooperation will not go beyond the limits of tolerance, or be against the principles of sovereignty and be to the detriment of one's own national interest and security'" (BBC, 1999). In fact, the Croatian government developed a "white paper"—as a political tool—containing thousands of pages of documents documenting its cooperation with the ICTY, including changes in legislation made to facilitate the cooperation, the chronology of cooperation, and specific initiatives (Vjesnik, 1999).

In 2000, while the remnants of the Tudjman nationalist regime strongly opposed cooperation with the ICTY, Stjepan Mesić was elected the new Croatian president and developed a different approach toward the ICTY that he had advocated while he was the opposition leader:

> [T]he extradition of generals and state officials is not a topic we should dwell on. We are not dealing with generals or officials here, because a person whom The Hague Tribunal wants becomes a war crime suspect—not a general, a minister, a captain, or a shoemaker, but a war crime suspect. Besides, the individualization of responsibility is a good thing for the Croatian nation, as it would be less than civilized to talk about the collective responsibility of us all (Vecernji list, 1999, p. 5).

Mesić argued for interstate and multiethnic reconciliation, respect for the rule of law, and accountability for past crimes (see, e.g., Akhavan, 2001). He emphasized cooperation with the ICTY and local courts as a means of addressing the issue of collective guilt and serving Croatian national interests, and thus attempted to shape public perceptions about the ICTY. Yet, even six months after Mesić became president, the results of a public opinion survey conducted by the local newspaper were summarized with the title "'Anti-Hague Atmosphere' Increasing in Croatia;" three-quarters of the respondents disapproved of the extradition of Croatian citizens to The Hague, and more than 60 percent believed that the ICTY was unfair (Jutranji list, 2000, p. 31).

The situation in Serbia was even more challenging. The ICTY had indicted a number of Serb political and military leaders, but was struggling to make arrests, particularly of the "big fish." The key figure in the wars in the former Yugoslavia, Slobodan Milošević, often had been treated by the West as an important political figure and a partner to be reasoned with during political negotiations. Hazan (2004, p. 146) noted:

> After reducing Vukovar to cinders in November 1991, after putting Bosnia-Herzegovina to fire and sword, after bombarding and laying siege to Sarajevo for more than three years, after deporting 740,000 Albanians from their province, President Milošević has finally been indicted. Until October 1998, the West still considered him an acceptable partner. . . . The Office of the Prosecutor never put to use the forces necessary to mount an indictment of the Yugoslav president. It is the legacy of Dayton: Peace with impunity as a bonus for Slobodan Milošević. . . . For eight years, the Western democracies continued to deal with him, to negotiate innumerable accords, to make him the guarantor of stability in the Balkans—all while he was its gravedigger. It took the war in Kosovo and the indictment by the ICTY to destroy his image as the indispensable fireman for a conflagration that he himself had set. It has taken the international court to put an end to the West's temptation to make deals with the man who has led his own people and others into war.

Milošević lost his aura in 1998. He was indicted by the ICTY, arrested, and eventually transferred to The Hague to face trial for war crimes and crimes against humanity. The circumstances leading to his arrest were complex: the new war in Kosovo, the strengthening of the opposition to his nationalist regime, lost elections, changing negotiation strategies of foreign political players, the creation of a context for wider public acceptance of the collective command responsibility of Serbian war crimes and crimes against humanity suspects, the recognition of the importance of joining the EU, and a real threat of the loss of billions of dollars in foreign aid (see Chapter 4) all eventually helped the ICTY arrest Slobodan Milošević. The ICTY likely has had very little direct effect on the politics and accountability for war crimes and crimes against humanity in the former Yugoslavia in general (see, e.g., McMahon and Miller, 2009) and the arrest of Milošević in particular.

However, the ICTY—primarily through its prosecutors—successfully managed to exercise power indirectly, through a network of international organizations and players. McMahon and Miller (2009, p. 34) describe how the accountability network worked:

> [B]y 1997 a transnational accountability network of governments and regional organizations had coalesced, making cooperation with the ICTY central to their own unique mission. The importance of the actors changed over time, depending on the country and the specific issue area; however, it is undeniable that without the support of the EU, NATO, and the U.S., it does not seem likely that the positive outcomes related to just liberal democracy [including "holding war criminals accountable"] in the Balkans would have taken place.

The accountability network supporting the ICTY—implemented primarily through conditioning membership in the EU and the granting of foreign aid—led toward the extradition of a larger number of defendants, including Milošević (see Chapter 4 for a detailed discussion). Thus, as a consequence of the power exercised by this accountability network, though once a key political player in the peace negotiations orchestrated by the international community, Milošević became *persona non grata.*

Public opinion polls conducted in Serbia in the aftermath of Milošević's political demise and eventual transfer to The Hague indicated that distrust of the ICTY and other negative attitudes toward it lingered in the public mind for quite some time. Even in 2003, 59 percent of the respondents thought that Serbia should not cooperate with the ICTY and 70 percent did not trust the ICTY as an impartial arbiter concerning Serb defendants (despite the fact that most respondents had little knowledge of the ICTY) (Arzt, 2006, p. 232).

With pressure from the West mounting and the opposition parties gaining strength, the post-2000 political landscape in Serbia, which included the appearance on the scene of Zoran Djindjić, a former prime minister of Serbia, and Boris Tadić, the current president of Serbia, resulted in more widespread adherence to pro-Western and democratic ideas. However, the nationalist agendas did not disappear from the political scene; to the contrary, in the 2008 presidential elections, the first runner-up to the current Serbian president, Boris Tadić of the Democratic Party (with 50.3 percent of the votes), was Tomislav Nikolić of the right-wing Serbian Radical Party (with 48 percent of the votes).

Despite the ICTY prosecutors' extensive efforts to utilize the accountability network and execute arrest warrants for Ratko Mladić and Radovan Karadžić, they remained at large for more than a decade after their initial 1995 indictments. After a decade-long political negotiation, Radovan Karadžić finally was arrested in Belgrade in the summer of 2008. His arrest seems to have been compelled by the European Union and its pre-conditioning of the EU membership for Serbia on the apprehension and transfer of war crimes and crimes against humanity suspects (see Chapter 4). The capture of Karadžić is seen by some members of the Serbian administration (e.g., Vladimir Vukčević, the

Serbian prosecutor for war crimes) as a clear sign of the political will to cooperate with the ICTY. At the same time, a deliberate message was sent to the constituency, arguing that the ICTY was a reality to be reckoned with: "We are not sending these people to the scaffold, but to the court. That is the only place where they can prove their innocence, or the prosecutors can prove their guilt. Whether we like it or not, The Hague is our reality" (Vjesnik, January 14, 2009). This sentiment, although still not particularly popular in Serbia, was gaining acceptance—a 2004 opinion poll suggests that most respondents viewed the ICTY as "an unavoidable and enforced precondition for Serbia's full return to the world community and simply the price that Serbia has to pay" (Bandović, 2004, p. 93). Another aspect of this reality, as Rasim Ljajić (the current president of the Serbian National Committee for Cooperation with the ICTY) recently argued, is that Serbia has suffered serious political and financial consequences for its failure to capture Ratko Mladić (Vjesnik, January 14, 2009).

The effect of the ICTY on Croatia and its acceptance of accountability for war crimes and crimes against humanity was also indirect. Whereas Croatia cooperated with the ICTY on the initial arrests, the crucial period that set the relationship between the ICTY and Croatia started with the sealed indictments for the Croatian generals Ante Gotovina and Rahim Ademi. Although the then-future Prime Minister Ivica Račan emphasized during his electoral campaign that he would improve the relations with the ICTY if elected, when the time came to transfer Gotovina and Ademi, the new government was put to the test. Ademi was transferred quickly, but the arrest of Gotovina was delayed and he eventually left the county in 2001 (McLean and Simons, 2005). As McMahon and Miller (2009, p. 22) argue, "[f]ailure to track Gotovina within the next few years became a major impediment for Croatia's relationship with the EU." In 2004, after Carla del Ponte, the ICTY's chief prosecutor at the time, accused the Croatian government of helping Gotovina escape the ICTY prosecution and remain at large, the prospect of Croatia's EU membership suddenly became problematic. Although Croatia received official candidate status in June 2004, the European Union postponed the scheduled March 17, 2005 start of negotiations with Croatia, citing the ICTY prosecutor's report on Croatia's inadequate efforts to capture Gotovina. Faced with pressure from the EU, the Croatian government, led by then Prime Minister Ivo Sanader, whose campaign prioritized EU and NATO membership, intensified cooperation with the ICTY on the Gotovina arrest (despite Gotovina's popularity in the country), and this eventually led to his arrest in the Spanish Canary Islands in December 2005. Negotiations with the EU did not continue until the ICTY prosecutor established Croatia's full cooperation with the ICTY in October 2005.

All four Serb representatives at the Dayton negotiations—Milošević, Krajišnik, Milutinović, and Stanišić—eventually were indicted by the ICTY (*Prosecutor v. Milošević*, 2001; *Prosecutor v. Krajišnik*, 2000; *Prosecutor v. Milošević* et al., 1999; *Prosecutor v. Milutinović* et al., 2006; *Prosecutor v. Stanišić and Simatović*, 2003) and stripped of their legitimacy, at least in the eyes of the international community. Former Croatian president Tudjman and former Bosnian president Izetbegović were both investigated by the ICTY's prosecutor, but they died before the investigations were completed.

Despite the ICTY's actions against them, a number of The Hague indictees have been viewed as heroes in their home countries, with their actions passionately debated and defended. For example, after Slobodan Milošević and Vojislav Šešelj (the head of the Serbian Radical Party) were indicted for war crimes and crimes against humanity and housed in the detention section of the ICTY, they created a stir in the subsequent December 2003 parliamentary elections in Serbia. They were each the standard bearer of the slate and the top candidate of their respective party (Socialist Party of Serbia and the Serbian Radical Party, respectively), and they each won a seat *in absentia* in the Serbian parliament (Los Angeles Times, 2003). Moreover, Šešelj coordinated the Serbian Radical Party election campaign via telephone, winning 27.5 percent of the votes in these elections (Voice of America, 2004). Thus, the government until the 2000s was dominated by a nationalist agenda and only recently—partly because of the financial incentives offered by the West (see Chapter 4)—has Serbia elected a more democratic and pro-Western leader. Therefore, it is not surprising that Milošević's 2001 arrest and transfer to The Hague, as an aftermath of losing the September 2000 elections and the political struggle that ensued, was a challenging undertaking. Milošević's arrest was opposed by the Serbian president Koštunica and supported by pro-West groups, including then Prime Minister Zoran Djindjić.

At the time, 47 percent of the respondents participating in a Social Science Institute survey opposed the transfer, while 37 percent of the respondents approved of it (Fabris Peruničić, 2001). The intensity of the reaction to the transfers was well illustrated by the public demonstrations that followed in their wake. The news of Milošević's arrest resulted in demonstrations involving several thousand people (BBC, 2001), and violent demonstrations accompanied the arrest of Radovan Karadžić in the summer of 2008 (Daily Mail, 2008). This is by no means surprising; a 2001 opinion poll conducted in Serbia revealed that 75 percent of the respondents named Ratko Mladić and Radovan Karadžić as the greatest defenders of the Serbian nation, and most respondents did not acknowledge a single war crime committed by Serbs (Perceptions in Serbia, 2001). Meanwhile, even the arrests of some of the comparably "smaller fish" have been accompanied by public outcry. For example, a large crowd gathered in Croatia (Simons, 2005) and Bosnia and Herzegovina (BBC, 2005) to protest the capture and the arrest of Ante Gotovina in December 2005.

THE ICTY, OTHER DECISION-MAKERS, AND WAR CRIMES

Whereas the ICTY and the local courts in Bosnia and Herzegovina and Croatia have concurrent jurisdiction, the ICTY "can claim primacy and may take over national investigations and proceedings at any stage if this proves to be in the interest of international justice" (ICTY, Mandate and Jurisdiction, 2008). The first three chief prosecutors of the ICTY—Richard Goldstone, Louise Arbour, and Carla Del Ponte—were strong advocates for the primary jurisdiction of the ICTY over war crimes and crimes against humanity in the former Yugoslavia and for subsequent international criminal courts, arguing that such courts often are the only means of assuring the security and independence needed to achieve international criminal justice. ICTY prosecutors have argued that, as supranational institutions, international criminal courts should assume powers of extraterritorial if not universal jurisdiction, exercising a primary jurisdiction that overtakes the sovereignty of nation-states.

When we began the first surveys in the mid- to late 1990s, the ICTY was the most prominent and active court addressing these war crimes. As time passed, local courts began trying a handful of cases. The most significant breakthrough came in mid-2002 with the passage of a law in the Bosnian Parliament establishing the Court of Bosnia and Herzegovina. In 2004, we modified the survey to reflect the reality that the ICTY was no longer the only court engaged in war crimes trials and asked the respondents to focus on the institution that should *primarily* carry out the trials. Regardless of the version of the survey used, the respondents could have selected the decision-maker of their choice from among the ICTY, local courts in the country in which the crimes were committed (Bosnia and Herzegovina, Croatia), local courts in the country of the offender's origin (Serbia, Croatia, Bosnia and Herzegovina), and the victims' families.

The respondents' answers were far from uniform, regardless of whether the question was asked in general terms or focused on a specific defendant (see Table 2.2). The respondents surveyed before 2003 (1997 Zagreb sample; 2000 Sarajevo sample) seemed much more convinced that the ICTY was the right choice: close to two-thirds of the respondents in both Zagreb and Sarajevo said that the ICTY should be the decision-maker in such cases, while the respondents surveyed in Sarajevo in 2003 and Vukovar in 2004 tended to be more evenly split between the ICTY and the local courts.

At the time of our two earliest surveys (1997 Zagreb; 2000 Sarajevo), the ICTY was the most prominent decision-maker in war crimes and crimes against humanity trials. However, the experiences of the ICTY's justice were limited because it had completed trials in only a handful of cases with nine defendants; at the same time, most of the "big fish" were still at large. Over the next several years, local courts became more prominent and the ICTY started processing more cases and a larger number of defendants. Over the next three years (2000–2002), an additional 25 defendants had trials completed, and in the years 2003 and 2004 there were 18 such defendants. Thus, with more trials and more cases to observe and discuss, the ICTY's justice became less abstract and more real.

The prospect of a shift in court jurisdiction was less immediate in 2000 than in 2003, when the Bush Administration began insisting on a completion strategy for the ICTY, involving the transfer of cases to the courts of the newly independent states of the former Yugoslavia. International criminal law, as reflected in the Treaty of Rome and now at the ICTY, encourages original and ultimately national sovereignty of jurisdiction, when and

TABLE 2.2

Respondent Designations of Appropriate Jurisdiction

	1997 Zagreb	2000 Sarajevo	2003 Sarajevo	2004 Vukovar	2004 Priština	2004 Belgrade	2005 Belgrade	*Chi-Square*	*Phi*
Jurisdiction in general[a]									
ICTY	68.8%	77.9%	43.9%	34.1%	65.6%	18.3%	27.3%	1539.4***	.744
Local courts (BiH & HR)	17.1%	17.6%	44.8%	44.2%	16.7%	6.4%	3.1%		
Offenders' courts	5.4%	0.3%	1.1%	14.2%	2.5%	67.5%	61.6%		
Victims' families	8.8%	4.2%	10.2%	6.8%	15.2%	7.8%	8.0%		
For Karadžić & Mladić[b]									
ICTY	76.8%	76.3%	41.0%	55.3%	74.0%	23.2%	30.7%	1473.7***	.748
Local courts (BiH)	8.9%	19.3%	45.5%	24.9%	12.8%	10.2%	7.4%		
Local courts (Serbia, RS)	2.0%	0.7%	0.9%	6.4%	0.4%	59.9%	60.2%		
Victims' families	12.2%	3.7%	12.6%	13.5%	12.8%	6.7%	1.8%		
For Blaškić[c]									
ICTY	70.6%	78.8%	44.6%	35.0%	76.9%	28.1%	33.0%	729.1***	.528
Local courts (BiH)	6.0%	18.1%	40.5%	33.9%	6.7%	22.8%	20.0%		

*** $p < .001$

[a] The question was worded as follows: "Who should try the persons accused of war crimes committed in the territory of the former Yugoslavia?" The possible answers were: "a) the courts in the territory of Croatia and Bosnia and Herzegovina where the crimes have been committed; b) the courts of the offender's country or country whose army force he was a member of; c) the International Tribunal in The Hague; d) the families of the victims; e) other _______."

[b] The question was worded as follows: "In your opinion, who should try Radovan Karadžić and Ratko Mladić?" The possible answers were: "a) courts in Bosnia and Herzegovina; b) courts in Serbia/the Serb Republic; c) the International Tribunal in The Hague; d) the families of the victims; e) other _______."

[c] The question was worded as follows: "In your opinion, who should have tried Tihomir Blaškić?" In the 2003 version, we added the explanation: "In your opinion, who should have tried Tihomir Blaškić (the commander of the regional headquarters of the HVO Armed Forces in central Bosnia as of June 1992)?" The possible answers were the same: "a) courts in Croatia; b) courts in Bosnia and Herzegovina; c) the International Tribunal in The Hague; d) the families of the victims; and e) other _______."

Continued

TABLE 2.2

Continued

	1997 Zagreb	2000 Sarajevo	2003 Sarajevo	2004 Vukovar	2004 Priština	2004 Belgrade	2005 Belgrade	*Chi-Square*	*Phi*
Local courts (HR)	17.0%	1.0%	4.7%	24.9%	6.2%	39.8%	40.0%		
Victims' families	6.4%	2.0%	10.1%	6.2%	10.2%	9.2%	7.0%		
For Landžo[d]									
ICTY	N/A	78.4%	43.0%	43.6%	76.9%	30.2%	32.9%	487.4***	.465
Local courts (HR)	N/A	5.5%	15.0%	3.7%	4.8%	2.3%	4.6%		
Local courts (BiH)	N/A	14.0%	32.4%	43.6%	7.5%	55.6%	53.5%		
Victims' families	N/A	2.1%	9.6%	9.2%	10.7%	11.9%	9.0%		
For Milošević[e]									
ICTY	N/A	N/A	43.6%	64.4%	70.6%	18.7%	27.4%	1516.2***	.841
Local courts (BiH & HR)	N/A	N/A	43.4%	19.7%	12.1%	0.8%	1.0%		
Local courts (Serbia, RS)	N/A	N/A	0.0%	0.0%	0.0%	71.3%	69.0%		
Victims' families	N/A	N/A	13.1%	15.9%	17.3%	9.2%	2.7%		

For Galić[f]									
ICTY	N/A	N/A	42.1%	44.4%	75.9%	26.7%	30.2%	1017.9***	.718
Local courts (BiH)	N/A	N/A	45.7%	46.3%	13.4%	12.7%	11.5%		
Local courts (Serbia, RS)	N/A	N/A	0.0%	0.0%	0.0%	51.8%	53.9%		
Victims' families	N/A	N/A	14%	9.3%	10.6%	8.8%	4.4%		
For Jokić[g]									
ICTY	N/A	N/A	42.3%	42.6%	77.7%	26.4%	30.9%	1145.0***	.744
Local courts (HR)	N/A	N/A	46.4%	43.9%	13.7%	5.0%	6.3%		
Local courts (Serbia, RS)	N/A	N/A	1.3%	8.2%	0.0%	61.0%	60.9%		
Victims' families	N/A	N/A	10.0%	5.4%	8.7%	7.6%	1.9%		

*** $p < .001$

[d] The question was worded as follows: "In your opinion, who should have tried Esad Landžo?" In the 2003 version we added the explanation: "In your opinion, who should have tried Esad Landžo (a guard at the Čelebići concentration camp)?" The possible answers were the same: "a) courts in Croatia; b) courts in Bosnia and Herzegovina; c) the International Tribunal in The Hague; d) the families of the victims; and e) other ______."

[e] The question was worded as follows: "In your opinion, who should try Slobodan Milošević?" The possible answers were: "a) courts in Bosnia and Herzegovina/Croatia; b) courts in Serbia/the Serb Republic; c) the International Tribunal in The Hague; d) the families of the victims; e) other ______."

[f] The question was worded as follows: "In your opinion, who should have tried Stanislav Galić (the major general who lead the Romanija Corps and maintained the siege of Sarajevo from 1992 to 1994)?" The possible answers were: "a) courts in Bosnia and Herzegovina/Croatia; b) courts in Serbia/the Serb Republic; c) the International Tribunal in The Hague; d) the families of the victims; e) other ______."

[g] The question was worded as follows: "In your opinion, who should have tried Miodrag Jokić (the admiral who led the shelling of Dubrovnik in 1991)?" The possible answers were: "a) courts in Croatia; b) courts in Serbia/the Serb Republic; c) the International Tribunal in The Hague; d) the families of the victims; e) other ______."

as circumstances allow. By 2003, planning had begun for the construction of a new War Crimes Chamber of the Court of Bosnia and Herzegovina to be located in Sarajevo, and the ICTY was beginning to arrange the transfer of cases. The responses to the questions in our surveys about where these prosecutions and sentencing decisions should take place indicate a rapid change and sharp conflict in the perceived justness of local and international jurisdiction for these crimes, rather than the evolutionary consensus that Slaughter (2004) foresaw.

Unlike the other groups of respondents, the respondents from both Belgrade surveys were convinced that the courts in the offenders' country/entity (e.g., courts in Serbia and Republika Srpska for Serb political and military leaders such as Radovan Karadžić, Ratko Mladić, and Slobodan Milošević, and Croatian courts for Tihomir Blaškić) should be the decision-makers in war crimes cases (see Table 2.2). The Belgrade respondents, almost exclusively of Serb ethnicity, also seemed to express consistent, although somewhat less uniform views regarding the cases involving defendants of other ethnicities (Landžo is a Muslim; Blaškić is a Croat). The Belgrade respondents expressed a preference that cases be tried by the courts in the countries of the defendants' origin (rather than the victims' origin). Given the political climate in these Serbian settings, this was a predictable choice. Indeed, in a political climate of strong opposition to cooperation with the ICTY, with popular political leaders indicted by the ICTY, and with the ICTY having processed mostly Serbs by 2005 (34 out of 50 people processed by 2005 were Serbs), the Belgrade respondents may have developed the view that only the local courts in Serbia could provide real justice to the Serb defendants, or at least be more lenient than the ICTY had been.

The only group surveyed post-2000 that (still) strongly supported the ICTY were the Priština respondents (see Table 2.2). For the respondents from Priština in 2004, the ICTY still might have been more abstract than it was for Serbs, Croats, and Muslims/Bosniaks, who already had several defendants "of their own" ethnicity processed and, most likely, convicted by the ICTY. Indeed, out of dozens of cases tried before the ICTY, there was only one case involving defendants from Kosovo. Even in this single case, two out of the three defendants were acquitted (see *Prosecutor v. Limaj et al.*, 2003).

We probed the respondents further by asking them to select the reason they thought the court they had chosen would be the fairest. The respondents could select one of the answers we offered or write in their own answer. Almost all of the respondents picked an answer from our list:

a) it is most familiar with the local conditions
b) it best understands the reasons that led to the war
c) the judges have experienced or witnessed war crimes themselves
d) the judges are removed from the local politics
e) the judges are the least susceptible to political influence
f) it is the most certain way the criminals would be punished

The respondents' selection of reasons was strongly related to the decision-maker they had picked (see Table 2.3). The respondents who selected the ICTY did so because they thought that the ICTY provides "the most certain way the criminals would be punished" and/or that the judges are the least susceptible to political influence ("judges removed from local politics," "judges least susceptible to political influence"). The respondents who opted for the victims' families also did so because they thought that this avenue would be most likely to lead to certain punishment.

On the other hand, the respondents who selected local courts, be they in the country in which the crimes were committed ("Local courts, BiH, HR") or in the country of the offender's origin ("Offenders' courts"), also occasionally picked their preferred decision-maker because of the certainty of punishment, although this reason was neither as uniformly chosen nor as dominant (Table 2.3). Rather, their decision to pick local courts appears to have been guided by local courts' familiarity, both with the local conditions in general ("most familiar with the local conditions") and the war in particular ("best understands the reasons that led to the war"). These choices may have different meanings across ethnic groups and countries. Respondents from Bosnia and Herzegovina and Croatia were more likely to pick local courts in Bosnia and Herzegovina and Croatia, and respondents from Serbia were more likely to pick "the courts of the offender's country or country whose army force he was a member of." These choices suggest that the respondents probably assumed that, relative to the ICTY, *their* local courts would treat members of *their* own group more leniently and members of the "*other*" ethnic group more harshly.

VIEWS ABOUT THE ICTY AND ITS FAIRNESS

To solicit their specific views about the ICTY, we asked respondents several questions about the ICTY and the fairness of its trials and decisions. We first asked a question about the fairness of the ICTY's decisions and procedures and then asked a more specific question targeting the ICTY's decisions (i.e., substantive justice) and another specific question targeting the ICTY's procedures (i.e., procedural justice).

The ICTY received overwhelming support from the respondents surveyed in 2000 or earlier, both for fairness in general and for the fairness of procedures and decisions (1997 Zagreb, 2000 Sarajevo). With the exception of the respondents from Kosovo, other groups surveyed in 2003 or later expressed either quite negative evaluations of the ICTY's fairness (2003 Sarajevo, 2004 Belgrade, 2005 Belgrade) or showed lukewarm support at best (2004 Vukovar). Such predominantly negative views appear to be related to the intensification of the ICTY's work in the post-2000 period, both in terms of the volume of cases and the number of defendants, and the resulting possibility for the respondents in the former Yugoslavia to move from a more abstract assessment of the ICTY to one supported by the observation of actual cases. The respondents from Kosovo once again

TABLE 2.3

Reasons for Selecting a Particular Decision-Maker

	Most familiar with local conditions	Best understands the reasons for war	Judges experienced or witnessed war crimes	Judges removed from local politics	Judges least susceptible to political influence	Conviction most certain	Court not fair	*Chi-Square*	*Phi*
ICTY								391.7***	.578
1997 Zagreb (N=57)	3.2%	31.2%	3.8%	21.7%	30.6%	9.6%	0.0%		
2000 Sarajevo (N=206)	1.5%	1.5%	1.5%	18.9%	12.1%	64.6%	0.0%		
2003 Sarajevo (N=174)	0.6%	5.7%	1.1%	16.1%	22.4%	54.0%	0.0%		
2004 Vukovar (N=141)	5.0%	4.3%	1.4%	34.0%	29.1%	26.2%	0.0%		
2004 Priština (N=304)	7.6%	14.5%	2.0%	1.0%	7.6%	64.8%	2.6%		
2004 Belgrade (N=70)	0.0%	1.4%	0.0%	37.1%	10.0%	50.0%	1.4%		
2005 Belgrade (N=120)	4.2%	3.3%	0.8%	25.0%	13.3%	50.8%	2.5%		
Local courts (BiH, HR)								124.3***	.459
1997 Zagreb (N=37)	43.2%	18.9%	5.4%	0.0%	0.0%	32.4%	0.0%		
2000 Sarajevo (N=50)	26.0%	26.0%	18.0%	0.0%	6.0%	24.0%	0.0%		
2003 Sarajevo (N=190)	50.0%	19.5%	10.0%	0.0%	0.0%	20.5%	0.0%		
2004 Vukovar (N=193)	37.8%	43.0%	3.6%	0.5%	3.6%	11.4%	0.0%		
2004 Priština (N=81)	18.5%	39.5%	16.0%	0.0%	0.0%	23.5%	2.5%		
2004 Belgrade (N=26)	26.9%	30.8%	11.5%	0.0%	11.5%	11.5%	7.7%		
2005 Belgrade (N=13)	23.1%	15.4%	23.1%	0.0%	0.0%	38.5%	0.0%		

Offenders' courts								98.3***	.404
1997 Zagreb (N=13)	23.1%	23.1%	46.2%	0.0%	0.0%	7.7%	0.0%		
2000 Sarajevo (N=1)	0.0%	0.0%	0.0%	0.0%	0.0%	100.0%	0.0%		
2003 Sarajevo (N=4)	0.0%	25.0%	0.0%	0.0%	0.0%	75.0%	0.0%		
2004 Vukovar (N=61)	32.8%	44.3%	6.6%	0.0%	3.3%	13.1%	0.0%		
2004 Priština (N=12)	33.3%	25.0%	8.3%	0.0%	0.0%	33.3%	0.0%		
2004 Belgrade (N=257)	20.2%	46.7%	5.8%	1.9%	6.6%	10.5%	8.2%		
2005 Belgrade (N=255)	23.9%	49.0%	2.0%	2.4%	5.9%	14.1%	2.7%		
Victims' families								85.7***	.663
1997 Zagreb (N=19)	5.3%	10.5%	0.0%	5.3%	0.0%	78.9%	0.0%		
2000 Sarajevo (N=12)	0.0%	0.0%	16.7%	0.0%	0.0%	83.3%	0.0%		
2003 Sarajevo (N=38)	5.3%	2.6%	7.9%	0.0%	0.0%	84.2%	0.0%		
2004 Vukovar (N=0)	0.0%	0.0%	0.0%	0.0%	0.0%	0.0%	0.0%		
2004 Priština (N=65)	4.6%	32.3%	9.2%	1.5%	1.5%	50.8%	0.0%		
2004 Belgrade (N=26)	0.0%	11.5%	3.8%	15.4%	7.7%	38.5%	23.1%		
2005 Belgrade (N=35)	0.0%	11.4%	2.9%	0.0%	8.6%	68.6%	8.6%		

*** $p < .001$

were an exception to this trend. As discussed earlier, until 2003, the ICTY's cases did not include any Albanians from Kosovo as defendants; there was only one case tried before 2005, involving three co-defendants, two of whom were acquitted. The Kosovo respondents' level of support for the ICTY was unsurpassed by other groups of respondents, regardless of whether they personally thought that the ICTY was the best choice for such trials (see Table 2.4).

The respondents' evaluations of the ICTY's fairness were related to their views about the appropriate decision-maker for war crimes (see Table 2.4). Not surprisingly, regardless of whether we asked the question about the ICTY's fairness in general, or focused on the fairness of its decisions or procedures, respondents who selected the ICTY as their decision-maker of choice also expressed much more positive evaluations of its fairness than respondents who selected other decision-makers did. The evaluations of the ICTY's fairness remained high for the respondents from Zagreb (1997), Sarajevo (2000), and Priština (2004), even among those respondents who thought that other decision-makers would be more suitable than the ICTY (see Table 2.4), suggesting that their choice of the appropriate decision-maker probably is not related to their views of the ICTY's fairness. On the other hand, the evaluations of the ICTY's fairness, both general and specific, were more negative among the respondents from most of the post-2000 samples (2003 Sarajevo, 2004 Vukovar, 2004 Belgrade, and 2005 Belgrade sample) who thought that another decision-maker would be more suitable than the ICTY (see Table 2.4).

As expected, the respondents' evaluations of the ICTY's fairness in decision-making and its procedural fairness are strongly related to their overall evaluations of the ICTY's fairness, with two exceptions (Table 2.4). For respondents from Sarajevo (2003) and Vukovar (2004), the overall assessment of the ICTY's fairness seems to be much more strongly related to their evaluations of the fairness of ICTY decisions than to their evaluations of the fairness of the ICTY's procedures. Although the ICTY intensified its activities in the post-2000 period, the respondents in Bosnia and Herzegovina and Croatia might have viewed decisions in some of the prominent cases (with a potentially large effect on public opinion) as questionable. For Sarajevan respondents, particularly poignant was the case of Biljana Plavšić (one of the key political leaders in the Serb community within Bosnia), who plea bargained in 2003 and, consequently, received a less serious sanction. For Vukovar respondents of Serb ethnicity, an important factor seems to have been the impression that the ICTY was targeting mostly Serbs. For Vukovar respondents of Croat ethnicity, it could have been a range of developments, namely, that in 2000 a Bosnian Croat, General Tihomir Blaškić, had been sentenced to 45 years, one of the harshest punishments handed down; that the Vukovar hospital case (*Prosecutor v. Mrkšić et al.*, 1997) resulted in relatively lenient sentences—a 20-year sentence for Colonel Mile Mrkšić (camp supervisor at Ovčara who had "aided and abetted the murder of 194 persons"), a 5-year sentence for Major Veselin Šljivančanin (head of security at the camp), and an acquittal for Captain Miroslav Radić; and that the ICTY justice was not fast enough for

TABLE 2.4

Respondents' Views of the ICTY and Its Fairness

	1997 Zagreb	2000 Sarajevo	2003 Sarajevo	2004 Vukovar	2004 Priština	2004 Belgrade	2005 Belgrade	*Chi-Square*	*Phi*
ICTY Fairness[a]									
% Fair	87.4%	85.9%	41.9%	53.6%	88.1%	22.9%	28.3%	800.8***	.526
ICTY Fairness by Decision-Maker of Choice									
ICTY									
% Fair	96.4%	99.6%	83.3%	85.0%	90.7%	90.7%	81.3%	55.6***	.213
Local courts (BiH, HR)									
% Fair	70.0%	34.0%	7.4%	39.6%	84.2%	26.9%	50.0%	172.3***	.538
Offenders' courts									
% Fair	84.6%	100.0%	40.0%	41.4%	83.3%	8.0%	9.8%	148.0***	.481
Victims' families									
% Fair	66.7%	50.0%	8.7%	26.7%	80.9%	25.0%	11.1%	90.3***	.607
ICTY Fairness of Procedures[b]									
% Fair	88.4%	92.4%	76.8%	58.1%	96.2%	26.9%	29.4%	964.5***	.577

*** $p < .001$

[a] The question was worded as follows: "Do you think that the International Tribunal conducts the trials correctly and fairly and makes just decisions?" The answers ranged on a four-point scale from "definitely yes" (i.e., very fair) to "definitely no" (i.e., very unfair). Categories "definitely yes" and "yes" were merged together, as well as categories "no" and "definitely no."

[b] The question was worded as follows: "Do you think that the procedure by the International Tribunal is fair?" The answers ranged on a four-point scale from "very fair" to "very unfair." Categories "very fair" and "fair" are merged together, as well as categories "unfair" and "very unfair."

Continued

TABLE 2.4

Respondents' Views of the ICTY and Its Fairness

	1997 Zagreb	2000 Sarajevo	2003 Sarajevo	2004 Vukovar	2004 Priština	2004 Belgrade	2005 Belgrade	*Chi-Square*	*Phi*
ICTY Fairness of Procedures by Decision-Maker of Choice									
ICTY									
% Fair	93.2%	99.6%	93.0%	80.7%	97.1%	93.3%	85.4%	66.6***	.233
Local courts (BiH, HR)									
% Fair	80.5%	60.4%	73.4%	47.4%	96.2%	42.3%	35.7%	80.0***	.370
Offenders' courts									
% Fair	92.3%	100.0%	60.0%	48.3%	100.0%	11.8%	9.7%	170.3***	.516
Victims' families									
% Fair	81.0%	91.7%	15.6%	34.5%	93.0%	16.7%	13.9%	125.0***	.716
ICTY Fairness of Decisions[c]									
% Fair	86.8%	87.4%	30.2%	38.1%	93.9%	26.7%	27.5%	961.0***	.579
ICTY Fairness of Decisions by Decision-Maker of Choice									
ICTY									
% Fair	93.2%	96.8%	57.9%	64.6%	96.5%	93.3%	82.9%	221.8***	.428

Local courts (BiH, HR)									
% Fair	75.6%	45.7%	7.5%	23.6%	87.8%	38.5%	35.7%	205.1***	.595
Offenders' courts									
% Fair	100.0%	100.0%	20.0%	26.3%	91.7%	11.8%	8.0%	153.9***	.492
Victims' families									
% Fair	81.0%	83.3%	6.7%	22.2%	90.1%	15.6%	8.3%	140.0***	.758
ICTY Fairness of Decisions: Duško Tadić (Serb)[d]									
% Fair	N/A	86.6%	21.1%	46.1%	41.1%	31.1%	35.7%	344.8***	.380
ICTY Fairness of Decisions: Tihomir Blaškić (Croat)[e]									
% Fair	N/A	31.1%	22.9%	11.9%	55.4%	54.6%	67.8%	425.6***	.413
ICTY Fairness of Decisions: Esad Landžo (Muslim)[f]									
% Fair	N/A	84.4%	41.7%	33.1%	38.7%	48.2%	45.3%	191.5***	.292
ICTY Fairness of Decisions: Stanislav Galić (Serb)[g]									
% Fair	N/A	N/A	6.4%	37.7%	33.9%	35.1%	38.0%	156.0***	.275

*** $p < .001$

[c] The question was worded as follows: "Do you think that the decisions/verdicts by the International Tribunal are fair?" The answers ranged on a four-point scale from "very fair" to "very unfair." Categories "very fair" and "fair" were merged together, as well as categories "unfair" and "very unfair."

[d] The question was worded as follows: "Do you think that the decision by the International Tribunal to sentence Duško Tadić (a guard at the Omarska concentration camp) to 20 years of imprisonment is fair?" The answers ranged on a four-point scale from "very fair" to "very unfair." Categories "very fair" and "fair" were merged together, as well as categories "unfair" and "very unfair."

[e] The question was worded as follows: "Do you think that the decision by the International Tribunal to sentence Tihomir Blaškić (the commander of the regional headquarters of the HVO Armed Forces in central Bosnia as of June 1992) to 45 years of imprisonment is fair?" The answers ranged on a four-point scale from "very fair" to "very unfair." Categories "very fair" and "fair" were merged together, as well as categories "unfair" and "very unfair."

[f] The question was worded as follows: "Do you think that the decision by the International Tribunal to sentence Esad Landžo (a guard at the Čelebići concentration camp) to 15 years of imprisonment is fair?" The answers ranged on a four-point scale from "very fair" to "very unfair." Categories "very fair" and "fair" were merged together, as well as categories "unfair" and "very unfair."

[g] The question was worded as follows: "Do you think that the decision by the International Tribunal to sentence Stanislav Galić (the major general who led the Romanija Corps and maintained the siege of Sarajevo from 1992 to 1994) to 20 years of imprisonment is fair?" The answers ranged on a four-point scale from "very fair" to "very unfair." Categories "very fair" and "fair" were merged together, as well as categories "unfair" and "very unfair."

Slavko Dokmanović, a former president of the Vukovar Municipality, who died before the case against him was completed.[5]

Overall, with a few exceptions, the respondents were unhappy with the ICTY's decisions and tended to view them as unfair (see Table 2.4). The 2000 Sarajevo respondents were the only group that was quite satisfied with two out of the three ICTY decisions reached by the time of the survey. The sentence of 45 years' imprisonment for Tihomir Blaškić[6] was highly displeasing to the respondents from both Sarajevo samples, as well as the Vukovar sample, but satisfying to the majority in the Priština and both Belgrade samples (Table 2.4).

THE ICTY, FAIRNESS, AND POLITICS

Since its inception, the ICTY often has been mired in politics. The creation of the ICTY itself was criticized for its origin in the narrow membership of the United Nations' Security Council rather than the more diverse and representative General Assembly (Robertson, 1999). The United Nations also was criticized for perpetuating a policy of "moral equivalency" that failed to respond militarily to Serb aggression to a sufficient degree while delaying action in creating and sustaining the ICTY (Guest, 1995; see also Power, 2002). The selection of the first ICTY chief prosecutor, Richard Goldstone, was a highly politicized and conflicted process that took more than a year (Scharf, 1997; Goldstone, 2000); this involved rejecting an Arab-American candidate, Cherif Bassiouni, whose intent was to make command responsibility for the siege of Sarajevo an early prosecutorial priority. The selection of judges for the ICTY, "no two of whom may be nationals of the same State" (Statute, 1993, Article 12), also was a highly politicized process that required balancing a wide range of international interests and demands for representation (Neier, 1998). This selection process often had little to do with the settings in which war crimes and/or crimes against humanity occurred—which may or may not be a good thing—but which in any event was a source of conflict among the parties involved, who usually wanted their own nations represented.

---

[5] As time progressed and the ICTY started to decide a large number of cases, we kept adding new cases in our questionnaire. The first case involved Duško Tadić (aSerb), a guard at the Omarska concentration camp, who was sentenced to 20 years' imprisonment. The second case involved a Croat, General Tihomir Blaškić, the commander of the regional headquarters of the HVO Armed Forces in central Bosnia, who initially was sentenced to 45 years' imprisonment (the Appeals Chamber in 2004 reduced his sentence to nine years). The third case involved Esad Landžo (a Muslim), a guard at the Čelebići concentration camp, who was sentenced to 15 years' imprisonment. Finally, the fourth case is the case of Major General Stanislav Galić (a Serb), the commander of the Romanija Corps that maintained the siege of Sarajevo from 1992 to 1994, who initially was sentenced to 20 years' imprisonment (the Appeals Chamber in 2006 sentenced him to life imprisonment).

[6] In 2000, Blaškić filed a notice of appeal and then submitted previously suppressed evidence in his defense. On July 29, 2004, the ICTY's Appeals Chamber reduced his sentence to nine years, essentially the time served, followed by his almost immediate release.

When our respondents were asked to assess the degree to which politics plays a role in the ICTY, most of them indicated a close relation. In particular, all samples are uniform in the view that politics plays an important role in the work of and the decisions by the ICTY, with at least two-thirds of the respondents in each sample saying so (see Table 2.5). However, there are also some disagreements on specific questions, particularly the assessment regarding the ICTY's ability to resist political pressures (with the respondents in the 1997 Zagreb, 2000 Sarajevo, and the 2004 Priština samples stating that the ICTY is able to resist political pressures), how independent the judges are, and whether the judges' nationality influences their decisions (see Table 2.5). For each of these questions, the respondents from the post-2000 samples (with the exception of Priština) were always more likely to evaluate the ICTY as less independent and more influenced by politics than the respondents from the pre-2000 samples or from the Priština sample were.

To explore further the relation between respondents' views of the ICTY and their perception of the politics involved in the ICTY's operation, we performed a logistic regression analysis in which the choice of the appropriate decision-maker (ICTY v. other decision-makers) is the dependent variable. The inclusion only of the respondents' demographic characteristics in the model shows ethnicity and education to be the key variables determining the choice of the ICTY as the appropriate decision-maker. Even when other variables are entered into the model, education remains significant. Specifically, the odds that the respondents who did not finish high school and respondents who graduated from high school, but did not graduate from college, would select the ICTY as the preferred decision-maker are .401 and .631 times lower, respectively, than those of college graduates.[7]

Compared to Croats, Albanians from Kosovo and Muslims/Bosniaks had a more positive view of the ICTY's fairness, while Serbs had a more negative view (Table 2.6). However, a gradual addition of further explanatory variables into the model (e.g., sample, fairness of decisions, fairness of procedures, political scale) eliminates the role of the respondents' ethnicity as a strong predictor of their views of the ICTY's fairness (Table 2.6).

Similarly, although belonging to a particular sample was a strong predictor of the selection of the ICTY as the decision-maker of choice, with the respondents from all non-Belgrade samples (1997 Zagreb; 2000 Sarajevo; 2003 Sarajevo; 2004 Vukovar; 2004 Priština) showing more positive views of the ICTY's fairness than the respondents from the two Belgrade samples (2004 Belgrade; 2005 Belgrade), the effect of the sample itself started to disappear with the inclusion of the respondents' views about procedural fairness and substantive fairness (Table 2.6). In the final model (Model 4, Table 2.6), belonging to a particular sample was only relevant for a few places. Specifically, the odds that the respondents from Vukovar and the respondents from the earlier Belgrade sample would

[7] The odds effects are obtained by exponentiation of the logistic coefficients.

TABLE 2.5

Respondents' Views of the ICTY and Politics

	1997 Zagreb	2000 Sarajevo	2003 Sarajevo	2004 Vukovar	2004 Priština	2004 Belgrade	2005 Belgrade	*Chi-Square*	*Phi*
ICTY Resists Political Pressure[a]									
% Does	72.2%	79.6%	47.4%	45.6%	75.7%	19.1%	21.6%	605.9***	.465
ICTY Judges' Independence Achieved[b]									
% Yes	82.4%	83.1%	47.4%	61.9%	80.4%	15.6%	25.5%	745.6***	.519
ICTY Politics Plays a Role[c]									
% Important	93.5%	51.7%	82.2%	78.9%	68.1%	93.7%	84.6%	275.0***	.311
ICTY Judges' Nationality Impacts the Decision									
% Yes	70.5%	8.5%	32.2%	29.6%	55.4%	51.9%	58.4%	355.2***	.358

*** $p < .001$

[a] The question was worded as follows: "Do you think that the International Tribunal in The Hague resists political pressure?" The answers ranged on a four-point scale from "definitely does" to "definitely does not." Categories "definitely does" and "does" were merged together, as well as categories "does not" and "definitely does not."

[b] The question was worded as follows: "Do you think that the independence of the judges of the International Tribunal in The Hague has been achieved?" The answers ranged on a four-point scale from "definitely yes" to "definitely no." Categories "definitely yes" and "yes" were merged together, as well as categories "no" and "definitely no."

[c] The question was worded as follows: "According to your opinion, what role will the politics play in the work and the decisions by the International Tribunal?" The answers ranged on a four-point scale from "very important" to "not important at all." Categories "very important" and "important" were merged together, as well as categories "not important" and "not important at all."

[d] The question was worded as follows: "Do you think that the nationality of a judge from the International Tribunal will influence the decision the judge will vote for?" The answers ranged on a four-point scale from "definitely yes" to "definitely no." Categories "definitely yes" and "yes" were merged together, as well as categories "no" and "definitely no."

TABLE 2.6

Logistic Coefficients from the Regression of the Decision-Maker of Choice on Respondents' Attitudes and Background Characteristics[a]

	Model 1			Model 2			Model 3			Model 4		
	B		s.e.	B		s.e.	B		s.e.	B		s.e.
Ethnicity[b]												
Muslims/Bosniaks	.435	***	.121	.313	a	.178	.158		.218	.287		.238
Serbs	−.788	***	.107	.485	**	.167	.141		.420	.111		.248
Albanians + Others	.595	***	.118	.399	a	.240	.018		.313	.087		.344
Gender[c]	.017		.081	.008		.085	.064		.104	.094		.120
Education[d]												
Below high school	−.1.062	***	.139	−1.031	***	.148	−.768	***	.184	−.913	***	.215
High school	−.624	***	.111	−.546	***	.118	−.466	**	.143	−.460	**	.161
Sample[e]												
1997 Zagreb				2.150	***	.235	.316		.301	.594	a	.330
2000 Sarajevo				2.306	***	.245	.692	*	.312	−.125		.347
2003 Sarajevo				.840	***	.204	.465	a	.273	.163		.301
2004 Vukovar				.676	***	.177	.056		.243	−.686	*	.277
2004 Priština				1.709	***	.265	.072		.347	.096		.385
2004 Belgrade				−.563	**	.167	−.724	**	.212	−.619	**	.233

* $p < .05$; ** $p < .01$; *** $p < .001$; [a] $p < .10$

[a] The question was worded as follows: "Who should try the persons accused of war crimes committed in the territory of the former Yugoslavia?" The possible answers were: "a) the courts in the territory of Croatia and Bosnia and Herzegovina where the crimes have been committed; b) the courts of the offender's country or country whose army force he was a member of; c) the International Tribunal in The Hague; d) the families of the victims; e) other ______." The dependent variable is coded as follows: 0 = other decision-makers; 1 = ICTY.

[b] Ethnicity is dummy coded with Croats as the omitted comparison category.

[c] Gender is coded as follows: 0 = males; 1 = females.

[d] Education is dummy coded with college graduates as the omitted comparison category.

[e] Sample is dummy coded with 2005 Belgrade as the omitted comparison category.

Continued

TABLE 2.6

Continued

	Model 1			Model 2			Model 3			Model 4		
	B		s.e.	B		s.e.	B		s.e.	B		s.e.
Fairness of decisions[f]							2.033	***	.162	1.527	***	.189
Punishment purpose[g]							−.017		.109	−.079		.126
Fairness of procedures[h]							1.145	***	.178	.593	**	.205
Political scale[i]										−.420	***	.036
Constant	.456	***	.125	−.885	***	.219	−1.988	***	.301	3.223	***	.545
Pseudo R^2	.128			.230			.467			.555		

* $p < .05$; ** $p < .01$; *** $p < .001$; [a] $p < .10$

[f] Fairness of decisions is coded as follows: 0 = unfair; 1 = fair.

[g] Punishment purpose is coded as follows: 0 = retribution; 1= deterrence (special and general).

[h] Fairness of procedures is coded as follows: 0 = unfair; 1 = fair.

[i] We created the political scale using the respondents' answers to four questions: "Do you think that the International Tribunal in The Hague resists political pressure" (four-point scale from "definitely does" to "definitely does not"); "Do you think that the independence of the judges of the International Tribunal in The Hague has been achieved?" (four-point scale from "definitely yes" to "definitely no"); "Do you think that the nationality of a judge from the International Tribunal will influence the decision the judge will vote for?" (four-point scale from "definitely yes" to "definitely no"); and "According to your opinion, what role will the politics play in the work and the decisions by the International Tribunal?" (four-point scale from "very important" to "not important at all"). The last two questions were recorded in the reverse order to fit the scale. The scale ranged from 4 to 16. The Cronbach's alpha is .612.

select the ICTY as their decision-maker of choice were .503 and .530 times lower, respectively, than those of the respondents from the 2005 Belgrade sample.

In the final model, the respondents' views about the ICTY as the appropriate decision-maker are also strongly related to how fair the respondents judged the ICTY's decisions to be, how fair they judged the ICTY's procedures to be, and how politically biased they viewed the ICTY's judges to be (see Table 2.6). The odds that the respondents who evaluated the ICTY's *decisions* as fair would select the ICTY as the appropriate decision-maker are 4.60 times higher than those of the respondents who deemed the ICTY's decisions to be unfair. Similarly, the odds that the respondents who evaluated the ICTY's *procedures* as fair would regard the ICTY overall as fair are 1.81 times higher than those of the respondents who think the ICTY's procedures unfair. Finally, a one-unit increase on the scale of perceived political influence decreases by 0.66 times the odds that the respondents evaluate the ICTY as fair overall. Thus, the respondents' selection of the ICTY as the appropriate decision-maker is related in a systematic way to their education, feelings that the ICTY's decisions are fair, that the ICTY's procedures are fair, and that the ICTY's judges are not politically biased. None of the remaining variables—including, most notably, ethnicity—are statistically significant at the .05 level. The influence of ethnicity is mediated by education and perceptions of political independence and procedural fairness.

CONCLUSION

Whereas the war in Croatia eventually ended with a sweeping military operation, the war in Bosnia and Herzegovina ended as a result of a series of negotiations that culminated in the signing of the Dayton Peace Agreement. The common feature is that in neither case was there a celebrated victor before whom the vanquished side pled on its knees for mercy. In fact, the international community put the ICTY in charge of trying members of *all* ethnic groups for the war crimes and crimes against humanity committed during these wars. Through its decisions and the sentencing of defendants representing former warring parties, the ICTY thus has been in the position to indicate symbolically who the "victors" and the "vanquished" are (see, e.g., Chambliss and Seidman 1982: 236). This makes the ICTY constituencies in these countries especially sensitive in their perceptions of the justness of these court decisions, be they dealing with "their own" as offenders or as the victimized.

When we first began the surveys in 1997, the ICTY was a novel international institution that had just embarked on the complex task of legal decision-making in cases involving war crimes and crimes against humanity. By the time the last survey was completed in 2005, the ICTY had completed trials against several dozen defendants. The perceptions of the ICTY among its constituencies probably shifted away from being almost purely theoretical to being substantively grounded in the actual decisions meted out and the processes employed by the ICTY. At the same time, local courts—particularly the Court of Bosnia and Herzegovina—gained more prominence in trying war crimes cases locally.

Our findings indicate a shift in public opinion regarding the ICTY. Compared to the pre-2003 surveys, the post-2003 surveys reveal substantially more negative attitudes toward the ICTY. The results of our multivariate analyses suggest that respondents' views about the fairness of the ICTY's decisions, together with their views of its procedural fairness and the role of political influence in shaping the ICTY, are crucial in shaping the overall views of the ICTY.

Prior research has suggested that "recognition of, and perhaps, a sense of responsibility for the commission of war crimes vary with national group and the history of the recent war" (Biro et al., 2004, p. 194). For the respondents from Serbia and of Serb ethnicity from other regions, the fact that two-thirds of the defendants with completed cases by 2004 were of Serb ethnicity could easily have resulted in doubts about the ICTY's fairness, if not open hostility toward the ICTY. This may especially be the case in light of the facts that nationalist ideas have been a powerful component of political life in the region, that denial of the scope of war casualties and the nature of the atrocities remained strong even after the discovery of a videotape documenting these horrors (see Chapter 4), and that cooperation with the ICTY, particularly with respect to the arrest of high-profile indictees, was achieved only after intense political negotiations and credible economic threats. Croats and Muslims/Bosniaks view themselves almost exclusively through their group identity as victims of the war (see, e.g., Stover, 2005, p. 114) or, at best, defenders of their countries. They do not accept that they could be both victims and aggressors (see, e.g., Stover, 2005) and that acknowledging individualized guilt could mitigate collective guilt (Biro et al., 2004, p. 195), and, therefore, are troubled by the fact that any members of their ethnic group (25 percent and 8 percent, respectively) have been tried by the ICTY. This is particularly true in cases in which defendants were sentenced to long-term imprisonment, such as the 45 years' imprisonment conviction of Bosnian Croat general Tihomir Blaškić (in 2004, the Appeals Chamber reversed the majority in the Trial Chamber's decision and sentenced Tihomir Blaškić to 9 years' imprisonment). The only sample that still remained optimistic about the ICTY even in 2004 was the Priština sample. By 2005, there was only one ICTY case involving three Albanian defendants, two of whom were acquitted. At the same time, Milošević was on trial for war crimes and crimes against humanity in Kosovo.

The decrease of confidence in the ICTY is mirrored by the increase of confidence in the local courts. The earliest surveys (1997 Zagreb; 2000 Sarajevo) suggested that the ICTY was the decision-maker of choice. By 2003, respondents were split between the ICTY and local courts. Finally, the last two Belgrade surveys (2004, 2005) indicated an almost absolute lack of confidence in the ICTY and an overwhelming preference for local courts, namely, the courts in the defendant's country of ethnic origin. At the same time, the respondents became more concerned with the link between politics and the ICTY.

The virtues that our respondents advocating local courts attribute to domestic Bosnian courts for war crimes revolve around their belief in these courts' understanding of, and familiarity with, the local setting. This familiarity and understanding involves political preferences. The respondents advocating the local courts increasingly resent what they perceive as international interpretations imposed on locally experienced problems. This is the sense in which all politics is locally defined (see O'Neill, 1994).

Although it may not be true that all politics are local, the lessons seem to be that the local dimension of international justice cannot be ignored and, it is important to note that, as Slaughter (2004) emphasizes, international criminal law and a global jurisprudence should not seek to do so. Moreover, the extent and severity of the atrocities committed and the ICTY's limited time and resources ultimately appear to *require* the involvement of the local criminal justice systems to address the widespread and systematic scale of violence that occurred during the wars in the former Yugoslavia. Yet, the local judicial system has been criticized for its lack of independence, as well as for its incompetence and corruption (see Human Rights Center, 2000: 145).

It seems likely that there is a predictable sequence to international efforts to restore a sense of domestic criminal justice and that, ultimately, settings and persons who have experienced major crimes against their people will wish to reclaim an indigenous role in the restoration of locally experienced justice (Karstedt, 1998). This may be no less true today with regard to the conflict in the former Yugoslavia than it was for Eichmann in Jerusalem. The struggle, as Arendt concluded, is to find a liberal legal balance between local, national, and international inclinations (Arendt, 1963). Finding this balance point is as much an ideological as it is an empirical matter, and it may inevitably involve conflict, as well as the negotiation, consensus, and harmonization envisioned by Slaughter (2004). As Gibson and Caldeira (1995) suggest, transnational courts are likely uniquely challenged in a way that will perpetuate more conflict and yield less diffuse support or legitimacy than national courts can generate.

3

ETHNICITY AND THE LEGITIMACY OF THE ICTY

BECAUSE WAR CRIMES AND CRIMES against humanity are ignited so often by ethnic and national hatreds, there is a persistent perception of prejudice and discrimination in attempts to address these disputes legally. The ICTY is seen by some as an Anglo-American- and European-inspired legal justification for NATO's intervention in the former Yugoslavia and, therefore, as inherently biased against the Serbs (Parenti, 2000). Others argue that neither the citizens of the former Yugoslavia nor the ICTY should be prejudged in this way. For example, a prominent contemporary historian, Mark Mazower (2000: 128–9), argues, in defense of the citizens of the former Yugoslavia, that the war in the 1990s "represented the extreme force required by nationalists to break apart a society which was otherwise capable of ignoring the mundane fractures of class and ethnicity." It is unclear what role, if any, contemporary ethno-national tensions play in the ICTY and in the response of citizens and victims to its actions in the new and old state settings.

In this chapter, we analyze the role of ethnicity in the formation of attitudes about the ICTY. Sampson and Bartusch (1998) propose that an ecological perspective involving normative orientations they call "cognitive landscapes" is essential to understanding perceptions of justice. We argue that this is as much or more the case in international as it is in domestic settings. In addition, we go a step further in suggesting that, in this international setting, it is skepticism about the independence of the ICTY that prominently accounts for disapproval of the ICTY among its constituencies. Ultimately, confidence in judicial independence is essential to the goals of democratization and the rule of law.

VIEWS ABOUT JUSTICE AND THE ENVIRONMENT

Sampson and Bartusch (1998) utilize the term "cognitive landscapes" to theorize the influence of the environment on the formation of attitudes about deviant behavior. They argue that a key source of variation in views of deviance and its control rests in the socio-ecological structure of neighborhoods and that the tolerance of deviance varies across structural and situational contexts. They suggest that the concept of "legal cynicism" captures the "anomie about law" and the apparent skepticism of American minority group members about the criminal justice system. Thus, their theory goes beyond a focus on individuals and is ecological in nature. Although Sampson and Bartusch devote their attention specifically to American neighborhood and ghetto experiences, the contextual conceptualization they provide has broader application in the arena of international justice.

Linking their work to earlier research by Kapsis (1978), Sampson and Bartusch argue (1998: 783) that individual and group perceptions of appropriate conduct are grounded in structural landscapes that define "defeated" and "defended" peoples and settings. Kapis (1978) found the level of anomie or "normlessness" to be higher in "defeated" communities—the ones least likely to exercise political influence and obtain the services they need—than in "defended" communities. Sampson and Bartusch (1998) further argue that "defeated" communities, characterized within the context of racial segregation and concentrated disadvantage, yield perceptions of legal injustice. Hagan and Albonetti (1982) find support for this view: compared to whites and members of the upper classes, blacks and members of the lower classes were more likely to perceive legal injustice. They conclude that "conceptions and perceptions of justice are determined in large part by the times, places, and positions in the social structure from which they are derived" (Hagan and Albonetti, 1982: 330).

Sampson and Bartusch's perspective goes further in predicting that sensitivity to inequities of political and power relationships is preeminently contextual and not reducible to the groups and individuals themselves. Thus, their fundamental hypothesis is that structural settings "where inability to influence the structures of power that constrain lives is greatest, also breed cynicism and perceptions of legal injustice" (Sampson and Bartusch, 1998, p. 783).

In the context of the former Yugoslavia and the ICTY, the application of the concept of "cognitive landscapes" implies that the structural landscape of the country's current national circumstance determines its localized attitudes toward the ICTY. The war in Bosnia and Herzegovina (BiH) ended with no declared victors and, by conducting trials and meting out sentences, the ICTY provides a legal framework to decide who the "defeated" and the "defended" are. Perceptions of the justice that the ICTY is delivering are colored by the degree to which each ethnic group is treated and viewed as "defended," as opposed to "defeated." Thus, the evaluations of the ICTY quite likely vary across countries and depend on how the ICTY is perceived to be treating the dominant and minority ethnic groups. A quick analysis of the ICTY cases completed by 2005 indicates that the Serbs typically are seen as offenders or the "defeated," Muslims/Bosniaks as victims or the "defended," and Croats somewhere in between: about two-thirds of the ICTY defendants have been Serbs, one-quarter have been Croats, and less than one-tenth have been Muslims/Bosniaks (see Table 2.1).

We also argue that the attitudes of an ethnic group are shaped differently within a country in which they are the dominant ethnic group, compared to the attitudes of that ethnic group in a country in which they constitute a minority. For example, we expect that Serbs who are removed from the localized structural circumstances of defeat in Serbia—for example, by living among the "defended" in Bosnia and Herzegovina or Croatia (HR)—may not be as embittered as Serbs residing in Serbia.

THE COGNITIVE LANDSCAPE OF THE CONFLICT IN THE FORMER YUGOSLAVIA

We provide a brief account of the ICTY to set the foundation for understanding how this institution is seen from several parts of the former Yugoslavia. The prosecution has asserted in ICTY cases that three wars in the former Yugoslavia took the following toll in the 1990s: at least several thousand deaths and 170,000 deportations in the early 1990s in Croatia, followed in the mid-1990s by more than 7,000 deaths and 200,000 to 300,000 deportations in Bosnia and Herzegovina, leading in the late 1990s to more than 4,000 deaths and 750,000 deportations in Kosovo. As leader of the former Yugoslavia, Slobodan Milošević was charged with advancing these events by supporting local Serb leaders in Croatia, Bosnia and Herzegovina, and Kosovo, while further creating government ministries in the former Yugoslavia to form links with these leaders outside Serbia. By 1991, Milošević had laid the groundwork for the wars that would follow.

Following Croatia's secession from the former Yugoslavia in 1991, several areas of Croatia dominated by Serbs separated from Croatia, and local Serb leaders used military and paramilitary units from the former Yugoslavia to murder, detain, and deport Croats and other non-Serbs. In the process, they largely destroyed the city of Vukovar and heavily damaged the city of Dubrovnik. Croatia later was able to push back militarily against the Serbs and used that opportunity to take control over portions of Bosnia.

Bosnia and Herzegovina was the second theatre of operations, and when the Muslims/Bosniaks and Croats in Bosnia and Herzegovina voted to separate from the former Yugoslavia, Radovan Karadžić simultaneously declared the formation of an independent Republika Srpska (RS), or Serbian Republic of Bosnia, and became its president. The ethnic cleansing of Prijedor, the siege of Sarajevo, and the massacre of Srebrenica, under the direction of Radovan Karadžić and General Ratko Mladić, were three of the most devastating of the Bosnian Serb aggressions. When the ICTY was unable to apprehend

Karadžić and Mladić, it had to content itself in the nearer term by prosecuting figures like Esad Landžo, a guard in a detention camp. Later, General Radislav Krstić was arrested by U.S. forces in Bosnia and convicted for his role in the Srebrenica genocide. In 2008, Karadžić was caught in Belgrade, the capital of Serbia, and transferred to The Hague, where he is on trial at the time of this writing.

Kosovo was the scene of the final war, which climaxed with NATO bombing in early 1999, an event that Milošević claimed as the pretext for the deportation of one-third of the Kosovo Albanian population. The events in Kosovo led finally to the ICTY indictment of Milošević in the spring of 1999. It took until the summer of 2001 to get Milošević removed from office, arrested, and transferred to the ICTY. At the time of this writing, Mladić still remains at large.

The wars in the former Yugoslavia did not end with the overpowering military victory of one ethnic group. While the fighting in Bosnia and Herzegovina was still going on, the international community facilitated peace negotiations, bringing all three ethnic groups to the negotiating table (see Chapter 2). The resulting Dayton Peace Agreement (1995) arguably established the groundwork for the future coexistence of the three ethnic groups, particularly in Bosnia and Herzegovina, but did nothing in terms of setting the stage for determination of criminal responsibility and/or civil liability for the atrocities committed during the war. In fact, the original agreement at Dayton was that the NATO-led troops would not pro-actively arrest people indicted for war crimes and crimes against humanity (Bass, 2000; McMahon and Miller, 2009).

As we discussed in Chapter 2, political leadership in all three countries—Bosnia and Herzegovina, Croatia, and Serbia—shaped public perceptions of the war and the ICTY. In all three countries, the top political leaders who controlled the country during the war remained in control for several years after the war had ended (Milošević in Serbia, Tudjman in Croatia, and Izetbegović in Bosnia and Herzegovina[1]). As the ICTY was accusing the top military commanders of committing war crimes and crimes against humanity, the ICTY was implicitly accusing the regimes—the Milošević regime in Serbia and the Tudjman regime in Croatia—of directly or indirectly approving the commission of war crimes and crimes against humanity. Both regimes had incentives to generate public opposition to the ICTY and the means to achieve it through the control of the media. The ICTY was viewed as challenging the regimes (see, e.g., Klarin, 2004), and the regimes generated the impression that cooperation with the ICTY amounted to not supporting the regime.

Under pressure from the West and with the strengthening of the opposition parties, nationalist agendas have not dominated the post-2000 political landscape in Serbia to the same extent they did before, during the Milošević regime (see Chapter 2). Yet, nationalist ideas remain strong, as the presidential and parliamentary elections have indicated,

[1] Izetbegović was the president of BiH until 1996 and then became a member of the Presidency of BiH.

with politicians from the Serbian Radical Party securing a substantial number of votes. With the economic incentives offered by the West and the possibility of joining the European Union, the rhetoric in everyday political life in Serbia gradually appears to be shifting in the direction of advocating the need to cooperate with the ICTY. Despite public rallies protesting the 2008 arrest of Radovan Karadžić (*Daily Mail*, 2008), there seems to be a much wider acceptance of the reality that support for, and cooperation with, the ICTY is a likely ticket to foreign aid and, eventually, membership in the European Union.

The Tudjman regime, which tightly controlled Croatia in the 1990s (Human Rights Watch, 1999), shaped the public view of the ICTY as well. After a decade in power, the Croatian Democratic Union lost the elections in 2000. At the same time, the ICTY started to investigate and prosecute cases of Croatian army generals, which generated discontent toward the ICTY and allowed the Croatian Democratic Union to strengthen its position. While the Croatian Democratic Union supported public rallies criticizing the ICTY, the new party leader, Ivo Sanader, gradually led the party away from the extreme nationalist views supported by Ivić Pašalić, the leader of the Croatian Democratic Union hardliners. During his two mandates as the prime minister, Sanader pushed for European Union membership, which both generated additional support among the voters and required Croatia's cooperation with the ICTY. The stumbling block for the beginning of negotiations with the European Union was the arrest of the indicted Croatian general Ante Gotovina. The Gotovina indictment stirred public opinion and indicated the diversity of opinions among politicians (i.e., four ministers, including the defense minister, resigned over the government's decision to cooperate with the ICTY; BBC, 2001). Toward the end of 2005, the ICTY reported that Croatia was cooperating fully; General Ante Gotovina was arrested in December 2005, and negotiations with the European Union commenced.

THE COGNITIVE LANDSCAPE AND VIEWS OF THE ICTY

The work of the ICTY is not likely to be seen similarly in different parts of the former Yugoslavia. To use a Sampson and Bartusch (1998) metaphor, the case-based historical edges and contours of the ICTY are sufficiently varied to make it a vivid institutional landscape onto which the sentiments of the various parties can be cognitively projected. To borrow further from Sampson and Bartusch's conceptualization, the Serbs constitute the "defeated" party in ICTY cases, whereas the Muslims/Bosniaks and Albanians are the "defended" parties, and the Croats find themselves located somewhere in between. This pattern has become more conspicuous as the ICTY has accumulated its judgments. In the process, the ICTY itself has assumed an important role in writing a legal war history of the former Yugoslavia. As the historian Robert Donia (2004: 11) notes, "These chambers have produced histories that are not only credible and readable, but indispensable to understanding the origins and course of the 1990s conflicts in the former

Yugoslavia." Richard Wilson (2005: 941) goes further in observing that "international tribunals such as the ICTY are altering the relationship between law and history."

In drafting this history, the judgments of the ICTY are helping to reshape the cognitive landscape of the former Yugoslavia. Public opinion surveys (International Institute for Democracy and Electoral Assistance, 2002) reveal a pattern of responses to the ICTY that range from high regard in Kosovo (83 percent approval), through acceptance in Bosnia and Herzegovina (51 percent approval), to rejection in Croatia (21 percent approval) and Serbia and Republika Srpska (4 percent and 8 percent approval, respectively). This pattern of approval has since declined in Bosnia and Herzegovina (Kutnjak Ivković and Hagan, 2006), but has not descended to the levels found in Serbia and Republika Srpska. Wilson (2005: 941-2) suggests that, in particular, we should hardly be surprised by the low approval in Serb areas, arguing that "any historical account which punctures nationalist mythologies is likely to be rejected as long as a region is dominated by nationalist politicians who have regularly denied responsibility for mass atrocities." As recently as the fall of 2002, the Republika Srpska government was in deep denial of its responsibility, insisting, for example, that only about a thousand Bosnian Muslim soldiers, rather than seven to eight thousand Bosnian Muslim civilians, had been killed at Srebrenica.

Such policies of denial in relation to events like the Srebrenica massacre have a radiating cultural effect that collectively influences the cognitive landscape of public opinion. Of course, this is what cultural propaganda is all about, and it is the kind of fuel that can drive genocidal violence in the first place. If this view of the cognitive landscape of attitudes toward efforts at international criminal justice is correct, we should be able to see testable signs of its operation. For example, we should find that the effects of such cultural policies and pronouncements are localized in their influence to the place of their origin and not more globally endemic or generic to the ethnic groups involved. That is, we should find that the Serbs in places like Belgrade are most affected in their views, while elsewhere in the former Yugoslavia the effect of being Serb might be culturally diffused and mitigated by countervailing cultural beliefs and victimization experiences shared with the locally defended, rather than defeated, groups. In that sense, members of an ethnic group who live in the country/federal unit in which they are the dominant ethnic group and in which nationalist mythologies are strong (e.g., Serbs in Serbia; Serbs in Republika Srpska; Croats in Croatia) would probably have a different view of the ICTY and its justice than the members of the same ethnic group who live in a country in which they are a minority (e.g., Serbs in Croatia; Serbs in the Bosnian Federation; Croats in Bosnia and Herzegovina). This is the thesis that we assess next.

ETHNICITY AND OUR SAMPLES

Over time, we collected seven samples across various parts of the former Yugoslavia. A common feature is that, in each of these seven samples, the dominant ethnicity in the sample matches the dominant ethnicity in the region or city where the sample was collected (see Chapter 1). As described in Chapter 1, Croats constitute the majority in the 1997 Zagreb sample and the 2004 Vukovar sample, Muslims/Bosniaks in the 2000 and 2003 Sarajevo samples, Serbs in the 2004 and 2005 Belgrade samples, and Albanians in the 2004 Priština sample (see Table 1.2).

The nature of the data is such that the four most recent samples (2004 Belgrade, 2004 Vukovar, 2004 Priština, and 2005 Belgrade samples) are representative of these cities. Thus, the ethnic composition of the sample matches the ethnic composition of these cities closely. Serbs are the most dominant ethnic group in the two Belgrade samples, Croats in the Vukovar sample, and Albanians in the 2004 Priština sample (see Table 1.2). The two Sarajevo samples, despite being convenience samples (see Chapter 1), are also close approximations of the ethnic composition of the city. Out of the three ethnic groups represented in the sample, Serbs are proportionate to their representation in the city, while Muslims/Bosniaks—the majority—are somewhat underrepresented and Croats—a minority—are somewhat overrepresented (see Chapter 1). This oversampling of Croats, a minority group, allows us to undertake statistical analyses comparing these three groups living in the same city. Finally, the 1997 Zagreb sample is not intended to represent the population of the Croatian capital (see Chapter 1). In fact, it is a convenience sample of displaced persons from Croatia and refugees from Bosnia and Herzegovina who had been receiving financial help in Zagreb at the time. However, most of the respondents in this sample are Croats and the sample matches the ethnic distribution of the population in both the country and the city of Zagreb (see Chapter 1).

The degree of ethnic homogeneity varies across the samples. The Belgrade and the Priština communities are the most homogeneous, with more than 90 percent of the respondents reportedly belonging to the same ethnic group. Out of the seven samples, the 2004 Vukovar and both Sarajevo samples are the most heterogeneous, thus reflecting the diverse ethnic composition of these cities. Both Vukovar and Sarajevo were ethnically diverse before the war, suffered tremendously during the war, and their residents have poignant stories to tell.

Vukovar is viewed as a symbol of Croatian resistance against heavily equipped Serb forces. When the heavily empowered Serb forces overtook the city on November 18, 1991, after several weeks of heavy fighting, the world media showed images of thousands of refugees carrying their possessions in plastic bags and being forced to leave the city, which lay completely destroyed. Wounded Croatian soldiers from the Vukovar Hospital were later killed by the Serb forces at the Ovčara farm (*Prosecutor v. Mrkšić* et. al., 1997).

The story of the city of Sarajevo is grim, too. The siege of Sarajevo lasted for nearly four years, from the spring of 1992 to late fall of 1995, and claimed the lives of thousands of soldiers and civilians, with countless others injured physically and/or psychologically. The basics of life—food and water, hygiene, heat, health care, sleep—were all affected by the siege (*Prosecutor v. Galić*, 2003):

> Civilians in BiH-held areas of Sarajevo deferred even basic survival tasks to times of reduced visibility, such as foggy weather... or night time, because they were targeted

> otherwise. Civilians would often collect wood at night, in particular, older people, "because they couldn't move as fast and they knew it was risky to travel during the day.". . . Schools were closed, and temporary neighbourhood schools were established in cellars, to minimize the distance that children had to travel to their classes, and therefore their exposure to sniping and shelling. . . . Many civilians lived for a long period of time in the cellars of their buildings in order to avoid the shells. . . . They learned to move around as little as possible,. . . rarely leaving their apartments:. . . some old people were "literally dying of malnutrition because they were too terrified to come out."

For much of this time, the UN Security Council had designated Sarajevo a "safe area." This was a cruel misnomer because, as Silber and Little (1995: 297) report, "The military and strategic reality facing Bosnia in the spring and early summer of 1993 was that the country was gradually being wiped off the map of Europe." More specifically, they reported that "a walk down any side street in Sarajevo provides visible evidence that nowhere was safe from the random mortar fire: the city's streets are pockmarked everywhere with the distinctive splatter of the mortar impact point. The local people called these imprints 'Sarajevo rose'—the color of blood. . . you could barely walk more than a few meters without passing one" (Silber and Little 1995: 310).

ETHNICITY, VIEWS ABOUT PUNISHMENT, AND ITS PURPOSE

A quick analysis of the ICTY cases completed by 2005 provides support for the view that Muslims/Bosniaks and Albanians are seen predominantly as victims or the "defended," Serbs as offenders or the "defeated," and Croats somewhere in between: about two-thirds of the defendants were Serbs, one-quarter Croats, and less than one-tenth Muslims/Bosniaks (see Table 2.1). We explore the degree to which our respondents' ethnicity is related to their perceptions of the appropriate punishment for committing war crimes and the reasons for the punishment, who the decision-maker in war crimes trials should be, and the fairness of the justice being delivered by the ICTY.

Although virtually all respondents, regardless of their ethnicity, said that those who committed war crimes and crimes against humanity should be punished, the rationale for the punishment varied. When asked to specify what they viewed as the purpose of punishing war criminals (Table 3.1), Croats and Muslims/Bosniaks were substantially more likely to cite retribution ("punishment of the offenders for the offenses they have already committed") as the key purpose of punishment than either Serbs or Albanians were. Serbs' views were divided between retribution and general deterrence ("deterrence of future perpetrators of war crimes in our country and in the world"), and Albanians' views were split among three purposes: retribution, general deterrence, and special deterrence ("deterrence of these punished offenders from committing new war crimes").

TABLE 3.1

Attitudes toward War Crimes and Their Punishment[a]

	Special deterrence	General deterrence	Retribution	*Chi-Square*	Phi
Ethnicity				233.3***	.290
Croats	8.8%	32.6%	58.6%		
Muslims/Bosniaks	3.2%	28.0%	68.8%		
Serbs	7.0%	43.5%	49.5%		
Albanians + Others	25.2%	34.7%	40.1%		
Croats (N=616)				43.9***	.267
1997 Zagreb (N=217)	12.4%	44.7%	42.9%		
2000 Sarajevo (N=39)	0.0%	33.3%	66.7%		
2003 Sarajevo (N=79)	1.3%	21.5%	77.2%		
2004 Vukovar (N=281)	9.3%	26.3%	64.4%		
Muslims/Bosniaks (N=474)				3.6	.087
2000 Sarajevo (N=206)	3.4%	31.1%	65.5%		
2003 Sarajevo (N=268)	1.9%	25.0%	73.1%		
Serbs (N=1,048)				47.6***	.213
2003 Sarajevo (N=48)	4.2%	10.4%	85.4%		
2004 Vukovar (N=148)	10.1%	31.1%	58.8%		
2004 Belgrade (N=395)	6.1%	43.5%	50.4%		
2005 Belgrade (N=457)	6.8%	51.4%	41.8%		
2000 Sarajevo (N=245)				1.4	.075
Croats (N=39)	0.0%	33.3%	66.7%		
Muslims/Bosniaks (N=206)	3.4%	31.1%	65.5%		
2003 Sarajevo (N=395)				6.1	.124
Croats (N=79)	1.3%	21.5%	77.2%		
Muslims/Bosniaks (N=268)	1.9%	25.0%	73.1%		
Serbs (N=48)	4.2%	10.4%	85.4%		

Continued

TABLE 3.1

Continued

	Special deterrence	General deterrence	Retribution	*Chi-Square*	Phi
2004 Vukovar (N=429)				1.4	.056
Croats (N=281)	9.3%	26.3%	64.4%		
Serbs (N=148)	10.1%	31.1%	58.8%		

*** $p < .001$

[a] The question was worded as follows: "According to your opinion, what is the purpose of punishing the war criminals?" The answers were: "a) deterrence of these punished offenders from committing new war crimes [i.e., special deterrence]; b) deterrence of future perpetrators of war crimes in our country and in the world [i.e., general deterrence]; c) punishment of the offenders for the offenses they have already committed [i.e., retribution]; d) ___________." Because of the small number of respondents who selected answer d), it was eliminated from the analysis.

If we look at the results from the "defended v. defeated" perspective, Muslims/Bosniaks, typically seen as "defended" and, thus, victims, were at the same time most likely to focus on past crimes and advocate predominantly retribution (68 percent), while Serbs, typically seen as "defeated" and, thus, offenders, were less likely to focus on past crimes, and instead advocated both retribution (49.5 percent) and general deterrence (43.5 percent).

A more revealing comparison of respondents' views requires that we have respondents of the same ethnicity from various sites. As it turned out, we had Albanian respondents only in the Priština sample and thus do not have different "cognitive landscapes" from which we can use to compare their views. Although there are a few Muslims/Bosniaks in the non-Sarajevo samples as well, their numbers are too small to allow for any meaningful comparison (Table 1.2). We present the perceptions of our Muslim/Bosniak respondents from the two Sarajevo samples, but only to establish the baseline for comparison of the views of the dominant ethnicity in the Sarajevo samples (i.e., Muslims/Bosniaks) with those of the ethnic minorities (i.e., Serbs and Croats). Because of the nature of the population distribution, and thus the composition of our samples, the exploration of our "cognitive landscapes" focuses on Serbs and Croats.

Further exploration of the role of ethnicity clearly shows that the views of Croats and Serbs depend upon their environments (Table 3.1). The Serbs from Belgrade, the most "defeated" environment in our study, tended to be the least likely to advocate retribution (50.4 percent and 41.8 percent; Table 3.1), while the Serbs from Sarajevo, the most "defended" environment, tended to be most likely to advocate retribution (85.4 percent). The Serbs from Vukovar, Croatia, placed somewhere in between (58.8 percent). The influence of cognitive landscapes is most apparent through a comparison of the views of the Serb respondents with the respondents of other ethnicities living in the same sites. The rationale for punishment expressed by the Serb respondents from Vukovar (58.8 percent retribution) is very similar to (and statistically not different from) the rationale for punishment expressed by the Croat respondents from Vukovar (64.4 percent retribution), just as the view of the Serb respondents from Sarajevo (85.4 percent retribution) is very similar to the views of the Croat (77.2 percent retribution) and Muslim (73.1 percent retribution) respondents from Sarajevo.

"Cognitive landscapes" shape Croats' attitudes about punishment purpose too. Whereas the respondents from the 1997 Zagreb sample were more likely to be split between the rationales of general deterrence (44.7 percent) and retribution (42.9 percent), the Croat respondents from the other three samples leaned more heavily toward the rationale of retribution (66.7 percent in 2000 Sarajevo, 77.2 percent in 2003 Sarajevo, 64.4 percent in 2004 Vukovar). A comparison of Croat views to the views of the other ethnic groups in the same sample further supports the "cognitive landscape" thesis: the Croats' views were quite similar to the views expressed by other ethnic groups from the respective site (66.7 percent Croats and 65.5 percent Muslims/Bosniaks in the 2000 Sarajevo sample; 77.2 percent Croats and 73.1 percent Muslims/Bosniaks in the 2003 Sarajevo sample; 64.4 percent Croats and 58.8 percent Serbs in the 2004 Vukovar sample; Table 3.1).

We next inquired about appropriate punishment. When asked to choose the appropriate punishment, Croats, Muslims/Bosniaks, and Albanians were most likely to select life imprisonment as their first choice (57.0 percent, 51.6 percent, and 56.1 percent, respectively; Table 3.2), while Serbs tended to lean toward less severe punishment and were about equally divided between life imprisonment (42.1 percent) and a more lenient punishment (36.9 percent).

Croat choices of the appropriate punishment for war crimes differed across the four samples, with the respondents from the 1997 Zagreb and 2000 Sarajevo samples split between the death penalty (42.8 percent and 33.3 percent, respectively) and life imprisonment (53.5 percent and 64.1 percent, respectively), and the respondents from the 2003 Sarajevo sample split among the death penalty (27.1 percent), life imprisonment (50.6 percent), and less serious punishment (22.4 percent). On the other hand, the Croats from the 2004 Vukovar sample leaned toward either life imprisonment (62.1 percent) or less serious punishment (26.3 percent; Table 3.2). Serb respondents' views also varied by site: the Serb respondents from the 2003 Sarajevo sample—the most "defended" place—were most likely among the Serb respondents to favor the death penalty (43.1 percent). Serb respondents from other sites were more evenly split between life imprisonment (47.8 percent in the 2004 Vukovar sample, 43.3 percent in the 2004 Belgrade sample, and 40.7 percent in the 2005 Belgrade sample) and less serious punishment (46.7 percent in the 2004 Vukovar sample, 43.6 percent in the 2004 Belgrade sample, and 32.1 percent in the 2005 Belgrade sample).

Croat views about the appropriate punishment were quite diverse across the four samples, and were related to local "cognitive landscapes" as well. Specifically, the choices of appropriate punishment made by Croats and Muslims/Bosniaks from the 2000 Sarajevo sample were almost identical (64.1 percent for life imprisonment among Croats and 64.4 percent for life imprisonment among Muslims/Bosniaks; Table 3.2). On the other hand,

TABLE 3.2

Views about Appropriate Punishment[a]

	Death penalty	Life in prison	Imprisonment or fine	*Chi-Square*	*Phi*
Ethnicity				247.9***	.311
Croats	27.4%	57.0%	15.6%		
Muslims/Bosniaks	39.7%	51.6%	8.7%		
Serbs	21.1%	42.1%	36.9%		
Albanians + Others	32.9%	56.1%	11.1%		
Croats (N=563)				85.1***	.389
1997 Zagreb (N=215)	42.8%	53.5%	3.7%		
2000 Sarajevo (N=39)	33.3%	64.1%	2.6%		
2003 Sarajevo (N=85)	27.1%	50.6%	22.4%		
2004 Vukovar (N=224)	11.6%	62.1%	26.3%		
Muslims/Bosniaks (N=504)				30.3***	.245
2000 Sarajevo (N=219)	33.3%	64.4%	2.3%		
2003 Sarajevo (N=285)	45.3%	42.8%	11.9%		
Serbs (N=871)				54.6***	.250
2003 Sarajevo (N=51)	43.1%	37.34%	19.6%		
2004 Vukovar (N=90)	5.6%	47.8%	46.7%		
2004 Belgrade (N=337)	13.1%	43.3%	43.6%		
2005 Belgrade (N=393)	27.2%	40.7%	32.1%		
2000 Sarajevo (N=258)				0.1	.007
Croats (N=39)	33.3%	64.1%	2.6%		
Muslims/Bosniaks (N=219)	33.3%	64.4%	2.3%		
2003 Sarajevo (N=421)				12.3*	.171
Croats (N=85)	27.1%	50.6%	22.4%		
Muslims/Bosniaks (N=285)	45.3%	42.8%	11.9%		
Serbs (N=51)	43.1%	37.3%	19.6%		

Continued

TABLE 3.2

Continued

	Death penalty	Life in prison	Imprisonment or fine	*Chi-Square*	*Phi*
2004 Vukovar (N=314)				12.9**	.203
Croats (N=224)	11.6%	62.1%	26.3%		
Serbs (N=90)	5.6%	47.8%	46.7%		

*$p < .05$; **$p < .01$; ***$p < .001$

[a] The question was worded as follows: "According to your opinion, what is the appropriate punishment for persons who committed war crimes and crimes against humanity?" The answers were: "a) the death penalty; b) life imprisonment; c) imprisonment for 21–50 years; d) imprisonment for 15–20 years; e) imprisonment for up to 15 years; f) monetary fine; g) __________."

although there is less reliance on life imprisonment in the 2003 Sarajevo sample regardless of ethnicity, Muslim/Bosniak respondents favored somewhat more serious punishment than Croat respondents did (Table 3.2). Similarly, the Croats in the 2004 Vukovar sample mostly favored life imprisonment (62.1 percent), while the Serbs in the same sample were split between life imprisonment (47.8 percent) and less serious punishments (46.7 percent).

ETHNICITY AND THE DECISION-MAKER FOR WAR CRIME TRIALS

There is a two-tier structure of jurisdiction over war-crime cases committed in the territory of the former Yugoslavia: the ICTY has primary jurisdiction and local courts have secondary jurisdiction (after the establishment of the Court of Bosnia and Herzegovina, the two-tier structure in Bosnia and Herzegovina became a three-tier structure). Initially, in the mid- to late 1990s, the ICTY was the most visible decision-maker and attracted major media attention. Local courts typically were reluctant to try war-crime cases, did not try them at all, or tried low-ranking officers. Over time, especially as the ICTY has continued to transfer an increasing number of cases to the local courts and prepared to close its doors, the spotlight has been shifting in the direction of local courts.

We asked our respondents whom they favored as the primary decision-makers of their choice in the war-crimes cases. The answers offered on the survey were the ICTY, local courts (either in Croatia or Bosnia and Herzegovina, where the crimes were committed, or in the offender's country of origin/military affiliation), or victims' families. Muslims/Bosniaks, Albanians, and Croats were most likely to pick the ICTY (59.3 percent, 60.3 percent, and 46.5 percent, respectively; Table 3.3), while the Serb respondents leaned toward the local courts in the offender's country of origin or the country for which the defendant fought (54.9 percent). These choices, particularly those made by the Serb respondents, fit the paradigm of "defended" and "defeated."

Further analyses indicate the mechanism of "cognitive landscapes" at work. The most prominent example involves the responses provided by Croat respondents (see Table 3.3). Whereas the Croats from the 1997 Zagreb and 2000 Sarajevo samples were most likely to pick the ICTY as the decision-maker of their choice (69.6 percent and 78.0 percent, respectively), the Croats from the 2003 Sarajevo and 2004 Vukovar samples were most likely to pick the local courts in Bosnia and Herzegovina and Croatia, respectively (53.5 percent and 52.1 percent, respectively; see Table 3.3). At the same time, the Croats' choices were strongly related to those made by others from the same sample. Croat respondents from the 2000 Sarajevo sample were as likely as Muslim/Bosniak respondents from the same sample to select the ICTY (78.0 percent and 76.7 percent, respectively; see Table 3.3.). Similarly, between 35 and 45 percent of the respondents from the 2003 Sarajevo sample, *regardless of their ethnic origin*, selected the ICTY (38.4 percent for Croats, 45.8 percent for Muslims/Bosniaks, and 35.8 percent for Serbs; see Table 3.3). The views of the Croats from the 2004 Vukovar sample, who constitute the majority in Vukovar, and the Serbs from the same sample, the minority in Vukovar, are substantially different, with the Croat respondents leaning more toward local courts in Bosnia and Herzegovina and Croatia, and the Serb respondents toward the ICTY.

The answers provided by the Serb respondents clearly show the influences of environment on their views about the appropriate decision-maker. Unlike the Serb respondents from Sarajevo and Vukovar, who were split between the ICTY and the local courts in Bosnia and Herzegovina and Croatia, the Serb respondents from both Belgrade samples—the most "defeated" site among our samples—indicated a very strong inclination toward the local courts in a defendant's country or the country in whose army the defendant fought (Table 3.3), and away from both the ICTY and the local courts in Bosnia and Herzegovina and Croatia. Compared to the Serbs in Belgrade, who expressed the perception that they needed to protect their own and advocated local courts in the country of a defendant's origin, the Serbs in Sarajevo—the most "defended" site—did not reflect such views and were congruent with other ethnic groups in the same sample, sharing the view that the ICTY or the local courts in Bosnia and Herzegovina and Croatia would be more appropriate decision-makers (see Table 3.3). Serbs in Vukovar, who constitute a strong ethnic minority but not the dominant ethnic group, were more likely to opt for the ICTY as the preferred decision-maker (47.6 percent) than were the Croats, who constitute the majority and tended to lean more toward the local courts in Bosnia and Herzegovina and Croatia (52.1 percent).

We probed further and asked specific questions about the appropriate decision-makers for the trials of Serb and Croat military and political leaders. We focused on Radovan Karadžić (the political leader of Bosnian Serbs), Ratko Mladić (the commander-in-chief of Bosnian Serbs), and Tihomir Blaškić (the commander of the regional headquarters of the HVO Armed Forces in central Bosnia). Whereas the percentages of the respondents

TABLE 3.3

Respondent Designations of Appropriate Jurisdiction[a]

	ICTY	Local courts (BiH & HR)	Offenders' courts	Victims' families	*Chi-Square*	*Phi*
Ethnicity					977.8***	.592
Croats	46.5%	37.6%	7.5%	8.3%		
Muslims/Bosniaks	59.0%	31.0%	1.5%	8.6%		
Serbs	28.1%	9.9%	54.9%	7.0%		
Albanians + Others	60.3%	18.2%	7.1%	14.4%		
Croats (N=626)					126.2***	.449
1997 Zagreb (N=217)	69.6%	16.1%	4.6%	9.7%		
2000 Sarajevo (N=41)	78.0%	22.0%	0.0%	0.0%		
2003 Sarajevo (N=86)	38.4%	53.5%	1.2%	7.0%		
2004 Vukovar (N=282)	28.0%	52.1%	11.3%	8.5%		
Muslims/Bosniaks (N=522)					50.8***	.312
2000 Sarajevo (N=227)	76.7%	17.6%	0.4%	5.3%		
2003 Sarajevo (N=295)	45.8%	42.4%	0.7%	11.2%		
Serbs (N=998)					267.4***	.518
2003 Sarajevo (N=53)	35.8%	52.8%	1.9%	9.4%		
2004 Vukovar (N=143)	47.6%	25.9%	22.4%	4.2%		
2004 Belgrade (N=375)	18.4%	6.1%	68.5%	6.9%		
2005 Belgrade (N=427)	27.2%	2.8%	62.1%	8.0%		

TABLE 3.3

Continued

	ICTY	Local courts (BiH & HR)	Offenders' courts	Victims' families	*Chi-Square*	*Phi*
2000 Sarajevo (N=268)					2.7	.101
Croats (N=41)	78.0%	22.0%	0.0%	0.0%		
Muslims/Bosniaks (N=227)	76.7%	17.6%	0.4%	5.3%		
2003 Sarajevo (N=434)					6.0	.117
Croats (N=86)	38.4%	53.5%	1.2%	7.0%		
Muslims/Bosniaks (N=295)	45.8%	42.4%	0.7%	11.2%		
Serbs (N=53)	35.8%	52.8%	1.9%	9.4%		
2004 Vukovar (N=425)					35.7^{***}	.290
Croats (N=282)	28.0%	52.1%	11.3%	8.5%		
Serbs (N=143)	47.6%	25.9%	22.4%	4.2%		

$^{***}p < .001$

[a] The question was worded as follows: "Who should try the persons accused of war crimes committed in the territory of the former Yugoslavia?" The possible answers were: "a) the courts in the territory of Croatia and Bosnia and Herzegovina where the crimes have been committed; b) the courts of the offender's country or the country whose army force he was a member of; c) the International Tribunal in The Hague; d) the families of the victims; e) other ______."

of various ethnicities who picked the ICTY as the primary decision-maker varied depending on the ethnic group and the specific question (i.e., a general question about the decision-maker v. specific questions for Karadžić/Mladić and Blaškić), in-depth analyses of the relation between the appropriate decision-maker and respondents' ethnicity across samples yielded results that were almost identical to the results associated with the question about the appropriate decision-maker in the abstract (see Tables 3.4 and 3.5). In all three cases, the views of one ethnic group (e.g., Croats) were quite similar to the views of the other ethnic groups (e.g., Serbs and Muslims/Bosniaks) in the same sample, thus suggesting the influence of environment on the respondents' views. At the same time, within each ethnic group (i.e., Croats, Serbs), the respondents' opinions varied across samples.

TABLE 3.4

Respondent Designations of Appropriate Jurisdiction for Karadžić and Mladić[a]

	ICTY	Local courts (BiH)	Local courts (Serbia, RS)	Victims' families	*Chi-Square*	*Phi*
Ethnicity					909.6***	.587
Croats	58.7%	23.2%	3.0%	15.1%		
Muslims/Bosniaks	56.9%	32.6%	1.1%	9.4%		
Serbs	34.5%	12.9%	48.7%	3.9%		
Albanians + Others	70.2%	13.1%	4.8%	11.9%		
Croats (N=631)					101.6***	.401
1997 Zagreb (N=224)	76.3%	7.1%	2.7%	13.8%		
2000 Sarajevo (N=42)	78.6%	21.4%	0.0%	0.0%		
2003 Sarajevo (N=88)	35.2%	53.4%	1.1%	10.2%		
2004 Vukovar (N=277)	50.2%	27.1%	2.5%	20.2%		
Muslims/Bosniaks (N=531)					50.1***	.322
2000 Sarajevo (N=232)	74.6%	20.3%	0.4%	4.7%		
2003 Sarajevo (N=299)	42.5%	44.1%	0.7%	12.7%		
Serbs (N=844)					196.6***	.483
2003 Sarajevo (N=53)	35.8%	49.1%	3.8%	11.3%		
2004 Vukovar (N=134)	60.4%	20.9%	15.7%	3.0%		
2004 Belgrade (N=288)	23.3%	11.1%	59.0%	6.6%		
2005 Belgrade (N=369)	30.9%	6.8%	61.0%	1.4%		

TABLE 3.4

Continued

	ICTY	Local courts (BiH)	Local courts (Serbia, RS)	Victims' families	*Chi-Square*	*Phi*
2000 Sarajevo (N=274)					2.3	.091
Croats (N=42)	78.6%	21.4%	0.0%	0.0%		
Muslims/Bosniaks (N=232)	74.6%	20.3%	0.4%	4.7%		
2003 Sarajevo (N=440)					6.7	.123
Croats (N=88)	35.2%	53.4%	1.1%	10.2%		
Muslims/Bosniaks (N=299)	45.2%	44.1%	0.7%	12.7%		
Serbs (N=53)	35.8%	49.1%	3.8%	11.3%		
2004 Vukovar (N=411)					44.4***	.329
Croats (N=277)	50.2%	27.1%	2.5%	20.2%		
Serbs (N=134)	60.4%	20.9%	15.7%	3.0%		

*** $p < .001$

[a] The question was worded as follows: "In your opinion, who should try Radovan Karadžić and Ratko Mladić?" The possible answers were: "a) courts in Bosnia and Herzegovina; b) courts in Serbia/Republika Srpska; c) the International Tribunal in The Hague; d) the families of the victims; e) other ______."

VIEWS ABOUT THE ICTY AND ITS DELIVERY OF JUSTICE

We asked our respondents to share with us their views of the ICTY and its meting out of justice. As our results show, all of them had heard of the ICTY, but their views most likely were based on indirect contact with the ICTY, through media reports, discussions with family, friends, and neighbors, and an occasional TV viewing of an actual trial. When asked to assess the fairness of the ICTY, about two-thirds of Croats, Muslims/Bosniaks, and Albanians (62.6 percent, 61.3 percent, 78.0 percent, respectively, Table 3.6) stated that they think the ICTY is fair. This is in sharp contrast with the Serbs' evaluations, two-thirds of whom thought that the ICTY is not fair (67.5 percent; Table 3.6).

However, in support of the "cognitive landscapes" paradigm, views of each of the three ethnic groups are not very homogeneous. Within each ethnic group, evaluations of the ICTY's fairness depended heavily on the specific sample (see Table 3.6). In some of the samples, the majority of an ethnic group would say that the ICTY is fair, while in other

TABLE 3.5

Respondent Designations of Appropriate Jurisdiction for Blaškić[a]

	ICTY	Local courts (HR)	Local courts (BiH)	Victims' families	*Chi-Square*	*Phi*
Ethnicity					380.7***	.381
Croats	48.7%	19.9%	23.8%	7.4%		
Muslims/Bosniaks	59.5%	2.7%	31.0%	6.8%		
Serbs	35.0%	34.6%	23.1%	7.2%		
Albanians + Others	70.6%	9.4%	9.9%	10.1%		
Croats (N=572)					141.5***	.497
1997 Zagreb (N=212)	71.7%	17.5%	3.8%	7.1%		
2000 Sarajevo (N=42)	78.6%	2.4%	19.0%	0.0%		
2003 Sarajevo (N=88)	39.8%	11.4%	40.9%	8.0%		
2004 Vukovar (N=230)	26.1%	27.8%	37.4%	8.7%		
Muslims/Bosniaks (N=534)					58.1***	.330
2000 Sarajevo (N=231)	77.9%	0.4%	19.0%	2.6%		
2003 Sarajevo (N=303)	45.9%	3.3%	40.9%	9.9%		
Serbs (N=922)					68.2***	.272
2003 Sarajevo (N=54)	35.2%	5.6%	48.1%	11.1%		
2004 Vukovar (N=133)	51.9%	18.0%	26.3%	3.8%		
2004 Belgrade (N=332)	28.0%	40.7%	22.3%	9.0%		
2005 Belgrade (N=403)	33.3%	40.2%	19.9%	6.7%		

TABLE 3.5

Continued

	ICTY	Local courts (HR)	Local courts (BiH)	Victims' families	*Chi-Square*	*Phi*
2000 Sarajevo (N=273)					2.9	.104
Croats (N=42)	78.6%	2.4%	19.0%	0.0%		
Muslims/Bosniaks (N=231)	77.9%	0.4%	19.0%	2.6%		
2003 Sarajevo (N=445)					11.1	.158
Croats (N=88)	39.8%	11.4%	40.9%	8.0%		
Muslims/Bosniaks (N=303)	45.9%	3.3%	40.9%	9.9%		
Serbs (N=54)	35.2%	5.6%	48.1%	11.1%		
2004 Vukovar (N=363)					25.2***	.263
Croats (N=230)	26.1%	27.8%	37.4%	8.7%		
Serbs (N=133)	51.9%	18.0%	26.3%	3.8%		

*** $p < .001$

[a] The question was worded as follows: "In your opinion, who should have tried Tihomir Blaškić?" In the 2003 version we added the explanation: "In your opinion, who should have tried Tihomir Blaškić (the commander of the regional headquarters of the HVO Armed Forces in central Bosnia as of June 1992)?" The possible answers were the same: "a) courts in Croatia; b) courts in Bosnia and Herzegovina; c) the International Tribunal in The Hague; d) the families of the victims; and e) other ______."

samples, the majority of the same ethnic group would say that the ICTY is *not* fair. This result is robust, regardless of whether the ethnic group in question is Croats, Muslims/Bosniaks, or Serbs. At the same time, and as before, these variations within ethnic groups are related to the views expressed by other ethnic groups from the same sample, thus suggesting cognitive landscapes at work. Specifically, the majority of Croats (82.9 percent) from the 2000 Sarajevo sample evaluated the ICTY as fair, as did an almost identical proportion of Muslims/Bosniaks (86.1 percent) from the same sample (see Table 3.6). Similarly, the majority of Croats (62.5 percent) from the 2003 Sarajevo sample reported that the ICTY is not fair, and the majority of Muslims/Bosniaks (57.8 percent) and Serbs (63.0 percent) from the same sample agreed. The only exception is the 2004 Vukovar sample: about one-half (52.1 percent) of Croats evaluated the ICTY as unfair, and only one-third (32.2 percent) of Serbs did the same.

TABLE 3.6

Respondents' Views of the ICTY and Its Fairness[a]

	Not fair	Fair	*Chi-Square*	*Phi*
Ethnicity			374.4***	.359
Croats	37.4%	62.6%		
Muslims/Bosniaks	38.7%	61.3%		
Serbs	67.5%	32.5%		
Albanians + Others	22.0%	78.0%		
Croats (N=616)			111.1***	.424
1997 Zagreb (N=228)	13.5%	86.5%		
2000 Sarajevo (N=41)	17.1%	82.9%		
2003 Sarajevo (N=85)	62.5%	37.5%		
2004 Vukovar (N=262)	52.1%	47.9%		
Muslims/Bosniaks (N=523)			107.2***	.447
2000 Sarajevo (N=224)	13.9%	86.1%		
2003 Sarajevo (N=299)	57.8%	42.2%		
Serbs (N=1,083)			95.6***	.294
2003 Sarajevo (N=51)	63.0%	37.0%		
2004 Vukovar (N=117)	32.3%	67.7%		
2004 Belgrade (N=443)	76.0%	24.0%		
2005 Belgrade (N=472)	72.1%	27.9%		
2000 Sarajevo (N=265)			0.3	.033
Croats (N=41)	17.1%	82.9%		
Muslims/Bosniaks (N=224)	13.9%	86.1%		
2003 Sarajevo (N=435)			0.9	.046
Croats (N=85)	62.5%	37.5%		
Muslims/Bosniaks (N=299)	57.8%	42.2%		
Serbs (N=51)	63.0%	37.0%		
2004 Vukovar (N=379)			13.9***	.188
Croats (N=262)	52.1%	47.9%		
Serbs (N=117)	32.3%	67.7%		

* $p < .05$; ** $p < .01$; *** $p < .001$

[a] The question was worded as follows: "Do you think that the International Tribunal conducts the trials correctly and fairly and makes just decisions?" The answers ranged on a four-point scale from "definitely yes" (i.e., very fair) to "definitely no" (i.e., very unfair). Categories "definitely yes" and "yes" were merged, as were categories "no" and "definitely no."

We also inquired separately about the fairness of decisions and the fairness of procedures. The results indicate that the fairness of decisions probably shapes overall evaluations of ICTY fairness to a larger extent than views about procedural fairness do (see Tables 3.6-3.8); across ethnic groups, the percentage of respondents who evaluated ICTY decisions as fair is smaller than the percentage of respondents who evaluated ICTY procedures as fair (see Tables 3.7-3.8). In fact, with the exception of two groups of Serbs (from the 2004 and 2005 Belgrade samples), every group of respondents evaluated the ICTY procedures as fair.

The only ethnic group that gave the ICTY decisions glowing evaluations were the Albanians (83.2 percent; Table 3.7). Slightly more than one-half of Croats and Muslims/Bosniaks felt the same way (54.2 percent and 55.4 percent, respectively; Table 3.7), while more than two-thirds of Serbs (68.8 percent) evaluated the ICTY decisions as unfair. This distribution of answers—with Albanians being the most positive, Serbs the most negative, and Muslims/Bosniaks and Croats somewhere in between—fits well within the paradigm of "cognitive landscapes." It is not surprising that Serbs, the ethnic group whose members constitute the majority of the defendants at the ICTY and who are viewed as the "defeated," are most likely to reject the decisions of the court that convicts "their own." It is surprising that the majority of Serbs in the 2004 Vukovar sample actually evaluated the ICTY decisions as fair (57.3 percent) and were even more likely to evaluate them as fair than Croats from the same sample were (29.0 percent; Table 3.7). One plausible explanation involves the "cognitive landscapes" concept: Serbs living in Vukovar constitute the minority in a Croatian town. Thus, they may be less burdened by the overall sense of being the "defeated" group that prevails in Serbia. At the same time, they may tend to distance themselves from the "singled-out" approach (i.e., instead of treating them as "defended," the ICTY treats them as somewhere between "defended" and "defeated") that the Croats may harbor when they think about the ICTY. Compared to public opinion in Serbia, public opinion in Croatia (in which Vukovar is located) may be very sensitive to the less numerous, but nevertheless long-term sentences meted out to Croat defendants. One prominent example is the case of Tihomir Blaškić. Initially, Blaškić was sentenced to 45 years of imprisonment in 2000 (*Prosecutor v. Blaškić*, 1996). On appeal, his sentence was reduced to nine years, which may be interpreted as a sign that the trial judges erred in a well-known, extensively commented-upon, and important case for Croats.

As was the case with the question of the ICTY's fairness overall, views about the fairness of the ICTY's decisions differed substantially within ethnic groups, depending on the specific sample. Whereas the overwhelming majority of Croats from the 1997 Zagreb and 2000 Sarajevo samples (87.7 percent and 82.9 percent, respectively) thought that ICTY decisions were fair, a strong majority in the 2003 Sarajevo and 2004 Vukovar samples (70.6 percent and 71.0 percent, respectively) evaluated ICTY decisions as unfair. This difference among the surveyed Croats could well be a consequence of the different "cognitive landscapes" in which they live. Although different from the views about ICTY

TABLE 3.7

Respondents' Views of the ICTY and Decision Fairness[a]

	Not fair	Fair	*Chi-Square*	*Phi*
Ethnicity			425.5***	.385
Croats	45.8%	54.2%		
Muslims/Bosniaks	44.6%	55.4%		
Serbs	68.8%	31.2%		
Albanians + Others	16.8%	83.2%		
Croats (N=616)			205.0***	.577
1997 Zagreb (N=228)	12.3%	87.7%		
2000 Sarajevo (N=41)	17.1%	82.9%		
2003 Sarajevo (N=85)	70.6%	29.4%		
2004 Vukovar (N=262)	71.0%	29.0%		
Muslims/Bosniaks (N=523)			174.9***	.578
2000 Sarajevo (N=224)	12.1%	87.9%		
2003 Sarajevo (N=299)	70.2%	29.8%		
Serbs (N=1,083)			45.7***	.205
2003 Sarajevo (N=51)	74.5%	25.5%		
2004 Vukovar (N=117)	42.7%	57.3%		
2004 Belgrade (N=443)	73.1%	26.9%		
2005 Belgrade (N=472)	72.9%	27.1%		
2000 Sarajevo (N=265)			0.8	.054
Croats (N=41)	17.1%	82.9%		
Muslims/Bosniaks (N=224)	12.1%	87.9%		
2003 Sarajevo (N=435)			0.4	.030
Croats (N=85)	70.6%	29.4%		
Muslims/Bosniaks (N=299)	70.2%	29.8%		
Serbs (N=51)	74.5%	25.5%		
2004 Vukovar (N=379)			27.5***	.269
Croats (N=262)	71.0%	29.0%		
Serbs (N=117)	42.7%	57.3%		

* $p < .05$; ** $p < .01$; *** $p < .001$

[a] The question was worded as follows: "Do you think that the decisions/verdicts by the International Tribunal are fair?" The answers ranged on a four-point scale from "very fair" to "very unfair." Categories "very fair" and "fair" were merged, as were categories "unfair" and "very unfair."

decision fairness held by Croats in the 1997 Zagreb and 2000 Sarajevo samples (87.7 percent and 82.9 percent fair, respectively), the Croats' views in the 2003 Sarajevo sample (70.6 percent not fair) are aligned with the views of both Muslims/Bosniaks and Serbs in the same sample (70.2 percent and 74.5 percent unfair, respectively). Similarly, Croats' extremely positive evaluations of the fairness of ICTY decisions in the earlier, 2000 Sarajevo sample (82.9 percent fair) closely match the views expressed by Muslims/Bosniaks from the same sample (87.9 percent fair).

Lastly, we asked respondents to evaluate the fairness of ICTY procedures. On the surface, it looks as if all ethnic groups except Serbs (36.9 percent) provided very positive evaluations of the ICTY's procedural fairness (71.9 percent Croats, 82.4 percent Muslims/Bosniaks, 86.0 percent Albanians; Table 3.8). However, and once again consistent with the paradigm of "cognitive landscapes," only the majority of Serbs in the two samples collected in Serbia (2004 and 2005 Belgrade) evaluated the procedures as unfair, while the majority of Serbs in two other samples collected outside of Serbia (the 2003 Sarajevo and 2004 Vukovar samples) evaluated the procedures as fair (Table 3.8). In fact, Serbs in Vukovar were more likely to evaluate the procedures as fair than Croats in the same sample were (71.8 percent v. 52.7 percent; Table 3.8). On the other hand, positive evaluations of the ICTY's fairness expressed by Serbs in the 2003 Sarajevo sample (74.1 percent fair) were quite similar to evaluations by Croats (79.5 percent fair) and Muslims/Bosniaks (76.5 percent) in the same sample.

Judicial independence is a crucial element of procedural justice. We explored whether the respondents' views of judges' political independence were related to their views of the ICTY. We created a scale of perceived judicial political independence to measure variation in respondents' views of the political neutrality of judges at the ICTY. Four items composing the ICTY judicial neutrality scale asked about judges' ability to resist political pressure, judicial independence, national bias, and the role political factors play in judicial decisions. We coded the scale, ranging from 4 to 16, in a way that assigns higher values for lack of political neutrality or judicial political independence. Perhaps not surprisingly, among all ethnicities, Serbs tended to view the ICTY as lacking political independence the most (11.92; Table 3.9), followed by Croats (10.20), and Muslims/Bosniaks (9.44). Further analysis suggests that the environment shaped respondents' views to a substantial degree. Indeed, Serbs in Belgrade scored the highest (12.40 in 2004 and 12.05 in 2005), while Serbs in Vukovar (9.66) scored among the lowest, and Serbs in Sarajevo scored in between (10.61). There is statistically significant variation across Croat and Muslim/Bosniak views too, as well as a very clear pattern of how their views differed. Croats in the 2000 Sarajevo sample had almost identical views about the ICTY's political independence as Muslims/Bosniaks from the same sample did (8.05 v. 8.03), which was quite different from the more skeptical and very uniform view of the ICTY expressed by Serbs, Croats, and Muslims/Bosniaks in the 2003 Sarajevo sample (10.61, 10.41, and 10.48, respectively; Table 3.9).

TABLE 3.8

Respondents' Views of the ICTY and Procedure Fairness[a]

	Not fair	Fair	*Chi-Square*	*Phi*
Ethnicity			575.4***	.445
Croats	28.1%	71.9%		
Muslims/Bosniaks	17.6%	82.4%		
Serbs	63.1%	36.9%		
Albanians + Others	14.0%	86.0%		
Croats (N=622)			96.3***	.393
1997 Zagreb (N=228)	9.6%	90.4%		
2000 Sarajevo (N=42)	11.9%	88.1%		
2003 Sarajevo (N=88)	20.5%	79.5%		
2004 Vukovar (N=264)	47.3%	52.7%		
Muslims/Bosniaks (N=535)			27.4***	.226
2000 Sarajevo (N=228)	6.6%	93.4%		
2003 Sarajevo (N=307)	23.5%	76.5%		
Serbs (N=1,101)			127.7***	.341
2003 Sarajevo (N=54)	25.9%	74.1%		
2004 Vukovar (N=131)	28.2%	71.8%		
2004 Belgrade (N=442)	71.5%	28.5%		
2005 Belgrade (N=474)	71.1%	28.9%		
2000 Sarajevo (N=279)			1.5	.074
Croats (N=42)	11.9%	88.1%		
Muslims/Bosniaks (N=228)	6.6%	93.4%		
2003 Sarajevo (N=449)			0.6	.037
Croats (N=88)	20.5%	79.5%		
Muslims/Bosniaks (N=307)	23.5%	76.5%		
Serbs (N=54)	25.9%	74.1%		
2004 Vukovar (N=395)			13.2***	.183
Croats (N=264)	47.3%	52.7%		
Serbs (N=131)	28.2%	71.8%		

*$p < .05$; **$p < .01$; ***$p < .001$

[a] The question was worded as follows: "Do you think that the procedure by the International Tribunal is fair?" The answers ranged on a four-point scale from "very fair" to "very unfair." Categories "very fair" and "fair" were merged, as were categories "unfair" and "very unfair."

TABLE 3.9

Perceptions about the Political Independence of the ICTY by Sample and Ethnicity (Means)[a]

Sample	Serbs	Croats	Muslims/Bosniaks
1997 Zagreb		10.38	
2000 Sarajevo		8.05	8.03
2003 Sarajevo	10.61	10.41	10.48
2004 Vukovar	9.66	10.37	
2004 Priština			
2004 Belgrade	12.40		
2005 Belgrade	12.05		
Total	11.92	10.20	9.44
F-test	40.06***	19.95***	130.16***

* $p<.05$; ** $p<.01$; *** $p<.001$

[a] Four items composing the ICTY political independence scale asked about judges' ability to resist political pressure, judicial independence, national bias, and the role played by political factors in judicial decisions. The alpha reliability coefficient for this scale is .70. The scale ranges from 4 (indicating perceptions about the ICTY's political neutrality) to 16 (indicating perceptions about the ICTY's political lack of neutrality).

ETHNICITY, THE ICTY, AND COGNITIVE LANDSCAPES IN A MULTIVARIATE FRAMEWORK

We further explored how views about the appropriate decision-maker were shaped across ethnic groups, with a further emphasis on cognitive landscapes. To do so, we focused our analyses on Croats and Serbs, that is, the ethnic groups included in several samples collected at different sites. Indeed, unlike Muslim/Bosniak and Albanian respondents, whose responses were collected almost exclusively at one site (Sarajevo for Muslims/Bosniaks and Priština for Albanians), Croats and Serbs had significant presence in several samples collected at different locations (Croats in 1997 Zagreb, 2000 Sarajevo, 2003 Sarajevo, 2004 Vukovar; Serbs in 2003 Sarajevo, 2004 Belgrade, 2004 Vukovar, 2005 Belgrade). Furthermore, and of critical importance to the ability to tease out the effect of cognitive landscapes, both Croat and Serb respondents constituted the dominant ethnic group in some samples (e.g., Croats in 1997 Zagreb, 2004 Vukovar; Serbs in 2004 and 2005 Belgrade) and a minority group in other samples (e.g., Croats in 2000 and 2003 Sarajevo; Serbs in 2003 Sarajevo and 2004 Vukovar).

In the first model (Model 1, Tables 3.10-3.11), featuring respondents' gender, education, and the sample to which respondents belonged, sample is a significant determinant of the respondents' choice of jurisdiction (ICTY or other decision-makers). However, the predictive value of the sample is largely diminished or eliminated completely when the model is expanded with other variables, namely, those directly related to the respondents' views of the ICTY (Model 2; Tables 3.10-3.11). For both Croats and Serbs, views about

TABLE 3.10

Logistic Coefficients from the Regression of Appropriate Jurisdiction on Croat Respondents' Attitudes and Background Characteristics[a]

	Model 1			Model 2		
	B		s.e.	B		s.e.
Gender[b]	−.002		.182	−.004		.240
Education[c]						
Below high school	−1.131	***	.296	−1.400	***	.402
High school	−.676	***	.243	−.795	*	.315
Sample[d]						
2000 Sarajevo	.349		.432	−.440		.534
2003 Sarajevo	−1.430	***	.276	−.572		.421
2004 Vukovar	−1.705	***	.202	−1.272	***	.322
Fairness of decisions[e]				1.396	***	.357
Punishment purpose[f]				.324		.249
Fairness of procedures[g]				.209		.377
Political scale[h]				−.294	***	.076
Constant	1.487	***	.260	3.163	**	1.041
Pseudo R^2	.241			.436		

* $p < .05$; ** $p < .01$; *** $p < .001$; [a] $p < .10$

[a] The question was worded as follows: "Who should [primarily] try the persons accused of war crimes committed in the territory of the former Yugoslavia?" The possible answers were: "a) the courts in the territory of Croatia and Bosnia and Herzegovina where the crimes have been committed; b) the courts of the offender's country or the country whose army force he was a member of; c) the International Tribunal in The Hague; d) the families of the victims; e) other ______." The dependent variable is coded as follows: 0 = other decision-makers; 1 = ICTY.

[b] Gender is coded as follows: 0 = males; 1 = females.

[c] Education is dummy coded with college graduates as the omitted comparison category.

[d] Sample is dummy coded with 1997 Zagreb as the omitted comparison category.

[e] Fairness of decisions is coded as follows: 0 = unfair; 1 = fair.

[f] Punishment purpose is coded as follows: 0 = retribution; 1= deterrence (special and general).

[g] Fairness of procedures is coded as follows: 0 = unfair; 1 = fair.

[h] We created the political scale using the respondents' answers to four questions: "Do you think that the International Tribunal in The Hague resists political pressure?" (four-point scale from "definitely does" to "definitely does not"); "Do you think that the independence of the judges of the International Tribunal in The Hague has been achieved? (four-point scale from "definitely yes" to "definitely no"); "Do you think that the nationality of a judge from the International Tribunal will influence the decision the judge will vote for?" (four-point scale from "definitely yes" to "definitely no"); and "According to your opinion, what role will the politics play in the work and the decisions by the International Tribunal?" (four-point scale from "very important" to "not important at all"). The last two questions were recorded in reverse order to fit the scale. The scale ranged from 4 to 16.

political independence and the fairness of the ICTY's decisions mediate the effect of the places where the data were collected. This suggests that the differences noted in the first model are incorporated in their views about the role of politics and the fairness of decisions. Thus, in that sense, in the case of the former Yugoslavia, the influence of cognitive landscapes can be interpreted as reflecting country-specific political evaluations of the ICTY and its work.

TABLE 3.11

Logistic Coefficients from the Regression of Appropriate Jurisdiction on Serb Respondents' Attitudes and Background Characteristics[a]

	Model 1			Model 2		
	B		s.e.	B		s.e.
Gender[b]	.198		.148	.384	a	.232
Education[c]						
Below high school	−1.199	***	.256	−.639		.421
High school	−.480	*	.200	−.213		.303
Sample[d]						
2004 Belgrade	−.821	*	.319	−.229		.485
2004 Vukovar	.753	*	.342	−.229		.533
2005 Belgrade	−.246		.311	.634		.480
Fairness of decisions[e]				1.669	***	.364
Punishment purpose[f]				−.728	**	.243
Fairness of procedures[g]				1.246	**	.388
Political scale[h]				−.419	***	.069
Constant	−.277		.332	2.309	*	.977
Pseudo R^2	.097			.632		

* $p < .05$; ** $p < .01$; *** $p < .001$; [a] $p < .10$

[a] The question was worded as follows: "Who should [primarily] try the persons accused of war crimes committed in the territory of the former Yugoslavia?" The possible answers were: "a) the courts in the territory of Croatia and Bosnia and Herzegovina where the crimes have been committed; b) the courts of the offender's country or the country whose army force he was a member of; c) the International Tribunal in The Hague; d) the families of the victims; e) other ______." The dependent variable is coded as follows: 0 = other decision-makers; 1 = ICTY.

[b] Gender is coded as follows: 0 = males; 1 = females.

[c] Education is dummy coded with college graduates as the omitted comparison category.

[d] Sample is dummy coded with 1997 Zagreb as the omitted comparison category.

[e] Fairness of decisions is coded as follows: 0 = unfair; 1 = fair.

[f] Punishment purpose is coded as follows: 0 = retribution; 1= deterrence (special and general).

[g] Fairness of procedures is coded as follows: 0 = unfair; 1 = fair.

[h] We created the political scale using the respondents' answers to four questions: "Do you think that the International Tribunal in The Hague resists political pressure?" (four-point scale from "definitely does" to "definitely does not"); "Do you think that the independence of the judges of the International Tribunal in The Hague has been achieved? (four-point scale from "definitely yes" to "definitely no"); "Do you think that the nationality of a judge from the International Tribunal will influence the decision the judge will vote for?" (four-point scale from "definitely yes" to "definitely no"); and "According to your opinion, what role will the politics play in the work and the decisions by the International Tribunal?" (four-point scale from "very important" to "not important at all"). The last two questions were recorded in reverse order to fit the scale. The scale ranged from 4 to 16.

The only exception indicating the location at which the sample was collected was relevant, once additional variables were entered into the model, is a comparison involving Croat respondents (1997 Zagreb sample v. 2004 Vukovar sample). Both samples were collected in Croatia, where Croats are the dominant ethnic group. The differences in the choice of the decision-maker could be explained by variables other than by sample-driven factors. On the one hand, the 1997 Zagreb sample included refugees and displaced persons from different, war-affected parts of Croatia. On the other hand, the most likely explanation is the passage of time and events that happened during the seven-year period between 1997 and 2004. In fact, our prior analyses indicate that the Croats in the latest two samples (2003 Sarajevo and 2004 Vukovar) were much less predisposed to select the ICTY than the two earlier samples of Croats (1997 Zagreb and 2000 Sarajevo) were, both in general and, particularly, for a Croat defendant (*Prosecutor v. Blaškić*, 1996). At the top of the list of relevant factors that could have affected respondents' evaluations of the ICTY are the actual operation of the ICTY, the types of cases tried, the ethnicity of the defendants/victims, and the outcomes of trials. Between 1997 and 2004, the ICTY made a number of decisions, both procedural and substantive, which were discussed intensely in the Croatian media, largely with a negative slant. The trial and the 2000 conviction and sentencing of Tihomir Blaškić to 45 years' imprisonment (ICTY, 2009) created a lot of negative sentiment toward the ICTY across Croatia and among Croats (and others) elsewhere. The majority of our respondents in the 2000 Sarajevo, 2003 Sarajevo, and 2004 Vukovar samples, all of which were collected before the 2004 reversal of the Blaškić decision by the Appeals Chamber (ICTY, 2009), evaluated the Blaškić trial as unfair, regardless of their ethnicity (see Table 2.4).[2] Moreover, the continuous debate between the Croatian government and ICTY representatives regarding the arrest of Naletilić, Martinović, Bobetko, and, especially, General Ante Gotovina (ICTY, 2009), who was viewed as a hero of the homeland war by some groups in Croatia, further colored views about the relationship between the ICTY and the Croats. Although we cannot measure the strength of the effect of these events on the respondents' evaluations of the ICTY, the fact nevertheless remains that these events likely affected how the respondents viewed the ICTY and how likely they were to pick the ICTY as the decision-maker of their choice.

In the second model, the extent to which Croats and Serbs tended to prefer the ICTY over other decision-makers was strongly related to their evaluations of the fairness of the ICTY's decisions and their views of the political independence of the ICTY judges (Tables 3.10-3.11). A one-unit increase on the scale of perceived political influence decreased the odds that the respondents would evaluate the ICTY as fair overall by 0.7 times for both Croats and Serbs.[3] On the other hand, believing that the ICTY decisions were fair increased the odds that the respondents would pick the ICTY as the preferred decision-making body by 5.3 times for Serbs and 4.1 times for Croats.

The evaluation of the ICTY's procedural fairness and views about the purposes of punishment mattered only for Serb respondents. The odds that Serbs who evaluated the

[2] The strong majority of our respondents from these four samples, regardless of their ethnicity, evaluated the original Blaškić decision as unfair (83.3% Croats and 64.8% of Muslims in 2000 Sarajevo sample; 85.2% Croats and 75.8% Muslims in 2003 Sarajevo sample; and 94.3% Croats and 72.0% Serbs in 2004 Vukovar sample).

[3] The odds effects are obtained by exponentiation of the logistic coefficients.

ICTY procedures as fair would pick the ICTY were 3.5 times as high as those of the Serbs who evaluated the ICTY procedures as unfair. Similarly, the odds that the Serbs who selected retribution as the purpose of punishment were 0.5 times as low as those of the Serbs who advocated for deterrence, be it general or specific.

Finally, our analyses indicate that gender is not a significant predictor of the respondents' choice of decision-maker for either Croats or Serbs (Tables 3.10-3.11). Although education was significant for both Croats and Serbs in the initial model—with college-educated respondents being more likely to select the ICTY—once the model was augmented with the political scale and other variables measuring ICTY fairness, the effect of education remained strong only for the Croat respondents, but disappeared for the Serbs. It seems that fairness of decisions, fairness of procedures, purpose of punishment, and the political scale mediate the effect of education for Serb respondents, but not for Croat respondents. In fact, education remains strong for the Croat respondents in the final model, whereas fairness of procedures and purpose of punishment do not reach levels of statistical significance.

CONCLUSION

To be seen as legitimate, justice delivered by the ICTY ultimately also must be seen as local justice. Global legal institutions may need to be particularly sensitive to localized democratic norms. Even though there often is an obvious and pressing need in wartime, and soon thereafter, for international legal assistance, the further challenge is to manage the tempo and terms of a return to local legal institutions. This point has been made before by Karstedt (1998) about two instances in twentieth-century German history, and we have shown that it appears to be true again most recently in the former Yugoslavia.

Individuals' views of the ICTY's legitimacy and fairness are likely affected by the environment in which they reside. Viewed through the theoretical lens of "cognitive landscapes" developed by Sampson and Bartusch (1998), we argue that the key sources of variation in views of the ICTY among its constituencies rest in the socio-political structure of the countries in which they reside. If this argument is extended to incorporate Kapsis's (1978) view of "defended" and "defeated" peoples and settings, the views of the ICTY shared by members of a society depend heavily on how members of the dominant ethnic group in a society evaluate the way the ICTY is treating members of their own ethnicity and members of other ethnicities. In a situation in which the ICTY symbolically communicates who the "defeated" and "defended" are, perceptions of the ICTY and its fairness are related to the actual decisions meted out by the ICTY, as evaluated through the filter of political commentary in the particular country.

Our prior analysis of ICTY decisions indicates that Serbs typically are seen as the "defeated," Muslims/Bosniaks and Albanians as the "defended," and Croats somewhere in between (see Table 2.1). Thus, we would expect that Serbs would be most critical of the ICTY, Muslims/Bosniaks and Albanians least critical, with Croats somewhere between these two extremes.

The results of our analyses provide very strong support for the "cognitive landscapes" paradigm. For example, when asked to pick the appropriate decision-maker for war crimes, the respondents from the "defended" areas—Muslims/Bosniaks from Sarajevo and Albanians from Priština—were the strongest supporters of the ICTY, while respondents from the "defeated" areas—Serbs from Belgrade—were the least supportive of the ICTY. Croats, who seem to be somewhere between "defeated" and defended" in the ICTY's decisions, were also somewhere between the two extremes in terms of their likelihood to pick the ICTY as the appropriate decision-maker. Similarly, Muslims/Bosniaks and Albanians, who were most likely to be viewed as victims, were also more likely to advocate the death penalty than the Serbs were, with the Croats' views again in between. The pattern sometimes changed and Albanians expressed the most positive attitudes, Serbs the most negative, while Muslims/Bosniaks' and Croats' attitudes fit somewhere between the extremes. Regardless of whether they evaluated the ICTY's fairness in general, the fairness of its decisions, or its procedures, the overwhelming majority of Albanians evaluated the ICTY as fair, as did the majority of Muslims/Bosniaks and Croats. By contrast, only a minority of Serb respondents reported positive evaluations.

However, although ethnicity undoubtedly is important in understanding the respondents' evaluations of the ICTY, the complexity of these issues far exceeds simple considerations of ethnicity. Evaluations of the ICTY's fairness are far from being uniform within the same ethnic group, and an in-depth understanding of the phenomenon necessitates inquiry beyond simple cross-ethnicity comparisons.

The concept of "cognitive landscapes" helps us understand ethnic variation in views across sample settings. The analyses show that Serbs' and Croats' assessments of the ICTY's fairness depend not only on their ethnicity, but also on their place of residence. For Croats, these assessments also depend on the time when the data were collected. More than three-quarters of Croats in the 1997 Zagreb and the 2000 Sarajevo samples evaluated the ICTY as fair, while the majority of Croats in the 2003 Sarajevo sample and the 2004 Vukovar sample evaluated the ICTY as unfair. About two-thirds of Serbs in the 2004 Vukovar sample evaluated the ICTY as fair, while two-thirds of Serbs in the 2003 Sarajevo sample and three-quarters of Serbs in the 2004 and 2005 Belgrade samples evaluated the ICTY as unfair.

The final piece of evidence in support of "cognitive landscapes" is that the diversity of views expressed by members of the same ethnic group often corresponds closely to the views expressed by members of other ethnic groups from the same site; the views within the same ethnic group were thus shaped differently depending on whether the respondents resided in the "defeated" or "defended" areas. For example, the overwhelming majority of both Croats and Muslims/Bosniaks in the 2000 Sarajevo sample evaluated the ICTY as fair, while the majority of Croats, Muslims/Bosniaks, and Serbs in the 2003

Sarajevo sample evaluated the ICTY as unfair. Furthermore, our results show that Serbs in Belgrade are most affected by the "defeated" set of views, while the effect of being Serb and defeated is apparently culturally diffused and mitigated in Sarajevo and Vukovar by countervailing cultural beliefs shared with the local, non-Serb groups. In fact, Serbs living in Vukovar expressed views of the ICTY that were even more positive than the views of Croats living in the same city.

As we argued earlier, dominant political groups in a country have the power to shape the cognitive landscapes of public opinion in that country and thus affect how respondents evaluate the ICTY and its work. Once these political views are taken into account, the place of residence may have no separate effect on the respondents' views of the ICTY. Indeed, our multivariate models of factors that shape the Croat and Serb choice of decision-maker clearly show that, with but one exception, the effect of the place of residence on the respondents' choice of the preferred decision-maker is fully mediated once views about the political independence of the ICTY and about the fairness of ICTY's decisions are taken into account. Believing that the ICTY is politically independent and evaluating the decisions meted out by the ICTY as fair are critical components in explaining Croat and Serb choices of the ICTY as the appropriate decision-maker for war-crime cases.

Overall, our results are consistent with Sampson and Bartusch's (1998) notion of "cognitive landscapes" and indicate that "defeated" communities generate more negative views of the justice delivered than "defended" communities do. Although our methodologies encompass different ecological units—neighborhoods in theirs and nations in ours—the common feature is that the environment in which the respondents live shapes their worldview, including their perceptions of the legitimacy of the courts and the justice they deliver. The fact that their members are less likely to exercise political influence and obtain the services and outcomes they want is common to the "defeated" communities, be they neighborhoods, counties, or nations. At the same time, we go beyond the groundwork established by Sampson and Bartusch (1998) and argue that members of these same "defeated" communities, when put in the environments that exhibit characteristics of the more "defended" communities, are less likely to express perceptions of injustice. In short, the specific political environments in which Serbs, Croats, and Muslims/Bosniaks live are of critical importance to the understanding of their evaluations of the ICTY and its delivery of justice.

The government should tell the people what the price of non-cooperation is. The price is the collapse of our country.

[SERBIAN PRIME MINISTER ZORAN DJINDJIĆ, DEMOCRATIC PARTY LEADER, JUNE 13, 2001]

I apologize to all the citizens of Croatia for the injustice done by my people, and I take responsibility for their actions.

[SERBIAN PRESIDENT BORIS TADIĆ, DEMOCRATIC PARTY LEADER, JULY 2007]

4

INDIVIDUAL AND COLLECTIVE RESPONSIBILITY

Structural Pre-Conditionality, Smoking-Gun Evidence, and Collective Responsibility

STRUCTURAL CONDITIONALITY IS the practice of powerful global actors providing financial assistance to countries with the explicit contingency that they take formally agreed-upon actions to reform their national economic, political, and legal systems (Kapur and Naim, 2005). It is an elaboration of the more circumscribed use of economic conditionality by the International Monetary Fund since the 1960s in Latin America (Babb, 2007; Babb and Carruthers, 2008). The terms of structural pre-conditionality may often be more vague than those of its more formal counterpart, but the scope and stakes of its application often are bigger.

Prominent practitioners of structural pre-conditionality notably include the European Union as well as the government of the United States. The precondition of structural reform often is experienced as an intervention into the domestic politics of the targeted, less powerful nations. It could also be understood as an instrument of soft power.

There is continuing debate about whether the strategy of economic conditionality produces intended results (e.g., Stiglitz, 1998), but there is little doubt that, beginning in the 1960s, this strategy became a well-recognized and growing component of international reform and development initiatives (Babb and Buira, 2005). In the 1980s, a more systemically and politically intrusive form of structural conditionality became a cornerstone of the World Bank's adjustment policies for developing economies, despite the increasing worry articulated by Sebastian Mallaby (2004: 182) that "the experience of structural adjustment in the 1980s suggested that conditions seldom worked."

The international community has used this practice of structural pre-conditionality to obtain cooperation by the governments of the former Yugoslavia, particularly Serbia, with ICTY requests. Although the ICTY has indicted members of the Serb, Croat, Muslim/Bosniak, and Albanian ethnic groups, Serbs constitute the majority of the defendants before the ICTY (see Chapter 2). Furthermore, the ICTY prosecutor has charged the sitting head of only one country with war crimes and crimes against humanity: Slobodan Milošević of Serbia (*Prosecutor v. Milošević*, 1999). In addition, several other key political figures from the Serb-governed areas of Bosnia and Herzegovina and Croatia have been charged, such as Radovan Karadžić (*Prosecutor v. Karadžić*, 2009), Biljana Plavšić (*Prosecutor v. Plavšić*, 2002), and Milan Babić (*Prosecutor v. Babić*, 2003). The sheer number of defendants before the ICTY and the prominence of the defendants indicted by the ICTY suggest that the ICTY typically views Serbs as the "defeated group," Muslims/Bosniaks as the "defended group," and Croats somewhere between these two extremes (see Chapter 3).

In this chapter we examine the use of structural pre-conditionality in the EU intervention, widely credited as leading to the arrest of Slobodan Milošević and his transfer to the ICTY. The visibility of the EU's hand in pre-conditioning movement toward an offer of EU membership to Serbia and the ICTY's Internet dissemination of a smoking-gun videotape (shown during the Milošević trial) offer a rare opportunity to assess strategies of political realism and liberal legalism in action simultaneously and transparently. In this case, both approaches presumably sought to advance public support for war crimes and crimes against humanity prosecutions. The precondition was the acceptance of collective responsibility for war crimes and crimes against humanity through the transfer of Serb politicians and soldiers to the ICTY. We analyze how this exercise of structural pre-conditionality mediated and contextualized Serbian politics in ways that established a political foundation first for the Milošević arrest and, subsequently, for the Karadžić arrest.

A MODEL OF STRUCTURAL PRE-CONDITIONALITY AND COLLECTIVE RESPONSIBILITY

The prosecution and punishment of Nazi war criminals at Nuremberg was an implicit precondition for the economic redevelopment of Germany after World War II and, as such, was a forerunner of structural pre-conditionality. The earlier failure to punish war crimes following World War I is thought to be one source of the political and economic calamities that led to the Second World War and its genocidal consequences (Bass, 2000). The connection between the Marshall Plan and the Nuremberg Tribunal was a historic model linking structural pre-conditionality with international criminal law for post-war economic development (Dezalay and Garth, 2006).

A more explicit and contemporary example of structural pre-conditionality in the context of war crimes and crimes against humanity was the transfer of Slobodan Milošević in 2001 to the ICTY. The United States, the European Union, and the World Bank joined in requiring Serbia to transfer Milošević to the ICTY as the precondition for several billion dollars in reconstruction aid and debt relief.

There was no mistaking the interventionist aspect of this use of structural pre-conditionality. U.S. Secretary of State Colin Powell threatened to boycott a donors' conference unless and until Serbia physically transferred Milošević to the ICTY. Powell cancelled scheduled dates for the conference until Serbian Prime Minister Djindjić observed, on June 13, 2001, that "the government should tell the people what the price of non-cooperation is. The price is the collapse of our country" (Fabris Peruničić, 2001: 8). The Serbian government hastily completed its investigation of Milošević by June 18. He was transferred to The Hague on June 29 when the rescheduled opening of the donors' conference was attended by Powell.

Both millions of dollars in financial support and membership in the European Union are powerful motivators that could drive politicians in Serbia to cooperate with the ICTY. However, Dobbels (2009) argues that, until 2005, the driving force behind the structural pre-conditionality for Serbia was primarily U.S. financial aid and that the European Union membership was put on the back burner (Dobbels, 2009: 9):

> Up until 2005, the condition of cooperation with the ICTY was not tied to any specific reward. After the fall of Milošević in 2001, there was a general reluctance in the EU to make the relations with Serbia dependent on cooperation with the ICTY. It was mentioned as one of the conditions in the SAP [Stabilization and Association Process], but the EU never explicitly linked the SAA [Stabilization and Association Agreement] to the fulfillment of the 'ICTY condition.' According to Carla del Ponte, the ICTY chief prosecutor from 1999 to 2008, the only external actor which had an impact on Serbia's cooperation before 2005 was the United States.

Cooperation with the ICTY was listed as a condition of the Stabilization and Association Process, but the EU did not condition the initiation of the Stabilization and Association Agreement on Serbia's full and unconditional cooperation with the ICTY (Dobbels, 2009: 9). On the other hand, the U.S. government established a review mechanism for enforcing cooperation from Serbia. Every year, according to Dobbels (2009: 9), Serbia's cooperation would increase as the deadline approached (Orentlicher, 2008: 30). In 2003, Serbia's cooperation increased even after the deadline had passed; Serbia arrested five suspects and extradited them to the ICTY. This by no means was a coincidence. Serbia had listened to the signals sent by the European Union. Specifically, at its Western Balkans summit in June 2003, the European Union and several potential candidate countries, including Serbia, agreed that providing justice was highly relevant and potential candidate countries pledged their "full and unequivocal co-operation" with the ICTY (EU-Western Balkans Summit Declaration, 2003). However, it was not until 2005 that this European Union pre-conditioning became prominent: On February 1, 2005, EU Enlargement Commissioner Olli Rehn explicitly warned Serbia that full and unconditional cooperation with the ICTY would be the main condition for a positive Feasibility Study assessing the country's readiness to take steps toward EU membership (*SETimes*, 2005; see also Dobbels, 2009: 10). A few months later, Carla del Ponte, then ICTY chief prosecutor, praised Serbia for its cooperation, which subsequently opened the doors for the Stabilization and Association Agreement (Independent, 2005). By the end of 2005, Serbia had extradited 14 indictees to the ICTY (Dobbels, 2009: 27), and it eventually arrested Karadžić in 2008. The arrest and transfer of Radovan Karadžić in August 2008, two weeks after the new, pro-European government took office, was a direct consequence of the government's realization that fuller cooperation indeed was required if Serbia wanted to become a full-fledged member of the EU (Orentlicher, 2008).

The coordination of Colin Powell's threat not to attend the donors' conference with a multilateral strategy of structural pre-conditionality brought about the Milošević transfer, and the EU membership pressure yielded Serbia's further compliance. Boyle and Meyer (2002: 82) observe that "the actual invocation of law is a dramatic step, infrequently taken, although the threat to invoke the law is omnipresent" (see also Meyer and Rowan, 1977; Hagan, 1989; Meyer et al., 1997). Structural pre-conditionality explicitly addresses the problem of noncompliance which Boyle and Meyer prominently associate with international policies and practices involving human rights and war crimes.

German chancellor Gerhard Schröder deftly described the successful example of Serbia's transfer of Milošević to the ICTY as a "dividend of democracy" (Black, 2001: 4), while the *Daily Telegraph* reported that "the west bribed Belgrade to hand over the tyrant" (*Daily Telegraph*, 2001: 21). Still, the *Telegraph* also praised the later-assassinated Serbian Prime Minister, Zoran Djindjić, for his courage and for avoiding bloodshed while accomplishing the transfer (*Daily Telegraph*, 2001: 21).

Meyer (1987: 65) notes that multinational corporations' use of monetary bribes and threats to manipulate states and regimes (for example, to complete sales and contracts) often is seen as the height of illegitimacy, yet when states and regimes use these tactics, they are accepted as legitimate. States effectively have a monopoly over the legal use of such inducements, tying them into legally binding structural agreements, with the result that they "bribe each other routinely, and employ all the standard political manipulations." The multinational sponsorship of the Serbian donors' conference was used to make the monetary manipulations appear more legitimate (see Ikenberry, 2001). However, the multinational involvement backed by U.S. leadership also made the conditions more enforceable and, in this sense, more coercive. Subsequently, the longer-term issue became Serbian accession to the European Union. Surprisingly little theoretical or empirical attention has been given to structural pre-conditionality in such circumstances.

Structural pre-conditionality in the context of war crimes and crimes against humanity intervention combines elements of political economic realism (e.g., when desperately needed aid or trade benefits are made contingent by powerful global actors) with liberal legalism (e.g., when transfers of defendants for trials follow filings of indictments and the issuance of warrants). As realists would predict, externally imposed economic conditions often strongly affect the politics of the targeted nation. The costs and benefits in social and political capital often are realized through the interpretation of key legal events and evidence used to justify the imposition of the structural conditions. The crucial elements in the Serbian example played out over a three-year time frame and through the public responses observed during the summer of 2005 (see Figure 4.1).

As noted, a key element was the requirement of the European Commission that Serbia make high-profile transfers of indicted and arrested war crimes and/or crimes against humanity suspects to the ICTY as a precondition for movement toward admission to the European Union. This was the "visible hand" with which the calculated political realism of the EU simultaneously promised and withheld much-needed economic support to Serbia. The challenge to this initiative was the opposition to these arrests and transfers by parts of the Serbian public.

A parallel element was the very public airing at the ICTY of a gruesome videotape displaying the violent participation of a feared Serbian paramilitary unit in the Srebrenica massacre. This "smoking gun" videotape evidence was seen throughout the former Yugoslavia in June of 2005 and, for the first time, visibly tied Slobodan Milošević's Serbian paramilitary forces to this massacre in neighboring Bosnia and Herzegovina. The ICTY expected this evidence could fulfill the liberal legal hope that a procedurally correct airing of unimpeachable evidence of direct participation in genocidal violence would turn Serbian public opinion in favor of its prosecutorial policies. These prosecutions attributed collective command responsibility for war crimes and crimes against humanity to well-known former political and military leaders.

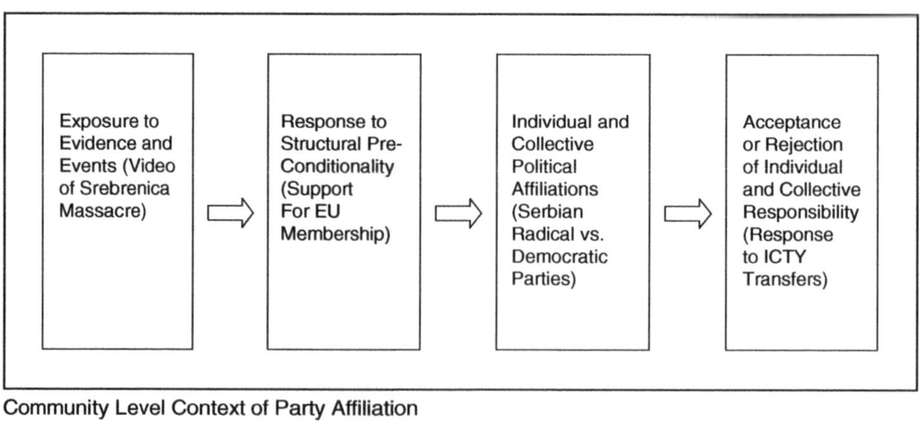

FIGURE 4.1 Model of the Effects of Structural Pre-Conditionality

The relative roles of this evidence and the conditional context in which it was presented can tell us a great deal about the ways and means by which elements of legal liberalism and political realism are mixed to oppose or create new forms of legal capital through international criminal law and its institutions. Our thesis is that the EU preconditionality mediated and contextualized the terms of domestic Serbian politics in ways that demonstrate the importance of strongly led, multilateral support for the use of this structural strategy of war-crimes intervention.

THE SMOKING GUN AND THE VISIBLE HAND

The assassination in March 2003 of Zoran Djindjić, the reformist Serbian prime minister who mobilized the transfer of Slobodan Milošević to the ICTY, was a chillingly realistic reminder of the risks of cooperation in war-crimes arrests and prosecutions. Djindjić was shot on the day he was to sign new warrants for high-level arrests (Simpson, 2003: 1). The Serbian Radical Party (SRS) capitalized on the anxiety following the assassination and formed a coalition with Milošević's old party. The SRS was led by Vojislav Šešelj, the former commander of the "White Eagles," a paramilitary group equipped by the Serbian Ministry of Internal Affairs during the war in Bosnia and Herzegovina. At the time, the public mood in Serbia was nationalistic and uncompromising. A May 2005 survey revealed that only about one-half of Serbs believed the massacre of 8,000 Muslims/Bosniaks in 1995 in Srebrenica actually took place (*Agence France Presse*, 2005), much less that Serbian forces participated in it.

Smoking-gun evidence of the Srebrenica massacre and Serbian involvement emerged in the form of a videotape obtained in December 2004 by the ICTY from a Serbian human rights activist. The videotape was shown as evidence in the Milošević trial on June 1, 2005, and then was seen more widely in Serbia through state-run as well as more liberal news media outlets and, for days afterwards, throughout the former Yugoslavia. The 12-minute videotape featured six prisoners who were executed individually and on camera, with the bullets seen entering the bodies and final shots delivered to the heads of the fallen victims (Wood, 2005b). Individual members of a paramilitary group known as the "Scorpions" and directly linked to the Serbian police service were clearly identified, later named from their appearance in the videotape, and prosecuted (Orentlicher, 2008). The videotape indelibly formed the connection between the massacre and the Serbian police service over which Milošević and his chain of command held clear authority. Daniel Williams wrote in the *Washington Post* (June 25, 2005) that the videotape "ripped away the veil of secrecy and denial of Serbian military operations in Bosnia during the 1992–1995 war.... No longer was it possible to label atrocity tales as Bosnian Muslim propaganda amplified by inventive foreign correspondents, as many Serbs had done for a decade." Still, the tape did not transform public attitudes in Serbia; one-third of a sample of surveyed Serbians remained convinced in a mid-June poll that the videotape was inauthentic (Kampschror, 2005).

As the ICTY was preparing to show the videotape in court, the EU announced that it was ready to start negotiations with Serbia on accession. The first steps were approved at an annual meeting of EU foreign ministers in April 2005. Over the preceding three months, the Serbian government had helped to transfer ten indicted suspects, mostly Bosnian Serbs, to the ICTY. The Serbian government linked these transfers directly to negotiations with the EU on a preliminary agreement that would be the first step toward membership. The EU's spokesperson nonetheless emphasized that full membership was conditional on the arrest of all indicted war crimes and crimes against humanity suspects, including the two most wanted suspects, Radovan Karadžić and Ratko Mladić. Even discussion of this precondition as a possibility represented a departure from earlier indications by the Serbian government that arrests would "enrage public opinion, destabilize the government and encourage Serbia's nationalist opposition" (Wood, 2005a).

The simultaneous appearance of the smoking-gun videotape evidence and the visibly and explicitly conditional offer of EU membership presents a rare opportunity to observe carefully the combined effect of political and economic pre-conditionality with eyewitness legal evidence on the acceptance of war crimes and crimes against humanity prosecutions. This public acceptance is a form of legal capital that liberal legal institutions require and are expected to nurture as a part of nation-building and democratization efforts. Yet, we have theorized above that structural pre-conditionality can be an intrusive wedge that mediates and contextualizes domestic politics. We now examine this process in relation to the pre-conditional offer of EU membership and the exposure to videotape evidence of the Srebrenica massacre during the summer of 2005 in the capital of Serbia.

THE BELGRADE SURVEY

The 2005 Belgrade survey was conducted by a Belgrade affiliate of Gallup International using a structured survey instrument we designed to measure attitudes toward the Srebrenica videotape, membership in the EU, and the work of the ICTY (see Chapter 1).[1] The survey was fielded after the March 2003 assassination of Zoran Djindjić, before the death of Slobodan Milošević in March of 2006, and about three years before the arrest of Radovan Karadžić in 2008.

[1] The survey is a multi-stage random-probability household survey of the adult population (18 years and older) of Belgrade in the first week of August 2005. The data include 507 respondents in 13 Belgrade municipalities sampled from 34 sampling points randomly chosen using a probability proportional to their share of voters, with 15 respondents randomly selected, using every fourth household surrounding each sampling point. The household response rate to the survey was 81.3 percent.

Because older and less-educated Serbs form a core source of support for nationalist policies hostile to the ICTY, it is essential that the characteristics of the sample closely mirror the characteristics of the general population. Indeed, our 2005 Belgrade sample closely replicates the demographic characteristics of the Belgrade municipality as accounted for by the 2002 census (Statistical Office, 2002; Statistical Office, 2003). Women constitute about one-half of both the sample and the 2002 census population in Belgrade (Table 4.1). The age demographics of the sample and the census population are similar: about one-third are individuals between the ages of 18 and 35 (35.7 percent and 32.2 percent, respectively), about another quarter are individuals between the ages of 36 and 50 (27.8 percent and 26.1 percent, respectively), and more than one-third are individuals above 50 years of age (36.5 percent and 41.7 percent, respectively; Table 4.1). The majority of both the sample and the Belgrade population have a high-school education (60 percent and 57.5 percent, respectively; Table 4.1). Furthermore, the overwhelming majority of the sample and the Belgrade population are Serb (Table 4.1).

POLITICAL PARTY AFFILIATION AND STRUCTURAL PRE-CONDITIONALITY

The political scene in Serbia is dominated by several parties and characterized by the fact that no party is powerful enough to control political events completely. Until recently, the Serbian Radical Party (SRS) formed a coalition with a wing of Milošević's old party. Vojislav Šešelj, who initially led the SRS, is being tried by the ICTY as the former

TABLE 4.1

Sample and Population Demographic Characteristics

	Belgrade Sample	Belgrade Municipality
Gender		
Women	48.1%	53.2%
Age		
18–35	35.7%	32.2%
36–50	27.8%	26.1%
50+	13.6%	14.0%
Education		
Below High School	26.4%	28.5%
High School	60.0%	57.5%
College	13.6%	14.0%
Ethnicity		
Serb	96.0%	92.9%

commander of the "White Eagles," a paramilitary group equipped by the Serbian Ministry of Internal Affairs during the war in Bosnia and Herzegovina. Until September 8, 2008, the SRS was led by Tomislav Nikolić. Nikolić parted ways with Šešelj and eventually formed his own party called the Serbian Progressive Party (SNS), which currently holds 21 seats in Parliament. SRS remains strongly opposed to cooperation with the ICTY and currently holds 57 seats in Parliament.

On the opposite end of the political spectrum is the Democratic Party (DS), led by Zoran Djindjić until his assassination, currently holding 64 seats in Parliament. The DS is currently led by Boris Tadić, who serves now as president of Serbia in a coalition with Milošević's old Socialist Party of Serbia (SPS). The Democratic Party of Serbia (DSS) is a party that just recently dropped out of the governing coalition. It currently has 21 seats in Parliament. Of the two leading Serbian political parties, the DS is more supportive of international criminal law and the ICTY. The SPS, in its new coalition with the DS (together holding 78 seats in Parliament), has displayed a new willingness to acquiesce in arrests and transfers to the ICTY.

G17+, originally established as a nonprofit organization in 1997 with support by the U.S. government through the National Endowment for Democracy, is led by Mladjan Djinkić, the Minister of Economy and Regional Affairs. In 2004, G17+ formed a minority government with DSS, but Djinkić led the G17+ out of the coalition in 2006, apparently because of the Koštunica's government's failure to catch the ICTY indictee, Ratko Mladić, and resume talks with the EU. G17+ currently has 24 seats in Parliament.

The issue of arresting and transferring indictees to the ICTY, particularly top political and military leaders, has remained highly sensitive and explosive. For a long time, Mladić and Karadžić have been viewed as national heroes among both the populace and elites in Serbia (Matić, 2004: 11–12), and the subsequent arrest and transfer of Karadžić to the ICTY in 2008 resulted in demonstrations across Serbia. However, the level of resistance toward cooperation with the ICTY has varied over time, with visible increases in public acceptance of the need to cooperate with the ICTY at the time of Milošević's extradition in June 2001—two-thirds approved the transfer (Matić, 2004: 11)—and after the Djindjić murder in 2003 (Šaponja-Hadžić, 2003). Whereas in December 2000, 72 percent of surveyed Serbs thought that the ICTY threatened the safety of Serbs, that percentage decreased to 40 percent in May 2003. At the same time, another survey (Bandović, 2004: 95-96) indicated that 59 percent of the respondents in 2003 still had strong animosity against the ICTY and insisted that Serbia should not cooperate with it.

The views of the ICTY and the extent of opposition to cooperation with the ICTY are related directly to the respondents' political views. The highest level of skepticism that the ICTY can hold unbiased trials is expressed among supporters of the SRS and DSS—78 percent and 79 percent, respectively (Belgrade Center for Human Rights, 2006: 44), and the lowest level of skepticism prevails among supporters of the DS and G17+ (52 percent and 45 percent, respectively). Similarly, supporters of the SRS and DSS overwhelmingly think it would be better to hold trials for war crimes in Serbia rather than at the ICTY (89 percent and 83 percent, respectively), compared, for example, to the mild preference expressed by the supporters of DS and G17+ (58 percent and 50 percent, respectively) (Belgrade Center for Human Rights, 2006: 54). Furthermore, opposition to Serbia's cooperation with the ICTY is by far the strongest among supporters of the SRS (46 percent said that Serbia should not cooperate, regardless of the costs) and the weakest among supporters of the DS (3 percent) and G17+ (8 percent) (Belgrade Center for Human Rights, 2006: 34). Among the respondents who said that the country should cooperate with the ICTY, the majority of SRS supporters (58 percent) and about one-half of DSS supporters (45 percent) argued that this should be done only to the extent necessary to avoid sanctions, while the DS and G17+ supporters tended to view cooperation either as the precondition of Serbia's reintegration into the world (46 percent and 50 percent, respectively) or as a way of achieving justice (28 percent and 30 percent; calculations made based on the data by the Belgrade Center for Human Rights, 2006: 34). Furthermore, about one-half each of supporters of SRS and DS (47 percent and 50 percent, respectively) said that their party's view of cooperation with the ICTY has an effect on whether they would vote for the party (Belgrade Center for Human Rights, 2006: 35).

The population of Serbia seems to be quick to criticize the ICTY, yet the majority typically reported being unfamiliar with the details of its work; a survey by the Belgrade Center for Human Rights indicated that 72 percent of the respondents in 2005 and 57 percent in 2006 reported knowing "little" or "very little" about the organization and operation of the ICTY (2006: 11). How much they thought they knew about the ICTY is related to their political views: supporters of the SRS seem to have been the most likely to say that they were familiar with the ICTY, while supporters of the DS were the least likely to say this. Specifically, while only 38 percent of the respondents supporting the SRS and 48 percent of the respondents supporting the DSS reported knowing nothing or very little about the work of the ICTY, 62 percent of the DS supporters and 61 percent of the G17+ supporters reported little or no knowledge of the ICTY (Belgrade Center for Human Rights, 2006: 15).

We explored political party affiliation among the respondents in our 2005 Belgrade survey. More than one-quarter of our sample (26.2 percent) supported the Serbian Radical Party (SRS), which is strongly opposed to cooperation with the ICTY. Nearly one-fifth (19.3 percent) supported the Democratic Party (DS), which is the most supportive of international criminal law and the ICTY. About one-tenth of our respondents (11.1 percent) were supporters of the Strength of Serbia Movement (PSS). Although PSS did not win any seats in the 2007 parliamentary elections, Bogoljub Karić, the party leader, came in third in the first round of the 2004 presidential elections. The Democratic Party of Serbia (DSS) is the final major party, with less than 10 percent support (8.5 percent). Supporters of G17+, Milošević's old Socialist Party of Serbia (SPS), and Vuk Drašković's Serbian Renewal Movement (SPO) had few supporters among our respondents (about 3 percent each).

Political party affiliation was directly related to respondents' choice of the appropriate decision-maker for war crimes and crimes against humanity, both in general and for specific cases (Table 4.2). When asked to select among the ICTY, local courts in Bosnia and Herzegovina/Croatia, local courts in Serbia/Republika Srpska, and families of the victims, between one-half and two-thirds of the supporters of G17+ and particularly the DS chose the ICTY as their preferred decision-maker (see Table 4.2). On the other hand, a miniscule percentage of the supporters of the SRS and SPS—the most radical parties and least supportive of the ICTY—made the same choice (Table 4.2). Supporters of the DSS and PSS were somewhere in between, with about 20 percent to 30 percent selecting the ICTY.

We also asked a series of specific questions about the ICTY, covering evaluation of its decision-making and procedural fairness, estimates of the ICTY's political independence, and the role the judges' nationality may play in the work and the decisions made by the ICTY (see Table 4.3). The results are quite uniform across the five questions: Supporters of the most pro-Western parties, DS and G17+, expressed the most positive views of the ICTY, while supporters of the most radical parties, SPS and SRS, expressed the most negative views of the ICTY (Table 4.3). For example, the majority of the respondents who supported the DS and G17+ evaluated both the ICTY in general and its decisions and procedures as fair, while only one in ten respondents who supported the SPS and SRS shared this assessment (Table 4.2).

We next focus specifically on the structural pre-conditionality of the EU membership offer and the dissemination of the smoking-gun videotape in building opposition or acceptance for the collective command responsibility of Serbian leaders. Political party affiliation was strongly related to the way respondents evaluated the necessity and importance of Serbia joining the EU (see Table 4.4). Supporters of the two most pro-Western parties, DS and G17+, overwhelmingly supported the idea that Serbia should join the EU, said they would vote for it if the referendum were held today, and thought EU membership an important issue. On the other hand, although supporters of the two most radical parties, namely, the SPS and SRS, recognized the importance of joining the EU and their hypothetical vote would have been in support of joining, their support for the idea was not as strong (see Table 4.4).

SMOKING-GUN EVIDENCE AND PERCEPTIONS OF ITS AUTHENTICITY

The videotape, shown first as evidence in the Milošević trial on June 1, 2005, and subsequently through state-run as well as more liberal news media outlets in Serbia, is the smoking-gun evidence of the Serbian involvement in the Srebrenica massacre. Although the videotape shows the executions of six men, it is evidence submitted to illustrate several points, one of which is that this killing was part of a larger, organized event in which several thousand boys and men were killed.

TABLE 4.2

Appropriate Decision-Maker by Political Party

	DS (N=88)	G17+ (N=14)	DSS (N=40)	PSS (N=51)	SPS (N=14)	SRS (N=124)	Undecided/ Would Not Respond (N=85)	*Chi-Square*	*Phi*
Appropriate Decision-Maker[a]									
% ICTY	63.6%	50.0%	27.5%	25.5%	7.1%	4.0%	17.6%	105.9***	.505
Decision-Maker for Milošević[b]									
% ICTY	59.8%	50.0%	30.3%	21.6%	9.1%	2.8%	16.3%	93.1***	.494
Decision-Maker for Karadžić and Mladić[c]									
% ICTY	64.4%	50.0%	30.3%	27.7%	9.1%	4.1%	18.9%	90.9***	.501
Decision-Maker for Galić[d]									
% ICTY	65.5%	53.8%	29.7%	26.5%	10.0%	5.5%	19.2%	94.0***	.497

*** $p < .001$

[a] The question was worded as follows: "Who should try the persons accused of war crimes committed in the territory of the former Yugoslavia?" The possible answers were: "a) the courts in the territory of Croatia and Bosnia and Herzegovina where the crimes have been committed; b) the courts of the offender's country or the country whose army force he was a member of; c) the International Tribunal in The Hague; d) the families of the victims; e) other ______."

[b] The question was worded as follows: "In your opinion, who should try Slobodan Milošević?" The possible answers were: "a) courts in Bosnia and Herzegovina; b) courts in Serbia/Republika Srpska; c) the International Tribunal in The Hague; d) the families of the victims; e) other ______."

[c] The question was worded as follows: "In your opinion, who should try Radovan Karadžić and Ratko Mladić?" The possible answers were: "a) courts in Bosnia and Herzegovina; b) courts in Serbia/Republika Srpska; c) the International Tribunal in The Hague; d) the families of the victims; e) other ______."

[d] The question was worded as follows: "In your opinion, who should try Stanislav Galić (the major general who was the commander of the Romanija Corps that maintained the siege of Sarajevo from 1992 to 1994)?" The possible answers were: "a) courts in Bosnia and Herzegovina; b) courts in Serbia/Republika Srpska; c) the International Tribunal in The Hague; d) the families of the victims; e) other ______."

Continued

TABLE 4.2

Continued

	DS (N=88)	G17+ (N=14)	DSS (N=40)	PSS (N=51)	SPS (N=14)	SRS (N=124)	Undecided/ Would Not Respond (N=85)	*Chi-Square*	*Phi*
Decision-Maker for Jokić[e]									
% ICTY	64.3%	58.3%	26.3%	28.6%	18.2%	6.3%	22.1%	86.0***	.475
Decision-Maker for Mrkšić, Radić, and Šljivančanin[f]									
% ICTY	66.7%	50.0%	25.6%	26.0%	8.3%	3.6%	19.0%	105.2***	.521
Decision-Maker for Stanković[g]									
% ICTY	67.1%	53.8%	32.5%	28.8%	7.7%	5.3%	16.5%	105.5***	.516

[e] The question was worded as follows: "In your opinion, who should try Miodrag Jokić (the admiral who led the shelling of Dubrovnik in 1991)?" The possible answers were: "a) courts in Croatia; b) courts in Serbia/Republika Srpska; c) the International Tribunal in The Hague; d) the families of the victims; e) other ______."

[f] The question was worded as follows: "In your opinion, who should try Mile Mrkšić, Miroslav Radić, and Veselin Šljivančanin (accused of participating in the criminal enterprise in which the Serb forces after the fall of Vukovar mistreated and killed non-Serbs from the Vukovar Hospital)?" The possible answers were: "a) courts in Croatia; b) courts in Serbia/Republika Srpska; c) the International Tribunal in The Hague; d) the families of the victims; e) other ______."

[g] The question was worded as follows: "In your opinion, who should try Radovan Stanković (accused of being a soldier in charge of a house in Foča in which Muslim women and girls were repeatedly raped and sexually assaulted)?" The possible answers were: "a) courts in Bosnia and Herzegovina; b) courts in Serbia/Republika Srpska; c) the International Tribunal in The Hague; d) the families of the victims; e) other ______."

TABLE 4.3

Views of the ICTY by Political Party

	DS (N=97)	G17+ (N=15)	DSS (N=43)	PSS (N=56)	SPS (N=17)	SRS (N=132)	Undecided/ Would Not Respond (N=103)	*Chi-Square*	*Phi*
ICTY Fair[a]									
% Yes	53.3%	60.0%	23.3%	25.0%	11.8%	9.1%	21.4%	75.0***	.403
ICTY's Decisions Fair[b]									
% Fair	58.8%	53.3%	20.9%	26.8%	5.9%	8.3%	17.6%	90.0***	.441
ICTY's Procedures Fair[c]									
% Fair	59.8%	46.7%	25.6%	26.8%	5.9%	9.0%	21.4%	82.9***	.423
Judge's Nationality Influences the ICTY Decision[d]									
% No	69.1%	53.3%	41.9%	34.5%	17.6%	27.3%	35.0%	49.3***	.327
Independence of the ICTY Achieved[e]									
% Yes	49.5%	60.0%	18.6%	23.2%	5.9%	10.6%	17.5%	64.4***	.373

*** $p < .001$

[a] The question was worded as follows: "Do you think that the International Tribunal conducts the trials correctly and fairly and makes just decisions?" The possible answers were: "a) definitely yes; b) yes; c) no; d) definitely no."

[b] The question was worded as follows: "Do you think that the *decisions/verdicts* by the International Tribunal are fair?" The possible answers were: "a) very fair; b) fair; c) unfair; d) very unfair."

[c] The question was worded as follows: "Do you think that the *procedure* by the International Tribunal is fair?" The possible answers were: "a) very fair; b) fair; c) unfair; d) very unfair."

[d] The question was worded as follows: "Do you think that the nationality of a judge from the International Tribunal will influence the decision the judge will vote for?" The possible answers were: "a) definitely yes; b) yes; c) no; d) definitely no."

[e] The question was worded as follows: "Do you think that the independence of the judges of the International Tribunal in The Hague has been achieved?" The possible answers were: "a) definitely yes; b) yes; c) no; d) definitely no."

TABLE 4.4

Joining the European Union by Political Party

	DS (Nv=97)	G17+ (N=15)	DSS (N=43)	PSS (N=56)	SPS (N=17)	SRS (N=132)	Undecided/ Would Not Respond (N=103)	*Chi-Square*	*Phi*
Vote on Referendum[a]									
% Yes to Join the EU	99.0%	100.0%	90.5%	87.5%	70.6%	59.8%	74.0%	64.6***	.374
Importance of Joining the EU[b]									
% Important	99.0%	100.0%	85.7%	87.5%	64.7%	60.6%	76.9%	60.7***	.362
Serbia Should Remain Independent and Not Join the EU[c]									
% Disagree	88.4%	86.7%	83.3%	69.1%	41.2%	45.4%	59.6%	60.2***	.363

*** $p < .001$

[a] The question was worded as follows: "If the referendum were held today, would you vote for Serbia and Montenegro to join the European Union?" The possible answers were: "a) definitely yes; b) yes; c) no; d) definitely no."

[b] The question was worded as follows: "In your opinion, how important it is that Serbia and Montenegro join the European Union?" The possible answers were: "a) very important; b) important; c) not important; d) not important at all."

[c] The question was worded as follows: "It is better that Serbia and Montenegro remain independent from outside pressures than join the European Union." The possible answers were: "a) strongly agree; b) agree; c) disagree; d) strongly disagree."

The smoking-gun videotape is probably one of the most widely disseminated pieces of evidence of the war crimes and crimes against humanity committed during the wars in the former Yugoslavia. However, only about 70 percent of the respondents from a representative national sample collected annually between 2004 and 2006 claimed to have heard about the "killings of a large number of Muslim civilians in Srebrenica" (Belgrade Center for Human Rights, 2006: 25).

The videotape did not transform public attitudes in Serbia; one-third of a sample of surveyed Serbians remained convinced in a mid-June 2005 poll that the videotape was inauthentic (Kamoschror, 2005), and only about one-half of the respondents in the Belgrade Human Rights survey believed that a large number of Muslim/Bosniak civilians were killed in Srebrenica (Belgrade Center for Human Rights, 2006: 25). In fact, the percentage of those who said they believed that the massacre in Srebrenica happened did not change substantially from the time of the two surveys conducted in July 2004 and April 2005, before the videotape had aired, to the time of the survey conducted in December 2006, one year after the videotape had aired (48 percent, 50 percent, and 50 percent, respectively) (Belgrade Center for Human Rights, 2006: 25).

We asked the respondents in our study—a representative sample of the Belgrade population—to answer several questions about the videotape and the massacre in Srebrenica. The survey was conducted in August 2005, two months after the videotape had been shown during the Milošević trial and had become widely available for public consumption. These two months provided plenty of opportunities for the respondents to see the videotape through various outlets, including TV stations and the Internet. Indeed, almost all respondents in our sample, regardless of their political party affiliation, said that they had heard about the videotape (see Table 4.5). Almost 70 percent of the respondents had heard about the videotape from TV stations ("RTS," "TV B92," "BK Telecom," "RTV Pink," and "RTV Studio B"), about 5 percent heard about it in the newspapers ("Politika," "Večernje novosti"), 8.5 percent learned of it from friends and relatives, and 13 percent from other media sources. In fact, more than two-thirds of the respondents also reported watching the videotape themselves (see Table 4.5).

Views about the authenticity of the videotape varied greatly with political orientation: respondents favoring DSS and the two most pro-Western parties, DS and G17+, were most likely to say that the videotape was authentic, while respondents from the two most anti-Western parties, SPS and SRS, were the least likely to say this (only a minority of the respondents who supported the SPS and SRS said that the videotape was authentic).

For more than four-fifths of our respondents, the videotape had no effect on how they viewed the war in the former Yugoslavia (see Table 4.5): less than one-fifth said that their opinion changed after they had watched the videotape. The extent to which the videotape had an influence on the respondents' views of the war is related to their political orientation. Whereas about one-third of the respondents favoring the most pro-Western parties, DS and G17+, reported changing their opinion, fewer than one in ten of our respondents favoring the least pro-Western parties, SPS and SRS, reported the same (see Table 4.5).

TABLE 4.5

Views about the Videotape by Political Party

	Sample	DS (N=97)	G17+ (N=15)	DSS (N=43)	PSS (N=56)	SPS (N=17)	SRS (N=132)	Undecided/ Would Not Respond (N=103)	*Chi-Square*	*Phi*
Heard about the Videotape[a]										
% Yes	93.7%	95.8%	86.7%	97.7%	94.6%	100.0%	92.4%	91.2%	5.87	.113
Seen the Videotape[b]										
% Yes	70.7%	80.2%	66.7%	83.7%	64.3%	100.0%	61.8%	66.7%	21.7**	.217
Believe Tape Is Authentic[c]										
% Yes	55.9%	80.0%	66.7%	71.4%	50.0%	17.6%	40.6%	53.8%	50.3***	.337
Opinion Changed after Watching the Videotape[d]										
% Yes	18.8%	30.9%	33.3%	21.4%	17.6%	5.9%	9.3%	19.4%	20.7**	.217

*** $p < .001$; ** $p < .01$; * $p < .05$

[a] The question was worded as follows: "Have you heard about the video of the executions near Srebrenica that has been aired recently as part of the Milošević trial?" The possible answers were: "a) yes; b) no."

[b] The question was worded as follows: "Have you seen the video?" The possible answers were: "a) yes; b) no."

[c] The question was worded as follows: "Do you believe that the video is authentic?" The possible answers were: "a) yes; b) no."

[d] The question was worded as follows: "Has your opinion about the war in the former Yugoslavia changed as a consequence of watching the video?" The possible answers were: "a) definitely yes; b) yes; c) no; d) definitely no."

COLLECTIVE RESPONSIBILITY

The Milošević regime (1987–2000) could be characterized as a "populist criminal regime" (see Dimitrijević, 2008: 8), in which normalization of crime occurs and there is "a high level of ideological and practical agreement about crime." Dimitrijević (2008: 9) describes as it as follows:

> Crime committed by these regimes can be identified as 'collective crimes'; acts committed by a significant number of group members in the name of all group members and against individuals identified as 'outsiders.' This type of crime cannot be committed by an individual, a random group or a collective understood as a mere sum of its members. It presupposes the collective intention to perpetrate a particular type of misdeed, collective awareness about the nature of the misdeed, organized effort to realize the intention (i.e., to carry out the chosen criminal action) and, finally, collective awareness about its consequences [footnotes omitted].

Thus, the construction of collective crime progresses through three stages. The third stage, particularly relevant for this chapter, is the joint, collective awareness of the consequences of the crime. Milošević and his regime projected the image of Serbia as a victimized nation with a desperate need to mobilize its resources on a nationalistic platform, protect its rights, and ultimately achieve the goal of establishing the "Greater Serbia." The BBC reported that "TV viewers here were fed a diet of propaganda which portrayed Serbs as the greatest victims of the conflict" (Prodger, 2005). The government, through massive propaganda, presented both its actions and their consequences as politically legitimate and morally right (see, e.g., Dimitrijević, 2008: 9). Consequently, the dominant view was either complete denial of the possibility that "our side" engaged in atrocities, or refusal to label such activities as criminal.

As discussed earlier, the international community was pushing Serbia to address its past and even preconditioned financial aid on cooperation with the ICTY. Although the situation potentially could have changed with the victory of the Serbian Democratic Opposition in the first post-Milošević elections, the political parties joined in electoral victory did not reach a clear agreement on what to do about the past. Eventually, despite attempts to confront the past and cooperate with the ICTY, the view of Serbia as a victim state persevered (see, e.g., Dimitrijević, 2008: 11–12). Not coincidentally, Zoran Djindjić, the first post-Milošević prime minister and leader of DS, the most dominant party in the coalition that won in the 2000 parliamentary elections, was assassinated in 2003.

Public opinion polls conducted in Serbia in the 2000s reflect this general attitude of Serbian victimhood with a broad denial of any victimization by the Serbs and a massive acceptance of Serb victimization. Indeed, several surveys by the Belgrade Center for Human Rights and the Strategic Marketing Group conducted in the period 2001–2006 show that, compared with the atrocities committed by the Serbs, respondents from representative national samples clearly were more likely to report hearing about atrocities involving Serbs as victims, more likely to believe that these events really happened, and more likely to label them as crimes (Belgrade Center for Human Rights, 2006: 25–31). In fact, only when Serbs were victims did the majority of the respondents in all surveys label these crimes as war crimes; the majority of the respondents were not willing to label atrocities involving non-Serb victims—some as prominent as the killings in Srebrenica, the seizure of Sarajevo, and the shelling of Dubrovnik—as crimes, and instead justified them as necessities of war (Belgrade Center for Human Rights, 2006: 25–31). Another relevant finding is the fact that the percentage of the respondents who had heard about particular events, believed that they really happened, or were willing to label them as criminal, remained the same over time and, in some instances, in fact, *decreased* over time (see, e.g., Belgrade Center for Human Rights, 2006: 29–31).

The topic of collective responsibility prompts us to explore in more detail public views about incidents in which Serbs were the perpetrators. One such prominent event is the killing of 8,000 Muslim/Bosniak men and boys in Srebrenica in 1995 and the subsequent airing of the smoking-gun videotape evidence. Even for such a prominent event, only about 70 percent of the respondents from a representative national sample collected annually between 2004 and 2006 claimed to have heard about the "killings of a large number of Muslim civilians in Srebrenica" (Belgrade Center for Human Rights, 2006: 25).

The percentage of the respondents who reported hearing about other atrocities involving non-Serb victims is smaller. Between 60 percent and 70 percent of respondents reported hearing that many civilians in Sarajevo were killed by snipers and that a large number of Albanian civilians were found in the mass graves in Batajnica, Suva Reka, and Perućac (Belgrade Center for Human Rights, 2006: 25). About 50 to 60 percent of respondents heard that Yugoslav People's Army (JNA) bombed Dubrovnik, that Sarajevo was under siege for more than 1,000 days, that Muslims/Bosniaks were abducted from the trains and cars in Štrpci and Sjeverin and subsequently killed, and that paramilitary units and JNA killed civilians in Vukovar (Belgrade Center for Human Rights, 2006: 25). Finally, between 25 and 45 percent of respondents reported hearing that, when NATO bombed Serbian troops in 1999, documents were taken away from the Albanians before they were cleansed from the area, that JNA soldiers looted and burned houses in the vicinity of Dubrovnik, and that paramilitary troops from Serbia were killing civilians in Bjeljina in 1992 (Belgrade Center for Human Rights, 2006: 25).

Even smaller percentages of the respondents reported that they believed these events really happened. Only about one-half of the respondents in the Belgrade Human Rights survey believed that highly publicized events, such as the killing of a large number of Muslim/Bosniak civilians in Srebrenica, actually happened (Belgrade Center for Human Rights, 2006: 25). When asked whether they believed that other, less-publicized events happened, the majority of the respondents were convinced that many civilians in Sarajevo were killed by snipers (57 percent in 2004, 58 percent in 2005, and 60 percent in 2006) (Belgrade Center for Human Rights, 2006: 25). Between 40 and 48 percent also believed that Sarajevo was indeed under siege for more than 1,000 days (Belgrade Center for Human Rights, 2006: 25). For all other events, less than one-third of the respondents reported believing these events had occurred, and, in fact, fewer than 20 percent of them believed that JNA bombed Mostar, that JNA soldiers looted and burned houses in the vicinity of Dubrovnik, and that paramilitary troops from Serbia were killing civilians in Bjeljina in 1992 (Belgrade Center for Human Rights, 2006: 25).

Finally, a still smaller percentage of the respondents recognized these atrocities as war crimes and labeled them as such; in no case did the majority of the respondents do so (Belgrade Center for Human Rights, 2006: 25). Between 30 and 45 percent recognized as war crimes the killings of a large number of Muslim/Bosniak men and boys in Srebrenica, the sniper killings of many civilians in Sarajevo during the siege, and the abductions of Muslims/Bosniaks from the trains and cars in Štrpci and Sjeverin and their subsequent murder (Belgrade Center for Human Rights, 2006: 25). Between one-quarter and one-third of the respondents recognized the killing of Albanian civilians in Batajnica, Suva Reka, and Perućac (Belgrade Center for Human Rights, 2006: 25) as war crimes. For all other atrocities, even as severe as keeping Sarajevo under siege for more than 1,000 days, killing civilians in Vukovar or Bjeljina, or bombing Dubrovnik, fewer than one in five respondents considered them war crimes; the rest reported viewing them as necessities of war (Belgrade Center for Human Rights, 2006: 25).

We asked our respondents—a representative sample of the Belgrade population in 2005—whether they believed that Serbs killed 8,000 men in Srebrenica: only about one-third of them reported such a belief (see Table 4.6). However, the degree to which respondents believed that the event indeed took place varied quite substantially with their political party affiliation. More than two-thirds of the respondents favoring the two most pro-Western parties, DS and G17+, said that they indeed believed that these events took place, while fewer than one-tenth of the respondents favoring the two least pro-Western parties, SPS and SRS, said the same (Table 4.6).

As discussed above, the smoking-gun videotape depicting the killing of six men in the Srebrenica area and linking Serbian troops with the genocide was shown during the Milošević trial. According to the BBC, the videotape was obtained by Nataša Kandić, a Serbian human rights activist from the Humanitarian Law Center in Belgrade, and passed on to the ICTY prosecutors (Prodger, 2005). Although Kandić was sure that "the video tape would finally convince Serbs of what happened in Srebrenica" (Prodger, 2005: 1), the videotape was far from convincing enough for the right-wing respondents in our study (see Table 4.5). Releasing the videotape to the ICTY prosecutor strengthened the prosecutor's case against Milošević and tied the Serbian Ministry of the Interior (the Scorpions militia that led the killing were a unit within the Ministry) to the Srebrenica genocide. However, only about one-third of our sample agreed with Kandić's decision to release the videotape to the ICTY prosecutor (see Table 4.6). The majority of the respondents who supported the two most pro-Western parties (DS and G17+), about two-thirds, agreed with Kandić. On the other hand, supporters of all the other parties (DSS, PSS, SPS, and SRS) mostly

TABLE 4.6

Command Responsibility by Political Party

	Sample	DS (N=97)	G17+ (N=15)	DSS (N=43)	PSS (N=56)	SPS (N=17)	SRS (N=132)	Undecided/ Would Not Respond (N=103)	*Chi-Square*	*Phi*
Believe Serbs Killed 8,000 Men[a]										
% Yes	31.6%	67.0%	66.7%	20.9%	30.4%	5.9%	10.5%	29.8%	99.8***	.463
Agrees with Giving the Videotape to the ICTY Prosecutor[b]										
% Yes	34.8%	63.9%	60.0%	23.3%	30.4%	11.8%	13.0%	42.6%	77.6***	.411
Command Criminal Responsibility—Heads of State and Military Commanders[c]										
% Agree	62.2%	78.9%	86.7%	60.5%	61.8%	17.6%	49.2%	68.3%	40.6***	.298

Command Criminal Responsibility—Milošević[d]										
% Agree	51.8%	80.4%	100.0%	48.8%	55.4%	11.8%	28.6%	53.8%	86.0***	.430
***Command Criminal Responsibility—Mrkšić* et al.**[c]										
% Agree	52.7%	78.4%	93.3%	53.5%	55.4%	17.6%	30.8%	54.8%	69.8**	.387
***Command Criminal Responsibility—Perišić* et al.**[f]										
% Agree	52.7%	82.5%	80.0%	37.2%	57.1%	29.4%	31.6%	55.8%	71.4***	.392

$^{*}p < .05$; $^{**}p < .01$; $^{***}p < .001$

[a] The question was worded as follows: "Do you believe that, during the war in the former Yugoslavia, the Serb forces executed about 8,000 thousand Muslim men and boys in Srebrenica?" The possible answers were: "a) definitely yes; b) yes; c) no; d) definitely no."

[b] The question was worded as follows: "Do you agree with the decision by Nataša Kandić from the Humanitarian Law Center to secure this video for the ICTY prosecutor?" The possible answers were: "a) strongly agree; b) agree; c) disagree; d) strongly disagree."

[c] The question was worded as follows: "Heads of states, as the highest-ranked military commanders, should bear command criminal responsibility for the war crimes committed under their command." The possible answers were: "a) strongly agree; b) agree; c) disagree; d) strongly disagree."

[d] The question was worded as follows: "Slobodan Milošević, as the highest-ranked military commander, should bear command criminal responsibility for the war crimes committed under his command." The possible answers were: "a) strongly agree; b) agree; c) disagree; d) strongly disagree."

[e] The question was worded as follows: "Mile Mrkšić, Miroslav Radić, and Veselin Šljivančanin, as the highest-ranked military commanders, should bear command criminal responsibility for the war crimes committed under their command." The possible answers were: "a) strongly agree; b) agree; c) disagree; d) strongly disagree."

[f] The question was worded as follows: "Momčilo Perišić and his eight co-defendants, as the highest-ranked military commanders, should bear command criminal responsibility for the war crimes committed under their command." The possible answers were: "a) strongly agree; b) agree; c) disagree; d) strongly disagree."

disagreed with Kandić. In fact, only one out of eight respondents supporting the two least pro-Western parties (SPS and SRS) agreed with her.

To assess the degree to which the respondents were able to separate collective responsibility from individual, command responsibility, we asked them two types of questions: one exploring whether they thought that the indictments of top military and political leaders implied the collective responsibility of all Serbs, and the other asking whether the top political and military leaders should be charged with command responsibility. The view that the ICTY indictments were a direct attack on the Serbs was readily detectable in their answers. Depending on the specific defendant(s) (e.g., Milošević, Mrkšić et al., Perišić et al.), between one-half and two-thirds of our respondents agreed that the initiation of ICTY trials against these defendants implied that the ICTY actually charged all Serbs with war crimes (see Table 4.7). However, the support for this view depended heavily upon political orientation, with respondents who supported the two least pro-Western parties (SPS and SRS) agreeing overwhelmingly (more than 75 percent) with this view (Table 4.7), and respondents who supported the two most pro-Western parties (DS and G17+) being the least supportive (less than 27 percent) of this view (Table 4.7).

When we sought the respondents' views about whether heads of state and other highly ranked military leaders should bear command criminal responsibility for the war crimes committed under their command, about one-half of the respondents agreed (see Table 4.6), with, once again, a sharp distinction along party lines (see Table 4.6).

MODELING THE ACCEPTANCE OF COLLECTIVE COMMAND RESPONSIBILITY

To explore the acceptance of collective command responsibility in a multivariate setting, we defined the dependent variable for each respondent, a surveyed adult citizen of Belgrade, as a scale of the acceptance of the collective command responsibility of Serbian political and military leaders for war crimes and crimes against humanity in the former Yugoslavia. To build the acceptance of collective command responsibility scale, we began by asking whether the respondent believed Serb forces executed 8,000 persons at Srebrenica, then whether Milošević should have been tried for command responsibility of war crimes, whether approval for the ICTY increased with his arrest, preference for lenience or severity in his sentencing by ICTY judges, and further acceptance of the transfers of the other co-conspirators (e.g., Mrkšić, Radić, Šljivančanin, Perišić).[2]

Because Milošević and others already had been on trial for two years or longer at the time of the Belgrade survey, raising potential doubt about causal sequence, we also conducted a secondary analysis assessing support for the ICTY's arrest and transfer of

[2] The responses to these items form a scale with a Chronbach's Alpha of .826, a score well above conventional thresholds, indicating that the various component items capture the same construct.

TABLE 4.7

Collective Responsibility by Political Party

	Sample	DS (N=97)	G17+ (N=15)	DSS (N=43)	PSS (N=56)	SPS (N=17)	SRS (N=132)	Undecided/ Would Not Respond (N=103)	*Chi-Square*	*Phi*
Indictment of Milošević Charges All Serbs[a]										
% Agree	60.7%	18.6%	20.0%	60.5%	69.6%	94.1%	85.7%	63.7%	127.7***	.525
Indictment of Mrkšić **et al.** ***Charges All Serbs***[b]										
% Agree	52.5%	14.4%	13.3%	53.5%	53.6%	88.2%	80.5%	51.0%	116.1***	.500
Indictment of Perišić **et al.** ***Charges All Serbs***[c]										
% Agree	50.8%	17.5%	26.7%	46.5%	50.0%	88.2%	75.2%	50.0%	88.0***	.432

* $p < .05$; ** $p < .01$; *** $p < .001$

[a] The question was worded as follows: "When the International Tribunal in The Hague initiated the trial of Slobodan Milošević, it actually charged all Serbs for war crimes." The possible answers were: "a) strongly agree; b) agree; c) disagree; d) strongly disagree."

[b] The question was worded as follows: "When the International Tribunal in The Hague initiated the trial of Mile Mrkšić, Miroslav Radić, and Veselin Šljivančanin (accused of participating in the criminal enterprise in which the Serb forces after the fall of Vukovar mistreated and killed non-Serbs from the Vukovar Hospital), it actually charged all Serbs for war crimes." The possible answers were: "a) strongly agree; b) agree; c) disagree; d) strongly disagree."

[c] The question was worded as follows: "When the International Tribunal in The Hague initiated the trial of Momčilo Perišić and other co-defendants (accused of being the commanders of the Serb forces that attacked the 'safe area' of Srebrenica), it actually charged all Serbs for war crimes." The possible answers were: "a) strongly agree; b) agree; c) disagree; d) strongly disagree."

Radovan Karadžić and Ratko Mladić, who were still at large at the time of the survey. The results are substantively similar.

Our measure of the effect of pre-conditional EU membership on this issue is a scale that asks respondents whether they would vote for EU membership, the importance they attach to EU membership, and, in the alternative, whether it is better for Serbia to remain independent than to join the EU. The respondents in our sample overwhelmingly indicated they would vote in favor of EU membership (79.9 percent) and that they regarded this membership as important (80.1 percent), while one-third (33.3 percent) endorsed remaining independent of the EU.[3]

The smoking-gun videotape potentially competed with the issue of EU membership in its salience in the minds of the Belgrade respondents. This is not surprising because the videotape was played and reported throughout the former Yugoslavia for several weeks after its showing at the ICTY. Our indicator of the effect of this videotape is measured with items that ask whether the respondents had heard about the videotape (92.9 percent), seen this videotape (70.6 percent), and believed the videotape was authentic (53.5 percent).[4]

Older and less-educated respondents form the foundation of nationalist sentiments and hostility to international intervention in Serbia. Therefore, we included measures of age and education as well as gender in our analysis.

We use hierarchical linear models [HLM] with robust standard errors to adjust for dependence within the neighborhood-clustered sample units. The HLM approach allows analysis of variation within and between the sampled neighborhoods (Raudenbush and Bryk, 2002). First, we estimate logistic regressions adjusted for dispersion to model the respondents' political party affiliations. Then, we estimate joined individual- and neighborhood-level OLS equations to model respondents' acceptance of the imposition by the ICTY of collective command responsibility on the Serbian leadership. We learn from the latter joint analysis not only about individual-level demographic, political and economic sources of variation in acceptance of Serbian collective command responsibility, but also about the influence on this acceptance of neighborhood-level political processes, with other individual-level variables taken into account.

Tables 4.8 and 4.9 present the logistic regression models of political affiliations. These models estimate the expected polarizing and mediating effects of the conditional offer of EU membership, as well as the smoking-gun video evidence and demographic characteristics, on party affiliations. The regressions focus on the two polar opposite parties: the pro-ICTY Democratic Party and the anti-ICTY Radical Party.

We estimate the logistic regressions with and without the support for the EU membership variable to capture its potential mediating effect. As expected, the videotape and EU

[3] The Chrobach's Alpha for this scale is .879.

[4] The Chronbach's Alpha score for this scale is .603.

TABLE 4.8

Logistic Regression Models of Democratic Party Affiliation, Adjusted for Dispersion

Variables	Eq. (1)	Eq. (2)
	b(SE)	*b(SE)*
Age	−.017 (.005)**	.245 (.097)**
Gender	−.189 (.192)	−.185 (.186)
Education	.311 (.103)**	.245 (.097)**
Exposure to Video Evidence	.475 (.185)**	.269 (.184)
Support for EU Membership		.369 (.063)***
Constant	−1.602	−1.772

variables have opposing effects in Tables 4.8 and 4.9, with exposure to the videotape and support for the membership offer increasing the likelihood of Democratic Party affiliation and decreasing the likelihood of Radial Party affiliation. The coefficients in the second columns of these tables indicate that the EU effect is especially strong in relation to Democratic Party support. In addition to its direct effect, its inclusion in the model mediates the effects of respondents' exposure to the videotape evidence. Among Democrats, support for EU membership reduces the effect of exposure to the videotape evidence by more than 40 percent and below statistical significance. The EU membership is an especially strong and determining force among those who affiliate with the Democratic Party. In turn, the importance of Democratic Party affiliation for the public acceptance of the collective command responsibility of Serbian leaders is revealed in Table 4.10. The results summarized in this table indicate that both exposure to the videotape evidence and support for EU membership, net of one another, significantly increases

TABLE 4.9

Logistic Regression Models of Radical Party Affiliation, Adjusted for Dispersion

Variables	Eq. (1)	Eq. (2)
	b(SE)	*b(SE)*
Age	.004 (.008)	.001 (.007)
Gender	−.494 (.210)*	−.436 (.217)*
Education	−.266 (.105)**	−.235 (.101)*
Exposure to Video Evidence	−.439 (.132)***	−.313 (.136)*
Support for EU Membership		−.287 (.055)***
Constant	−1.119	−1.154

TABLE 4.10

Unstandardized Hierarchical Linear Models of Acceptance of Collective Command Responsibility

	Model 1			Model 2			Model 3			Model 4		
	B		s.e.	B		s.e.	B		s.e.	B		s.e.
Individual Level Effects												
Age	−.018		.016	−.015		.016	−.009		.015	−.008		.015
Gender	.527		.473	.668		.447	.620		.410	.664		.393
Education	.808	***	.178	.720	***	.176	.638	***	.167	.612		.166
Party Affiliation												
SRS	−3.098	***	.829	−2.799	***	.791	−1.925	**	.759	−1.871	**	.759
DDS	−1.250	*	.644	−1.633	**	.599	−1.674	**	.645	−1.678	**	.632
DS	3.094	***	.650	2.818	***	.670	2.116	***	.638	2.049	**	.650
SPS	−.399		.829	−.372		.881	−.431		.855	−.379		.837
Exposure to Video Evidence				1.183	***	.320	.871	**	.307	1.020	**	.271
Support for EU Membership							.693	***	.123	.696	***	.122
Cross-Level Neighborhood Interaction												
Exposure to Video Evidence * SRS affiliation in the Neighborhood										−3.224		2.322
Exposure to Video * DS Affiliation in Neighborhood										4.952	*	2.411
Constant	18.158			18.160			18.158			18.099		
Pseudo R^2												

Note: Insignificant main effects of neighborhood-level exposure to video evidence and party affiliation in neighborhood are not shown to conserve space.
* $p < .05$; ** $p < .01$; *** $p < .001$

the acceptance of the collective command responsibility involved in transfers to the ICTY. Again, support for EU membership has a strong role, while also mediating about one-third of the effect of exposure to the smoking-gun videotape evidence. The effect of being a Democrat on acceptance of ICTY-imposed Serbian collective command responsibility is especially strong and statistically significant, with an effect that is larger than the negative effect of being a Radical on acceptance of this responsibility. The strong and opposite directions of the political party effects confirm the influence of the structural pre-conditionality strategy, at the same time indicating that this influence is a polarizing as well as a mediating factor.

Finally, there is a significant and potentially important cross-level interaction effect on the acceptance of Serbian collective responsibility in the last column of Table 4.10 of living in a Democratic Party neighborhood and being exposed to the videotape evidence. This effect indicates that, net of individual-level influences in the final model, living in a neighborhood with higher numbers of Democratic Party members increases the effect of exposure to the videotape on acceptance of Serbian responsibility for the genocide. This reinforcing neighborhood effect of Democratic Party membership is summarized graphically in Figure 4.2. Living in a neighborhood that is about 40 percent, as compared to about 6 percent, Democratic increases the effect of higher videotape exposure scores. In the former neighborhood, hearing about, seeing, and believing the videotape evidence (which results in the highest possible score) increases acceptance of collective command responsibility by about two scale points, or more than 10 percent. This effect is modest, but it is multiplicative in form, and small percentage differences often alter the outcomes of elections. A further implication is that this multiplicative effect of Democratic neighborhood affiliation could be enhanced, for example, with strengthened outside support of the kind U.S. Secretary of State Powell provided five years earlier in the successful transfer of Milošević.

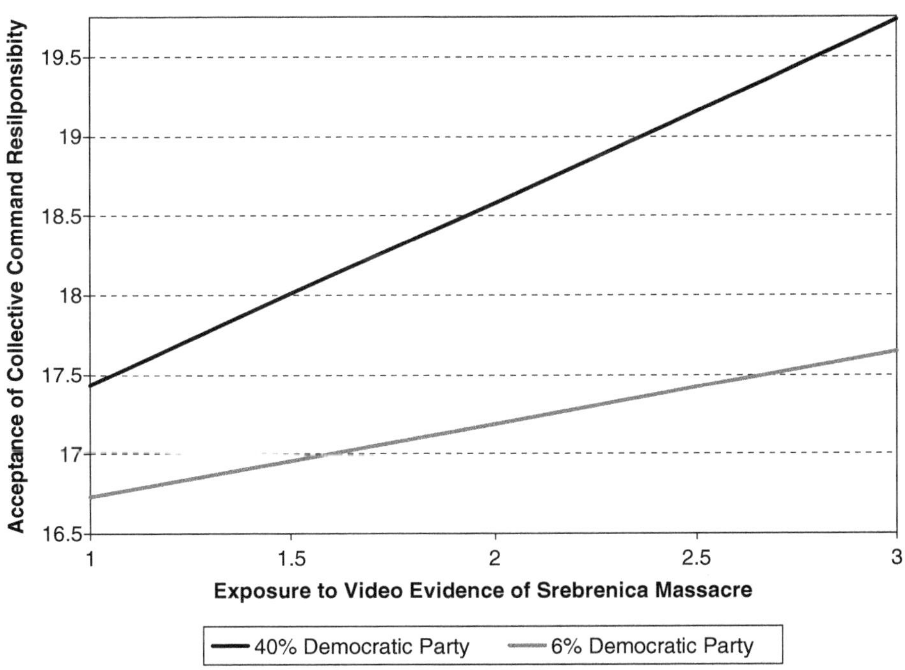

FIGURE 4.2 Cross-Level Interaction Effect of Neighborhood Democratic Party Membership and Exposure to Videotape Evidence of Srebrenica Massacre on Acceptance of Collective Command Responsibility of Serbian Leadership

CONCLUSION

What we have called structural pre-conditionality is the centerpiece of the European Union's efforts to produce arrests and transfers of defendants to the ICTY in The Hague. The transfer of Milošević and the 2008 arrest of Karadžić are likely to give new encouragement to the use of structural pre-conditionality policies for war-crimes intervention and other international purposes.

The strategy of EU structural pre-conditionality did not work quickly in the case of Karadžić. The Serbian Democratic Party failed to deliver on its pledge to arrest and transfer Karadžić to the ICTY in 2007, with the Karadžić arrest taking over three years to finally happen, and Ratko Mladić remains at large at the time of this writing. The deterrence doctrine, on which so much of the work of the ICTY is based, demands celerity in punishment, and this delay is not helpful for that purpose.

Furthermore, the Belgrade Survey indicates that the EU structural pre-conditionality strategy, as political realists would predict, is a wedge issue that polarizes affiliation between the rival Serbian political parties that most strongly support and oppose transfer of suspects to the ICTY. As the realists would further predict, we also found that the offer of EU membership is a salient mediator of the influence of the smoking-gun videotape evidence of Serbian-led involvement in the Srebrenica genocide. We found additional evidence that the degree of Serbian Democratic Party affiliation at the neighborhood level magnifies the effect of videotape evidence of the Srebrenica massacre on public acceptance of the Serbian leadership's collective command responsibility for the genocidal violence in the former Yugoslavia. This is further evidence of the kind of local cognitive landscape effect identified in the previous chapter.

I only hope that trials will be fair and just, that everyone will get a deserved punishment for crimes committed, regardless of ethnicity!
[RESPONDENT FROM THE 2004 VUKOVAR SAMPLE].

5

DISTRIBUTIVE AND PROCEDURAL JUSTICE

THE WAR IN THE FORMER YUGOSLAVIA created thousands of victims of war crimes and crimes against humanity. A key purpose of the International Criminal Tribunal for the former Yugoslavia (ICTY) is to render justice to these victims (ICTY, 2006). By providing justice, the ICTY expects also to achieve another part of its mission—"to contribute to the restoration of peace" (ICTY, 2006) and, at the same time, to reestablish interethnic communication and stability.

Many victims—Muslims/Bosniaks, Croats, Serbs—have testified in the cases tried before the ICTY (ICTY, 2009):

> The Tribunal's courtrooms have heard hundreds of victims tell what are often painful and tragic stories about what they saw and experienced. People of all walks of life—farmers, doctors, housewives, local politicians, mechanics, students, school children and many others—were victims of horrific crimes. Many of them were victims simply because they were of a different ethnicity from their attackers. Many victims who testified before the Tribunal courageously related how they were either beaten, tortured, raped, sexually assaulted, forced from their homes, watched how their family members were murdered, or how they saw others fall victim to these terrible crimes.

Yet, compared to the estimated numbers of victims—more than three million refugees, 200,000 to 250,000 people killed, another 50,000 tortured, and 20,000 raped (Bassiouni, 1994)—the hundreds of victims who have testified before the ICTY are only a small portion. Most of the victims will not get to The Hague to confront their assailants and hold them accountable. Most of the victims will never get an opportunity to tell of their pain and suffering in that setting. For most of them, The Hague is a distant and remote force. Their experience is limited to occasionally viewing the proceedings on the Internet, reading media accounts of the sentences, or hearing politicians interpret the events at The Hague. The contact they have with the ICTY is indirect, sporadic, and far removed.

This chapter explores what people who view themselves as victims of war crimes and crimes of humanity and who will never see firsthand the inside of the ICTY courtroom, think about the justice delivered by the ICTY. We will focus on their views about distributive and procedural justice, both in general and more specifically, and study the correlates of their perceptions of ICTY fairness. We will examine basic propositions of the procedural justice theory in a new and novel setting (a transnational court), with new types of respondents (victims directly affected by the war, but not able to participate in the proceedings) and very serious crimes (i.e., war crimes, crimes against humanity).

THE ICTY'S SUBSTANTIVE AND PROCEDURAL RULES

To understand the context of the victims' views, we will first explore the legal environment of the ICTY. A short description of the legal rules governing the work of the ICTY will be beneficial for three reasons. First, it will provide the reader with a basis to assess the balance between the due process rights given to the defendant and the rights established to protect the victims and to allow the prosecutors to do their job. Second, it will allow the reader to gain a more thorough understanding of the context in which the victims, who are subjects of civil-law jurisdictions, respond to the ICTY. Third, it will familiarize the reader with the basic rights involved in our later analysis of victims' views.

The ICTY is in charge of prosecuting "persons responsible for serious violations of international humanitarian law committed in the territory of the former Yugoslavia since January 1, 1991" (Article 1, *Statute*, 2006). However, unlike a typical criminal code, the ICTY's *Statute* does not create crimes; it merely lists the crimes that already exist in the body of international conventional and customary laws. These serious violations of international humanitarian law can be grouped as: (1) grave breaches of the 1949 Geneva Conventions (Article 2, *Statute*, 2006); (2) violations of the laws or customs of war (Article 3, *Statute*, 2006); (3) genocide (Article 4, *Statute*, 2006); and (4) crimes against humanity (Article 5, *Statute*, 2006). The former Yugoslavia ratified these conventions and, thus, the defendants at the ICTY have little basis to claim that their actions do not constitute crimes.

By design, the choice of punishments for such severe violations of international law is limited. Specifically, the only punishment at the ICTY's disposal is imprisonment (Article 24, *Statute*, 2006). The *Rules of Procedure and Evidence* (Article 101, 2010) do not provide the minimum length of the prison sentence, just the maximum ("including the remainder of the convicted person's life"). While determining the appropriate sentence, the ICTY takes into account several factors, including the severity of the offense and the individual circumstances of the convicted persons (Article 24, Section 2, *Statute*, 2006), as well as other factors which could be meaningfully claimed as aggravating or mitigating circumstances (Article 101, *Rules of Procedure and Evidence*, 2010). The only factor specifically listed as a mitigating circumstance (Article 101, *Rules of Procedure and Evidence*, 2010) in accordance with the common-law tradition, but novel for citizens from civil-law jurisdictions, is "substantial cooperation with the Prosecutor before or after conviction." According to Morris and Scharf (1995: 279–280):

> The reduction of sentence based on cooperation with the Prosecutor represents a compromise between the judges who favored the U.S. proposal for granting full or limited testimonial immunity in exchange for meaningful cooperation with the Prosecutor, and those who opposed conferring any kind of immunity on the perpetrators of the crimes referred to in the Statute as a matter of international law and policy. The proposal was intended to encourage low-level offenders who actually committed the heinous acts to turn 'State's evidence'.

Procedures for guilty pleas were barely mentioned in the original versions of both the *Statute* and the *Rules of Procedure and Evidence* (Article 20, *Statute*, 2010; Rule 62, *Rules of Procedure and Evidence*, 2010; see also Clark, 2003). However, after legal problems emerged with the original plea in the Erdemović case (see Clark, 2003; Cook, 2005), the ICTY formally established a procedural framework for accepting guilty pleas (Rule 62*bis*, *Rules of Procedure and Evidence*, 2010). The right to plea bargain was initially incorporated in the ICTY set of procedural rules as a mitigating possibility (for "substantial cooperation with the Prosecutor before or after conviction;" Article 101, *Rules of Procedure and Evidence*, 2010).

In the first few years of the ICTY's existence, few cases were plea bargained. Under pressure from the UN and the Bush administration to expedite its process and develop a completion strategy, plea bargaining became a regular practice at the ICTY (see Cook, 2005: 475). In fact, Scharf (2004: 1074) wrote that "between 2001 and 2003, the Tribunal approved 12 plea bargains, clearing 40 per cent of the cases from its crowded docket." Since the Erdemović case and the first use of plea bargaining (see Erdemović case), the ICTY has treated guilty pleas as a mitigating circumstance (see Clark, 2003).

The *Statute* (Articles 18–29) of the ICTY establishes its criminal procedures. However, Article 15 of the *Statute* also authorized the ICTY judges—a heterogeneous group of legal scholars and practitioners from around the world—to develop further rules of procedure and evidence. As the ICTY's work has evolved, the judges have amended the rules to address unresolved issues, such as cooperation of various states, arrest conditions, subpoena orders, and witness protection (see Jorda, 2006). Since their adoption in 1994, the ICTY has amended its *Rules of Procedure and Evidence* 44 times by the time of this writing (*Rules of Procedure and Evidence*, 2010).

The procedural rules at the ICTY reflect a multitude of influences. For example, whereas the rules of the pretrial phase are based on inquisitorial precedents (procedures typical of civil-law countries), the trial is based primarily on adversarial rules (the procedure typical of common-law countries), with some added elements of inquisitorial procedure. Adversarial procedures place responsibility for evidence collection in the hands of prosecuting and defending parties. The judge has a passive role; the trial depends primarily on decisions reached by the prosecutor and defense (see, e.g., Reichel, 2006). In contrast, in inquisitorial procedure, the prosecutor initiates the case *ex officio*. The court has the duty to collect and present the evidence and thus has an active role both in evidence collection and in the examination of evidence (see, e.g., Reichel, 2006).

At the ICTY, the pretrial procedure commences with an investigation conducted by the Office of the Prosecutor (Article 18, *Statute*, 2006). The prosecutor questions victims, witnesses, and suspects. The prosecutor collects evidence and conducts on-site investigations (Article 18, *Statute*, 2006; Rules 39(i), 42, and 43, *Rules of Procedure and Evidence*, 2010). The prosecutor can request states to arrest a suspect or an accused, seize physical evidence, and take the necessary measures to prevent the escape of the suspect or the accused, injury to or intimidation of victims or witnesses, or destruction of the evidence (Rule 40, *Rules of Procedure and Evidence*, 2010). Thus, the prosecutor (or investigators working for the prosecutor) is the first party with whom the victim will have any contact.

Based on the results of the investigation, the prosecutor prepares the indictment and forwards it together with the supporting material to the Registrar for confirmation by a judge (Article 18, *Statute*, 2006; Article 47, *Rules of Procedure and Evidence*, 2010). A judge may issue an arrest warrant for the accused upon the confirmation of the indictment (Article 19, *Statute*, 2006; Articles 47H and 55, *Rules of Procedure and Evidence*, 2010). Generally, the prosecutor makes confirmed indictments public (Article 52, *Rules of Procedure and Evidence*, 2010). However, in the interest of justice, the judge or the trial chamber can decide to "seal" the indictment (Article 53, *Rules of Procedure and Evidence*, 2010). Because the ICTY does not have its own police or police powers, it depends on the will of various states and international organizations (e.g., United Nations Protection Force [UNPROFOR], Stabilisation Force [SFOR]) to make arrests instead for it.[1] The sealing of the indictment increases the element of surprise and vulnerability and thus may increase the chance of an arrest by either international forces or the forces of

[1] However, getting access to the suspects remains one of the most severe challenges that the ICTY faces to date, despite the mechanisms put in place to entice states and international organizations to cooperate with the prosecutor and the ICTY (e.g., the states have an obligation to cooperate with the ICTY and to execute arrest warrants; the UN Security Council has the authority to impose sanctions against any state that fails to do so; Article 29, Statute, 2006, Article 58, Rules of Procedure and Evidence, 2006; see Gallant, 1994; Sharp, 1997).

a particular country. Nevertheless, two of the "big fish" in Bosnia and Herzegovina (BiH)—Ratko Mladić and Goran Hadžić —remain at large, despite their actual arrest and transfer to the ICTY being made a condition of European Union membership for Serbia.

Article 20 of the *Statute* (2006) provides for the charging and transfer of detained suspects to the ICTY. Probably because of the severity of the charges and the difficulty in making an arrest in the first place, the general rule is that the accused will remain in the custody of the ICTY (Rules 64 and 65, *Rules of Procedure and Evidence*, 2010). Provisional release is not a right guaranteed to a defendant, but rather an exception to the rule. In a few cases, the ICTY has agreed to grant a provisional release (see, e.g., Simić, Bulletin No. 21, 2006) or a house arrest (see, e.g., Blaškić, *Prosecutor v. Blaškić,* 1996).

The next step in the process includes the initial hearing. A judge reads the charges to the defendant in court, the defendant is asked to enter a plea, and, if the defendant pleads not guilty, the trial date is set. As in common-law systems, a guilty plea at the ICTY results in waiving the trial and proceeding directly to the sentencing stage. In recent years, up to 40 percent of the cases have been plea bargained.

The trial encompasses a number of other accusatory elements. The burden is on the prosecutor to prove beyond a reasonable doubt that the defendant committed the crimes as described in the indictment. The prosecutor and the defendant may call witnesses and present evidence; unless decided otherwise by the trial chamber in the interest of justice, the order of their presentation follows the typical common-law format (prosecution, defense, prosecution rebuttal, defense rejoinder: Rule 85, *Rules of Procedure and Evidence*, 2010). Unlike common-law courts, the trial chamber may play an active role (similar to the courts in civil-law systems) in decisions about what evidence will be presented before the chamber; the trial chamber has the power to order each party to produce additional evidence and to summon witnesses *proprio motu* (Rules 85, 89–98, *Rules of Procedure and Evidence*, 2010). Although the examination of witnesses predominantly follows the common-law model (examination-in-chief, cross-examination, and re-examination done by the parties), the chamber, in the civil-law tradition, may also take an active role by asking questions of witnesses.

The ICTY guarantees the defendant a number of rights during the trial stage. These guarantees include: the right to be informed about the charges; the right to be present at trial; the right to remain silent (the right against self-incrimination); the right to prepare a defense; the right to counsel; the right to be provided with a counsel, if indigent; the right to call witnesses; the right to examine witnesses; the right to be a witness; and the right to the free assistance of an interpreter (Article 21, *Statute*, 2006). The prosecutor also has certain duties; specifically, the prosecutor has to disclose copies of the supporting material to the indictment, copies of the statements by witnesses who will testify at the trial, and copies of other statements; the prosecutor must also allow the defense to examine any material evidence, especially exculpatory evidence. The ICTY guarantees defendants fair, speedy, and public trials (Articles 20 and 21, *Statute*, 2006).

Although the ICTY's rules do not contain provisions relating to the participation of victims in the proceedings (see, e.g., May, 2006) like typical civil-law criminal justice systems do (and the former Yugoslavia did), victims and witnesses are provided with a certain set of rights in the proceedings before the ICTY. To balance victims' and defendants' interests, the general rule is that all witnesses have to testify and be available for examination and cross-examination (Rule 85, *Rules of Procedure and Evidence*, 2010). To increase the victims' willingness to testify at the trials, there are rules guaranteeing protection to the victims and witnesses. For example, the identity of victims and witnesses may not be disclosed in some cases (Rule 69, *Rules of Procedure and Evidence*, 2010). However, to balance the interests of the defense and the witness, the discretion to grant anonymity "must be exercised fairly, and that only in exceptional circumstances can the Trial Chamber restrict the right of the accused to examine or have examined witnesses against him" (*Prosecutor v. Tadić*, 1995; see also Momeni, 1997; Lakatos, 1995; Leigh, 1996). Moreover, the judges may order appropriate measures for the privacy and protection of victims and witnesses, such as expunging their names and any identifying information from the public records, or testimony through image- or voice-altering devices, in closed sessions, or on closed-circuit televisions (Rule 75, *Rules of Procedure and Evidence*, 2010).

After all the evidence has been presented, the prosecutor and the defense provide their closing statements (Rule 86, *Rules of Procedure and Evidence*, 2010) and the presiding judge of the Chamber declares that the hearing is closed. The next step in the proceedings is a private deliberation by the trial chamber. A finding of guilt may be reached only when a majority of the Trial Chamber is satisfied that guilt has been proved beyond reasonable doubt (Rule 87, *Rules of Procedure and Evidence*, 2010). The judges also determine the penalty for each finding of guilt at the same time. Not surprisingly, and in accordance with the purposes of the ICTY, the rules mandate pronouncement of the decision in public and in the presence of the defendant.

DISTRIBUTIVE AND PROCEDURAL JUSTICE

Tyler (1990, 2000) suggests that citizens' views of justice derive from feelings of fairness. What matters is both *distributive justice* (the fairness of outcomes) and *procedural justice* (the fairness of the procedures). In other words, citizens are concerned about fair outcomes arrived through a fair procedure. In the context of the ICTY, then, the fairness of both decisions and procedures matters.

Distributive justice relies on equity (Tyler, 2000: 118) and equality (Deutsch, 1975). In terms of equity, fairness means that rewards should be proportional to contributions (Tyler, 2000: 118). In the language of criminal law, the severity of the punishment should be proportionate to the gravity of the crimes committed. In the context of war crimes and crimes against humanity, the defendants are potentially guilty of committing the most serious crimes, including murdering, abusing, raping, and/or mistreating many victims.

The choice of punishments for such severe violations of international law is limited. The death penalty is not allowed, and the only punishment at the ICTY's disposal is imprisonment (Article 24, *Statute*, 2006), which can range from imprisonment for just one day to lifetime imprisonment (Article 101, *Rules of Procedure and Evidence*, 2010). If the victims seek retribution as the main goal of punishment, adhering to the ancient Hamurabi's maxima, "An eye for an eye, and a tooth for a tooth," the lack of the death penalty may leave them dissatisfied (regardless of how proportionate the ICTY decisions might be).

In terms of equality—equal application of the laws resulting in similar punishments for similar crimes—victims also could view the outcomes in similar cases (e.g., a low-level concentration camp guard sentenced to 15 years' imprisonment) differently, depending on the defendants' and their own ethnicity. Regardless of the ICTY's efforts to be as objective as possible, the victims could still view the same or very similar decisions as unfair when they involve "our" defendants compared to "their" defendants. At the same time, they may have the tendency to overestimate the victimization of "our" victims compared to "their" victims. The ICTY's overall report card may be susceptible to a tendency of people to "exaggerate the importance or value of their contributions to groups" (Tyler, 2000: 118), which in this case might be the severity of their victimization.

According to Leventhal's theory (1976; 1980; see also Tyler, 1990), *procedural justice* consists of six components: (1) representation, (2) consistency, (3) impartiality, (4) accuracy, (5) correctability, and (6) ethicality.

Representation (Leventhal, 1976, 1980) or participation (Tyler, 2000: 121) refers to the extent to which the parties in a legal dispute believe that they have appropriate input into the process, not necessarily in terms of determining the outcome of the dispute, but in the sense of having opportunities to present their side of the story to the decision-makers. "Having a voice" can assume importance in a variety of settings. These settings can include plea bargaining (Houlden, 1980) and sentencing hearings (Heinz and Kerstetter, 1979), as well as mediation (Kitzmann and Emery, 1993; MacCoun et al., 1988; Shapiro and Brett, 1993), especially if the parties believe that their statements have a direct influence on the outcome of the case (see, e.g., Shapiro and Brett, 1993).

Although the ICTY has performed a vital role by giving hundreds of victims a chance to testify (see ICTY, 2008), most of the victims of war crimes and crimes against humanity will never get a chance to tell their side of story to the ICTY judges. The reasons are at least twofold. First, the victims are too numerous and many have perished. The siege of Sarajevo alone, which lasted from the spring of 1992 to late fall of 1995, claimed the lives of thousands of soldiers and civilians, with countless others injured physically and/or psychologically. It is impossible for all victims and their families to have their voices heard during the ICTY trials. In fact, a truth commission might serve these purposes better.

Second, the ICTY procedure, which combines adversarial and inquisitorial elements, defines the victim's role more in adversarial terms. In civil-law systems, victims have an active role. They have extensive rights with respect to the prosecution (they can initiate private prosecution or become subsidiary prosecutors) and, thus, a larger degree of control over the trial (see Erez and Bienkowska, 1993). For example, the procedural rules in the former Yugoslavia—the regime in which most of the victims grew up and with which they are most familiar—allowed the victim to move away from the passive role of a crime victim and become an active participant in the process. Compared to the victims in civil-law countries, victims in the common-law tradition, like the victims at the ICTY, have only a passive role in the trials. They are mostly observers and, at most, witnesses, with no formally recognized role in the process. Erez and Bienkowska (1993: 48) summarize this procedure from the perspective of victims:

> Studies of victims before the law in several countries (e.g., Kelly, 1984; Shapland et al., 1985) have suggested that victims' grievances are as much with the system's procedures, particularly victims' lack of involvement in the decision-making process, as with the supposed injustice of the outcome . . .. However, the most important grievance mentioned by the victims has been their lack of 'standing' and voice in the proceedings. As one victim who testified before the presidential committee established to study the situation of victims in the USA expressed it, 'Why didn't anyone consult me? I was the one who was kidnapped, not the State of Virginia.'

Research suggests that the problem lies more with the lack of voice or standing than the injustice of the outcome (see, e.g., Kelly, 1984a, 1984b). A study by Heinz and Kerstetter (1979) shows that victims appreciate the opportunity to speak at sentencing hearings, regardless of whether their arguments influence the actual sentences. Recent research (Buzawa and Hotaling, 2006) supports the importance of victims having a voice in order that they feel satisfaction with the process. For example, in domestic violence cases, satisfaction increases when the victim experiences some control over the process. In fact, when "the victim had a low sense of control, satisfaction with the system decreased significantly" (Buzawa and Hotaling, 2006: 2). The effect of this sense of control, according to Tyler and Lind (1992: 144), is "probably the most widely replicated finding in procedural justice research." That ICTY rules provide no room for any active involvement other than serving as a witness probably leaves many victims with a sense that the procedures are unfair because they likely feel they have no voice in, or control over, the process.

Yet, recent studies involving participants in various settings (Lind, et al., 1997; Tyler and Blader, 2000; Tyler and Huo, 2002) find control elements have little independent effect beyond other procedural elements, namely, the quality of the decision-making and the quality of treatment. Instead, control elements—particularly the control over the process—have an indirect influence in that they affect victims' levels of trust and judgments about the quality of decision-making procedures, the quality of the treatment received, and outcome favorability (Tyler and Huo, 2002: 86). For victims, their lack of standing may strongly affect how they view the court. In their case, it is not about whether the judges recognized them as important participants, but whether they entered the courtroom at all and, if so, whether their role was active in any aspect.

The ICTY is not interested in hearing stories, which is something that victims may be willing to share with the ICTY; the short answers providing factual and direct responses to the prosecutor's or defense attorney's questions is something that the victims may experience as unpleasant. Thus, the judges may have a tendency to cut the storytelling short and focus on the answers to specific questions, as was noted in the analysis of the Krstić transcripts (Dembour and Haslam, in Stover, 2005: 132) and in the videotapes and transcripts of trials that Stover explored (Stover, 2005: 132). The insensitive, inappropriate, or paternalistic behavior of judges, when compounded with tough cross-examination, may damage the witness's court experience. The cross-examination and adversarial nature of the trial may contribute to victims feeling that the ICTY does not treat victims with respect, that the judges do not protect witnesses, and that the ICTY does not appreciate the efforts involved in testifying.

Consistency refers to "similarity of treatment and outcomes" (Tyler, 1990: 118), which can occur across people and across time. For the procedure to be fair across people, the same rules should apply to everyone. Assuming that the ICTY is trying to the best of its abilities to be consistent across defendants of various ethnicities, the victims may still perceive the ICTY as unfair. If we further assume that the victims downplay the seriousness of crimes committed by "our" defendants compared to the seriousness of their own victimization caused by "their" defendants (see the equity theory discussion), victims might still perceive the ICTY as unfair.

Impartiality (Paternoster, et al., 1997: 168), *neutrality* (Tyler and Lind, 1992; Tyler, 2000: 122), or *objectivity* occurs when the decision-makers do not allow the personal characteristics of the parties or favoritism of one party to influence decisions and treatment during the process. Simply put, neutrality involves honesty and lack of bias (Tyler and Lind, 1992: 141). The ICTY judges come from different states and legal traditions. The concern with fairness is noticeable in the way the *Statute* determines qualifications for the judges (Article 13, *Statute*, 2006):

> The judges shall be persons of high moral character, impartiality and integrity who possess the qualifications required in their respective countries for appointment to the highest judicial offices. In the overall composition of the Chambers due account shall be taken of the experience of the judges in criminal law, international law, including international humanitarian law and human rights law.

The issue of impartiality could play a crucial role in victims' evaluations of the ICTY's fairness: the war itself was fought largely along ethnic lines and the ICTY must make decisions involving defendants of all three ethnicities. The issues of defendants' ethnicity, judges' nationality, and international politics interconnect in victims' views of the ICTY. Although the UN—a heterogeneous world organization—established the ICTY and tried to eliminate potential political bias by requiring that no two judges be citizens of the same state (Article 12, *Statute*, 2006), the fact nevertheless remains that politics and backgrounds play a role in the work of the ICTY. To a Muslim/Bosniak victim, the test of the ICTY's fairness may center on, for example, whether a UK or French judge treats the defendants of Serb ethnicity differently from a Pakistani or Saudi Arabian judge. As prior research suggests (see, e.g., Lind and Lissak, 1985), doubts about judges' impartiality may exacerbate the challenges to the fairness of the procedures. It seems that in legal settings, the issues of consistency, honesty, and impartiality are key (see Tyler and Lind, 1992: 158).

Ethicality (Patternoster, et al., 1997: 168), *treatment with dignity and respect* (Tyler, 2000: 122), or *standing or status recognition* (Tyler and Lind, 1992) imply that the evaluations of procedural fairness will be affected by views as to whether the decision-makers treat the participants with dignity and with respect for their rights. Although a number of procedures protect victims when they testify before the ICTY (see, e.g., Rules 69 and 75, *Rules of Procedure and Evidence*, 2010), most victims will never reach the stage at which these procedures will apply to *them*. Rather, they will never stand before the ICTY and, as a result, will feel that their stories do not count. They will watch from the margins at the way the ICTY judges start from the presumption of innocence and treat the defendants with respect and dignity by allowing them to exercise their legally prescribed rights. Despite the fact that, by behaving in this way, the ICTY judges are acting in accordance with the rules (and thus behaving ethically), the overall effect on the non-testifying victims could still be negative.

Accuracy of the procedure (Paternoster et al., 1997) or a decision (Tyler, 1990: 119) refers to the ability of the decision-makers to make competent decisions publicly, based on reliable and valid information. A couple of factors might lead victims to regard the ICTY procedures as legitimate. First, the people serving as ICTY judges presumably should be selected only if they qualify to serve at the highest courts (i.e., "persons of high moral character, impartiality, and integrity, who possess the qualifications required in their respective countries for appointment to the highest judicial offices," Article 13, *Statute*, 2006). Second, the ICTY's rules and regulations are public and the trials are public and broadcast around the world. On the other hand, the existence of the rule that allows the same judges to serve both during the indictment stage and either during the trial or during the appeal is problematic. Moreover the ICTY trials can last for many months, even years, as the prosecution presents numerous witnesses and experts in each case. This can test victims' patience.

The fact that the appellate decision does not always plainly confirm the trial chamber's original decision is a double-edged sword. The disparity in views may signal to the victims that the trial chamber is not able to make competent decisions, particularly if these appellate decisions dramatically alter the original decision. This was a problem in the Blaškić case (in this case the sentence was reduced from 45 to 9 years; ICTY, 2009) and the Šljivančanin case (in this case the sentence was increased from 5 to 17 years; ICTY, 2009). Stover (2005: 134) interviewed victims testifying in the five Lašva Valley cases (one of which is the Blaškić case) before the appellate chamber made the decision and speculated that their overall satisfaction with their experience at the ICTY would probably drop by 20–25 percent in the aftermath of the quashing of the verdicts in the Blaškić and Kupreškić cases.

Correctability (Tyler, 1990: 119; Patternoster, et al., 1997: 168) refers to the existence of avenues to address unfair or incorrect decisions. For correctability, appellate procedures themselves must be viewed as procedurally fair. The ICTY is composed of trial chambers and the appellate chamber and thus provides a forum, separate from the decision-maker during the trial, to address grievances. On the other hand, the rule that allows a decision-maker to play two roles (e.g., the judge controlling the indictment and a trial judge; the judge controlling the indictment and an appellate judge) in the same case (Rule 15, *Rules of Procedure and Evidence*, 2010) clouds this aspect of procedural fairness. However, just as they have no standing during the trial, victims have no standing during appeals. Unlike defendants, to them the existence of the appellate chamber may mean relatively little, unless the appellate chamber reverses the decision in favor of "our own" or against "one of them."

Despite the existence of more than half a dozen factors, Tyler (2000: 121) emphasizes that the four key factors affecting people's evaluations of procedural fairness are participation, neutrality, trustworthiness of authorities, and treatment with dignity and respect. Whereas the basic propositions of the procedural justice theory have been supported in various contexts, from work settings to plea bargaining, standing and trust seem to be the most important in the legal environment (Tyler and Lind, 1992: 150). Tyler (2000: 123) argues that cultural backgrounds may affect the factors that individuals use to define fairness. Victims' judgments also may be affected by the social standing of their opponents. Studies have indicated that people put less emphasis on fairness when dealing with someone outside of their own ethnic or social group and are more concerned with personal favorability of the outcome, but when the issue involves a member of their own group, fair treatment becomes more important (Tyler et al., 1998). If this argument is applied to the ICTY trials, the victims might put more emphasis on the outcome of the case when the ICTY tries defendants of ethnicities different from theirs but more emphasis on the procedures when the ICTY tries defendants of the same ethnicity as theirs.

VICTIMS OF WAR CRIMES AND CRIMES AGAINST HUMANITY, INTERNATIONAL CRIMINAL TRIBUNALS, AND DISTRIBUTIVE AND PROCEDURAL JUSTICE

Since World War II, thousands of people have been victims of war crimes and crimes against humanity. Yet, very few have testified before international criminal tribunals, be they temporary (e.g., The Nuremberg Tribunal, the Tokyo Tribunal, the ICTY, the ICTR) or permanent (e.g., International Criminal Court). Scientific research on the subject is quite limited, as Eric Stover (2005: 17) vividly describes:

> Little, if anything, is known about the experiences of victims and witnesses who have testified before international war crimes tribunals. What we do know is

> anecdotal, based largely on accounts given to the press by past witnesses. A review of the English literature covering the hundreds of war crimes trials held after World War II reveals not a single empirical study of witnesses and their perceptions of the trial process . . .. In fact, little mention is made of witnesses beyond their appearance at trial and the probative value of their testimony in determining the verdict.

The situation has improved slightly in the last few years with the publication of Eric Stover's (2005) seminal work, *The Witness*. It is the only published empirical study to date that provides an in-depth exploration of victims' experiences with testifying before the ICTY. Stover interviewed 87 victims or witnesses who testified in one of the seven trials at the ICTY. The overwhelming majority of the witnesses (72 percent) were Bosnian Muslims who testified in the five Lašva Valley cases, in which Bosnian Croats were accused of committing war crimes and crimes against humanity. About one-quarter of the respondents (23 percent) were Croats who testified in the trial of Slavko Dokmanović, former mayor of Vukovar, Croatia (HR), and just five (5 percent) were Bosnian Serbs who testified in the Čelebići prison camp case (Stover, 2005: xi). Although Stover's choice of cases and the related ethnic distribution of victims and offenders (mostly Bosnian Muslim victims of Bosnian Croats) do not necessarily match the nature of the cases tried before the ICTY (e.g., 67 percent of defendants in completed cases are of Serb ethnicity; see Chapter 2), it is by far the most comprehensive study on the topic.

Stover provided a detailed qualitative account of what it means to be a witness in such a case, including pretrial fear and the factors affecting the witnesses' motivation to testify; their views about their rights to testify and the benefits thereof; actual experiences in the courtroom; their return home and the consequences of testifying; and, finally, their general evaluations of their overall experience. While the majority of Croats and Serbs in the study did not fear for their safety, Bosnian Muslims expressed a greater degree of such fear (Stover, 2005: 74). Despite the fact that the decision to testify is by no means an easy one to make, one of the strongest findings from the research is the common view—shared by 90 percent of the witnesses of all ethnicities—that it was their moral duty to testify (Stover, 2005: 76). In addition, a number of them wanted to share their stories, have memories of dead family members acknowledged before the ICTY, confront the people who committed the atrocities, and learn what happened to their family members—in other words, to go beyond the pure fact-finding function of the ICTY. Indeed, Stover (2005: 87) reports that several witnesses ended up being angry when the judges prevented them from telling a more contextual account of the event.

Witnesses' interactions with the ICTY, including the prosecutor's office and the office for the protection of witnesses and victims, were generally evaluated as positive (Stover, 2005: 91), although witnesses mentioned a number of complaints, from logistical ones to substantive ones. Even things that may look trivial to an outsider carry a lot of weight in the eyes of the victims and may affect their views of the ICTY's fairness or impartiality. For example, although the three languages spoken in the region (Croatian, Serbian,

Bosniak) are similar, they are not the same language. Consequently, if the language spoken by the ICTY escorts provided for the victims coming to The Hague to testify is the same as the language of the defendant in the case in which the witness is testifying, as several witnesses complained, this can make the witnesses feel quite uncomfortable (see, e.g., Stover, 2005: 91), raise serious doubts about the ICTY's ability to understand the events, and probably affect how the witnesses perceive the ICTY.

Unlike the inquisitorial procedure in which the judges question witnesses, as was the case in the former Yugoslavia, ICTY rules put more emphasis on the adversarial aspect of the proceedings. Thus, the investigators and the prosecutors are the key persons in contact with the witnesses. The quality of pretrial preparation varied greatly, from very minimal to much more extensive, with witnesses carrying the prosecutors' business cards with them (Stover, 2005: 84). Prosecutors who were evaluated positively had some common features (Stover, 2005: 90):

> While witnesses spoke highly of the support provided by the counseling staff of the VWS, their real need was to be actively engaged with the prosecutors who, after all, were their primary link to The Hague tribunal. Indeed, prosecutors and investigators who created a supportive atmosphere for the witnesses were the ones who took the time to orient witnesses to the layout and procedures of the courtroom, to coach them on what to expect from the defense, and to debrief them in a substantive way on the value and effects of their testimony on the case as a whole.

The link between how prosecutors treated witnesses and their satisfaction with the experience is very direct: "When prosecutors paid more attention to the needs of the witnesses, a higher degree of witness satisfaction resulted" (Stover, 2005: 90). Not informing the witness about what would really happen in the courtroom seems to have been a crucial omission.

When asked to evaluate their overall experience with testifying before the ICTY, three-quarters (77 percent; Stover, 2005: 103) evaluated their experience as positive and most said that they would testify again. The follow-up comments depended upon the specifics of the case. The witnesses testifying in the Dokmanović et al. case—Croats testifying in the case with Serb defendants—evaluated their experience as positive, yet felt that justice was not done until one of the key players in the case, Veselin Šljivančanin, the major who ordered the evacuation from the Vukovar hospital, was brought before the ICTY. Unlike the witnesses in the Dokmanović case, the five Serbs testifying in the Čelebići case expressed negative views of the ICTY. They "deeply distrusted" the ICTY (Stover, 2005: 103). Their views were probably related to the outcome in the case and thus touch upon the issue of distributive justice: one of the defendants was acquitted and other defendants received what they perceived to be light sentences (Stover, 2005: 104).

The Lašva Valley witnesses—Bosnian Muslims testifying against Bosnian Croats—were not as uniform in their view, although the majority still evaluated their experience as positive (Stover, 2005: 104). Those who were unhappy with their experience attributed their dissatisfaction to factors that procedural justice theory probably would not consider salient. Yet, these reasons resonated with victims, who said that testifying drained them emotionally or that they suffered negative consequences from testifying and thus were unhappy with their experience. After the appeals chamber quashed the convictions of three defendants (Mirjan Kupreškić, Zoran Kupreškić, and Vlatko Kupreškić), Stover asked his assistant to re-interview the witnesses. According to Stover (2005: 106), four reported being too angry to talk to anybody and eleven were "shocked and disappointed .... Most of the witnesses lost confidence in the ICTY. They feel betrayed. They consider their testifying before the ICTY a waste of time and energy, but, still they do not regret it entirely because ... they see it as their civic duty. But all of them said that next time they would think twice before deciding to testify again." Equity, one of the basic propositions of distributive justice theory, was thus violated, as those whom the witnesses clearly saw as guilty received no punishment at all for the crimes they had committed.

The sense of acknowledgement most felt in the courtroom gradually faded away as they went back home and returned to their lives. Whereas most witnesses seemed to express the desire to be in contact with the ICTY, only about one-half received a simple "thank-you" note and most of them had no contact with the ICTY at all (Stover, 2005: 96). When asked to describe how they felt post-trial, the word "abandonment" was used frequently (Stover, 2005: 96).

Although Stover's study (2005) provides a valuable insight into victims' perspectives of the ICTY and its trials, for the overwhelming majority of the victims, the stark reality is that they will never testify before the ICTY and their impression of the ICTY justice, be it distributive or procedural, will come only from indirect sources. Although a few studies surveyed citizens of the former Yugoslavia (e.g., Arzt, 2006; Biro et al., 2004; Human Rights Center, 2000; Stover, 2005; Stover and Weinstein, 2004), these studies did not explore the issue of distributive and procedural justice in depth. Rather, they typically studied the general level of support for, or trust in, the ICTY and did not ask questions about specific decisions or procedural rules. We now present the analysis of our data and explore how respondents who view themselves as victims reason about the ICTY, its decisions, and procedures.

THE RESPONDENTS AND VICTIMIZATION

The data we use in the analyses that follow are from all seven samples, but we initially include only the respondents who reported being victims of war crimes and crimes against humanity.[2] The percentage of respondents from each sample who viewed themselves

[2] The wording of the identifying question was: "Do you consider yourself a victim of war crimes or crimes against humanity?" Possible answers were "yes" and "no." This question was used in subsequent logistic regression analyses to measure victimization status.

as victims of war crimes and crimes against humanity varied greatly across samples (Figure 5.1; Table 1.4): three-quarters of the respondents from the Zagreb and two Sarajevo samples reported being victims, compared to about one-half of the respondents from the 2004 Priština and 2004 Vukovar samples, and about one-quarter of the respondents in two Belgrade samples.

We also asked a separate question inviting our respondents to describe their victimization to us. Whereas their willingness to provide the description varied across the samples (from 90 percent in the Zagreb sample, to 0 percent in the two Belgrade samples), the descriptions yield a poignant picture of human suffering and loss. Here are excerpts from their descriptions:

The 1997 Zagreb sample (Kutnjak Ivković, 2001):

I lost my father, mother, mother-in-law; our house has been leveled to the ground [woman born in 1967].

I am a mother of a child killed in Vukovar hospital.

My father died defending Vukovar. One brother was killed in Nuštar. One lost his legs. I was expelled [born in 1960].

I've seen everything; I was in the concentration camp 'Manjača,' where I received beatings and beatings . . .

I am a displaced person from Vukovar. I was in town all the time during the attacks on Vukovar with two little kids. My husband, father, and brother were in the concentration camp 'Sremska Mitrovica'. Today, we live in a very small refugee room in Zagreb [born in 1966].

The 2000 Sarajevo sample (Kutnjak Ivković, 2001):

During this war we suffered not only from material losses, but also from psychological stress. To live for four years in the largest concentration camp—how is that?

I resided in Sarajevo during the entire war. [I experienced] an indescribable fear and inexpressible hunger, all the way to shooting pain. All cannot be described in five lines, but it fit into my war diary.

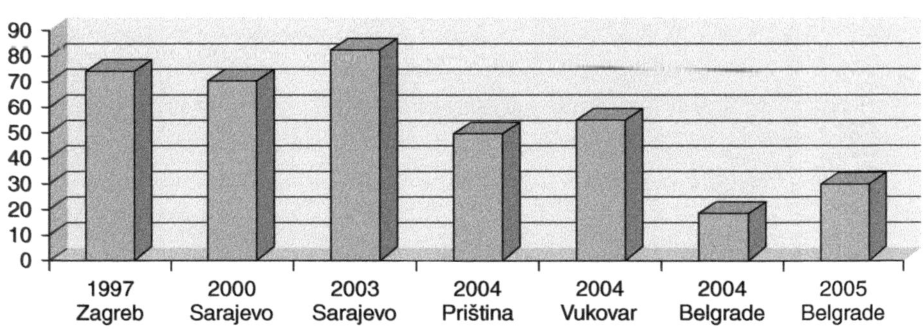

FIGURE 5.1 Percentage by Sample of Respondents Reported Being Victimized

I lived in the besieged city of Sarajevo during the war. Hunger, fear of grenades, snipers . . . Suffering was all around me.

Hungry, thirsty, frozen, and no freedom; I had only courage.

Serbs expelled my parents and me, killed my cousins and friends, raped my neighbors (the Bosnjaks), plundered my property, looted and burnt my parents' house, killed my fiancée, [and] made us homeless in our own town and state.

The 2003 Sarajevo sample (Kutnjak Ivković and Hagan, 2006)

I witnessed all the horrors that happened in the besieged city of Sarajevo. Many of my friends and neighbors were killed or wounded. We picked our fellow citizens' body parts from the streets. Horrific!

Murders of immediate and extended family . . . devastated the city and state . . . Spent all the time in Sarajevo with my family—hunger, thirst, poverty, sickness.

Interruption of normal life. Hunger, thirst, fear for own life and lives of family members, cousins, and fellow citizens.

We had no water, electricity, food, or luck to die at the beginning [of the siege of] Sarajevo.

I was wounded by a sniper bullet from the aggressors' posts (Serb). I am a civil victim of the war. I became a paraplegic [after being] wounded in the spine.

The 2004 Vukovar sample:

[I was] forced to leave my house, 11 years in exile, damaged health, destroyed house. They took everything from me. My life was torn apart, destroyed completely!

Regarding war crimes, firstly my house was burned down, secondly my two sons were taken away and to this very day I have no information about them. I think more should be done for all sufferers from Vukovar.

My children were wounded in the war, my son is an invalid. My house was destroyed and looted. My husband was in a detention camp in Mitrovica. I got diabetes due to fear that I went through.

I consider myself a war victim because my family had to leave our home. I stayed to defend my town and survived heavy shelling. I was in constant danger of being hit by a grenade or bullet. I was captured when Vukovar fell. I was imprisoned for 270 days. I experienced horror, torture, and humiliation. I watched my friends die of severe beating. It's impossible to describe all the horror I've been through on this small piece of paper. I could write a book because all that torture and pain cannot be described in just a few words.

[I] lost a son who was a defender. After that, in 1997, daughter-in-law died leaving 2 children behind. House was destroyed. My sister and brother were slain. Horrible!

The 2004 Priština sample:

The Serbian police beat me up and stole 400DM from me at the train station. Also, they wrote on my identity card that I shouldn't come back anymore and that I should go to Albania.

> We have experienced various forms of mistreatment, like being forced out of our homes. We have stayed in the forests for a long time without eating or drinking. On the way [to the forest] we saw people who had been killed.
>
> I have two dead uncles. The uncle's son has disappeared, my aunt's son was shot and massacred, and my father's uncle has disappeared.
>
> I will never forget the day when they killed my brother's daughter. It was a very tough and black day.
>
> My uncle was shot and my house burned down to the ground.
>
> The 2004 and 2005 Belgrade samples:
>
> Bombing of our country is one of the most severe crimes in history, and no one shall be responsible.
>
> NATO countries should also face the charges for crimes against the Serbs

We have no means of checking the accuracy of the respondents' victimization and we rely on their self-reports. We provided no motivation to the respondents to overestimate their victimization because we neither offered any benefits if they claimed to be victims, nor had we the means of doing so. However, it is still possible that some respondents overreported their victimization. When we compare the descriptions in five samples, provided by respondents viewing themselves as victims (1997 Zagreb, 2000 Sarajevo, 2003 Sarajevo, 2004 Vukovar, 2004 Priština) with the two Belgrade samples (2004 Belgrade, 2005 Belgrade), the nature of the reported experiences typically differ. The respondents from the non-Belgrade samples focused on their own experiences (e.g., assaulted, imprisoned, property stolen), while the respondents from the two Belgrade samples tended to view their victimization as part of a larger victimization of Serbia by NATO.

On the other hand, victims possibly could have underreported their victimization, for the same reasons that victims of other, more traditional crimes may tend to do so. For example, all respondents in the Zagreb sample were either refugees or displaced persons waiting to receive their monthly check from the Croatian government. They had been expelled from their homes by force or a threat to use force. The sheer fact that they are refugees or displaced persons qualifies them, regardless of their own perceptions about their victimization status, to be classified as victims.[3] Many of them were also directly affected by the war as they were injured, held in concentration camps, had family members killed or missing, or had their property destroyed completely. Similarly, we

[3] Roch (2005, p. 15), for example, concludes upon the analysis of differences between forced displacement and indirect displacement (not under a direct use of force, but a threat to use force) and the legal consequences of these differences (i.e., whether both of these categories may be classified as war crimes and, if so, under which conventions), that forced displacement constitutes war crimes and that indirect displacement "should and does fall within the definition as intended by Geneva IV, because the language implies that the victim is moved involuntarily from his "area of habitual residence," regardless of whether he is physically moved or is chased away by fear" [footnotes omitted].

asked our respondents from both Sarajevo surveys where they resided in the city during its siege (1992–1995). The majority of the respondents responded positively and they should readily be considered victims. The siege of Sarajevo claimed the lives of thousands of soldiers and civilians, with countless others injured physically and/or psychologically. People who survived the 44 months of the siege of Sarajevo were victims of a campaign of sniping, artillery, and mortar attacks, all part of a widespread or systematic attack directed against the civilian population. The specific crimes causing suffering and indignity were numerously defined (e.g., *Violations of the Laws or Customs of War*, Article 3; Crimes Against Humanity, Article 5), and the survivors of the siege of Sarajevo were judged to have endured inhumane treatment for a period of close to four years (see *Prosecutor v.Galić*, 2003).

The choice of procedural justice questions was limited as these victims did not participate in the proceedings before the ICTY and thus have no personal experience with the ICTY judges. We could not ask questions about their feelings of trust in the motives of the particular authority who handled their case (e.g., "considered my views," "tried hard to do the right thing by me," "tried to take my needs into account," "cared about my concerns"; Tyler and Huo, 2002: 68) because the victims have no direct experience with the ICTY. In addition, we could not ask direct questions about status recognition by the ICTY because the victims were not parties in the case; they had no standing during the trial. But we could (and we did) ask questions about whether they approve of various victims,' defendants,' and prosecutors' rights.

Procedural justice also involves the perceived quality of decision-making procedures ("neutrality"; Tyler and Huo, 2002: 52). Because of their lack of involvement with the ICTY judges, we could not ask about whether the judges treated them the same as they did other victims. Instead, we asked the respondents about the judges' perceived neutrality. We composed a political neutrality scale based on the questions about judges' ability to resist political pressure, judicial independence, national bias, and the role played by political factors in judicial decisions.

THE RESPONDENTS' DECISION-MAKER OF CHOICE

According to Article 9 of the ICTY's *Statute*, the jurisdiction of the ICTY is *concurrent* with jurisdiction of the national courts. However, the *Statute* determines that the ICTY, as an organ of a superior legal order, has primacy over national courts. If the primacy of the ICTY were not predetermined, the accused would be permitted "to select the forum of his choice, contrary to the principles relating to coercive criminal jurisdiction" (*Prosecutor v. Tadić*, 1995). The primacy of the ICTY over national courts is further enhanced with the two rights given to the ICTY. First, the ICTY may request from the national courts, regardless of the stage in the trial conducted by a national court, to defer the case to the competence of the ICTY (Rule 9, *Rules of Procedure and Evidence*, 2010). Second, the *Statute* provides the ICTY with the option of trying the accused even after the national proceedings are completed. The first three ICTY chief prosecutors—Richard Goldstone, Louise Arbour, and Carla Del Ponte—have been strong advocates for the primary jurisdiction of the ICTY over war crimes and crimes against humanity in the former Yugoslavia and for subsequent international criminal courts, arguing that such courts are often the only means of assuring the security and independence needed to achieve international criminal justice.

Although the ICTY remains the most visible decision-maker for cases involving war crimes and crimes against humanity committed in the 1990s in the territory of the former Yugoslavia, over time local courts gained more prominence: local courts in Croatia became more active and specialized and local courts in Bosnia and Herzegovina and Serbia have been established to address war crimes and crimes against humanity (e.g., the War Crimes Chamber of the Court of Bosnia and Herzegovina and the Special Court for War Crimes of the District Court in Belgrade). As part of its completion strategy, the ICTY also has started transferring cases to the Court of Bosnia and Herzegovina and to the local courts in Croatia. Consequently, as the reality changed, we also revised a question so that, instead of asking respondents to identify the appropriate decision-maker who should try people responsible for war crimes and crimes against humanity, the question asked them to identify the decision-maker who should *primarily* try such cases.

Like our respondents overall (see Chapter 2), the subsets of our samples who viewed themselves as victims did not overwhelmingly support the ICTY (see Table 5.1). Whereas the respondents from the pre-2003 samples (1997 Zagreb sample, 2000 Sarajevo sample) and the respondents from the 2004 Priština sample favored the ICTY over other types of decision-makers, the respondents from other post-2000 samples favored local courts over the ICTY. Specifically, the respondents in the 2003 Sarajevo and 2004 Vukovar sample were split between the ICTY and the local courts in Bosnia and Herzegovina and Croatia, while the respondents from the two Belgrade surveys typically selected the courts in the countries of the defendants' origin and disregarded the ICTY as the decision-maker of choice. As discussed earlier, probably as a consequence of different political and social environments, as well as more information becoming available over time about the specific decisions made and procedures utilized by the ICTY (see Chapter 2), victims' views varied substantially across time and place.

As the war was fought across ethnic lines, we also wanted to explore how ethnicity and views about the ICTY are related, especially for the victims. We carried out an in-depth analysis of the ICTY's legitimacy and ethnicity in Chapter 3. In this chapter, we explore how the victims' views of the ICTY depend upon their ethnicity. A superficial exploration of the topic (see Table 5.1) would lead us to believe that the Muslims/Bosniaks and Albanians seem to be stronger proponents of the ICTY than either the Croats or the Serbs are. The Croats were more evenly split in their views of the appropriate decision-maker between the ICTY and local courts in Bosnia and Herzegovina and Croatia (see Table 5.1), while the Serbs tended to pick the courts in the countries of the defendants' origin more often than they did the ICTY.

TABLE 5.1

Victim Designations of Appropriate Jurisdiction

	ICTY	Local courts (BiH & HR)	Offenders' courts	Victims' families	*Chi-Square*	*Phi*
Jurisdiction in general[a]						
1997 Zagreb	76.9%	13.9%	1.7%	7.5%	786.7***	.760
2000 Sarajevo	74.8%	18.8%	0.5%	5.9%		
2003 Sarajevo	42.4%	45.3%	1.1%	11.3%		
2004 Vukovar	29.8%	50.0%	11.9%	8.3%		
2004 Priština	65.0%	16.9%	2.5%	15.6%		
2004 Belgrade	20.5%	6.8%	68.5%	4.1%		
2005 Belgrade	11.3%	5.7%	69.8%	13.2%		
Jurisdiction in general[a]						
Croats (N=441)	47.8%	38.5%	5.2%	8.4%	378.8***	.529
Bosniaks/Muslims (N=434)	55.8%	33.2%	0.9%	10.1%		
Serbs (N=204)	30.4%	17.6%	44.6%	7.4%		
Albanian + Others (N=276)	62.7%	19.2%	4.3%	13.8%		
Croats (N=441)						
1997 Zagreb	77.4%	13.4%	1.2%	7.9%		
2000 Sarajevo	77.3%	22.7%	0.0%	0.0%		
2003 Sarajevo	35.3%	55.9%	0.0%	8.8%		
2004 Vukovar	23.1%	55.9%	11.3%	9.7%		
Bosniaks/Muslims (N=434)						
1997 Zagreb	71.4%	28.6%	0.0%	0.0%		
2000 Sarajevo	73.5%	18.7%	0.6%	7.2%		
2003 Sarajevo	44.2%	43.0%	0.8%	12.0%		
Serbs (N=204)						
2003 Sarajevo	28.1%	56.3%	3.1%	12.5%		
2004 Vukovar	56.3%	22.9%	16.7%	4.2%		
2004 Belgrade	20.9%	7.5%	68.7%	3.0%		
2005 Belgrade	11.8%	3.9%	70.6%	13.7%		

TABLE 5.1

Continued

	ICTY	Local courts (BiH & HR)	Offenders' courts	Victims' families	*Chi-Square*	*Phi*
Others (N=276)						
2003 Sarajevo	78.6%	14.3%	7.1%	0.0%		
2004 Vukovar	29.4%	64.7%	5.9%	0.0%		
2004 Priština	64.8%	16.9%	2.5%	15.7%		

*** $p < .001$

[a] The question was worded as follows: "Who should try the persons accused of war crimes committed in the territory of the former Yugoslavia?" The possible answers were: "a) the courts in the territory of Croatia and Bosnia and Herzegovina where the crimes have been committed; b) the courts of the offender's country or the country whose army force he was a member of; c) the International Tribunal in The Hague; d) the families of the victims; e) other ______."

However, a more thorough exploration of the relation between views about the ICTY and ethnicity (see Table 5.1) supports our conclusion from Chapter 3 about the complexity of this relation. When we examine the answers by the respondents from the same ethnic group, despite the fact that all of them view themselves as victims and belong to the same ethnic group, the reality is that their views must have been also shaped by factors that go beyond ethnicity—such as the political and social environment—the notion we call "cognitive landscapes" (see Chapter 3). We have a substantial number of Croats in four samples (1997 Zagreb, 2000 Sarajevo, 2003 Sarajevo, 2004 Vukovar) and Muslims/Bosniaks in three samples (1997 Zagreb, 2000 Sarajevo, 2003 Sarajevo). Although they belong to the different ethnic groups who fought against each other, the views of the Muslims/Bosniaks and Croats in our samples seem to follow similar themes. Both Muslims/Bosniaks and Croats in the pre-2003 samples wholeheartedly supported the ICTY, while in 2003 and 2004 less than one-half of both Muslims/Bosniaks and Croats favored the ICTY. The Croats leaned more toward the local courts in Bosnia and Herzegovina and Croatia, while the Muslims/Bosniaks were split between the ICTY and the local courts in Bosnia and Herzegovina and Croatia.

The analysis of the Serb responses (see Table 5.1) further illustrates the point about the complexity of victims' views about the ICTY and the danger of oversimplification of ethnicity. Views about the appropriate decision-maker varied greatly across ethnic groups. Like the Croats from the 2003 Sarajevo sample, the Serb respondents from the same sample—who thus lived in Bosnia and Herzegovina—preferred the local courts from Bosnia and Herzegovina and Croatia, while the majority of the Serb respondents from Vukovar in Croatia—who constitute a minority in Croatia—preferred the ICTY over the local courts (see Table 5.1). Finally, the two surveys from Belgrade project a different picture: Serb respondents from both Belgrade surveys consistently favored the courts in the defendants' country of origin and strongly opposed the idea of utilizing the local courts in Bosnia and Herzegovina and Croatia or the ICTY to try the defendants for war crimes and crimes against humanity. For the respondents from Belgrade, this option (selecting the courts from the country of the defendants' origin) would come closest to a realistic possibility that Serbia, rather than Bosnia and Herzegovina or Croatia, would have jurisdiction over these cases. Our analyses of ethnicity and choice of decision-makers for specific defendants (see Tables 5.2 and 5.3) yielded a similar conclusion about the complexity of the interplay between respondents' views about the appropriate decision-maker and their ethnicity.

Victims' views also depended upon who the defendant was (see Tables 5.2 and 5.3). We present the analyses for three high-ranking defendants who are of Serb and Croat ethnic origin. The first question inquired about the appropriate decision-maker for Radovan Karadžić (the political leader of Bosnian Serbs) and Ratko Mladić (the top military leader of Bosnian Serbs), both of whom are Serbs. The second question asked about the decision-maker for Tihomir Blaškić (the commander of the regional headquarters of the HVO Armed Forces in central Bosnia), who is a Croat.

The general question about the appropriate decision-maker for war crimes and crimes against humanity and the specific question about the appropriate decision-maker for Karadžić and Mladić yielded similar results. The responses about the appropriate decision-maker by all but one group of the respondents remained quite similar regardless of whether the question asked about the decision-maker in general or for specific defendants. Unlike all the other groups of respondents, victims from Vukovar, who preferred local courts over the ICTY in general, turned out to be more sympathetic toward the ICTY when confronted with specific defendants, "the big fish" Karadžić and Mladić. In this case, the majority of the respondents actually selected the ICTY as the decision-maker of their choice (Table 5.2). On the other hand, when the specific defendant was Blaškić, a Bosnian Croat, the respondents from Vukovar and Belgrade (both samples) had quite heterogeneous opinions; their answers were almost equally spread across not two, but three choices: the ICTY, local courts in Bosnia and Herzegovina, and local courts in Croatia.

PERCEPTIONS OF THE ICTY'S FAIRNESS

The notion of the declining trust in the ICTY could also be observed in the respondents' answers about the ICTY's fairness. The results summarized in Table 5.4 reinforce this growing disillusionment. With the exception of the respondents from the 2004 Priština sample, there is a highly significant drop from an overwhelming majority (87 percent in the 1997 Zagreb sample, 85 percent in the 2000 Sarajevo sample) to a strong minority agreement (40 percent in the 2003 Sarajevo sample, 48 percent in the 2004 Vukovar sample) and, finally, to a weak minority agreement (26 percent in the 2004 Belgrade sample and 17 percent in the 2005 Belgrade sample) that the ICTY is fair. Simply put,

TABLE 5.2

Victim Designations of Appropriate Jurisdiction for Karadžić and Mladić

	ICTY	Local courts (BiH)	Local courts (Serbia, RS)	Victims' families	*Chi-Square*	*Phi*
Jurisdiction for Karadžić & Mladić[a]						
1997 Zagreb	80.1%	6.6%	0.6%	12.7%	817.6***	.779
2000 Sarajevo	72.8%	22.3%	0.5%	4.4%		
2003 Sarajevo	39.4%	45.5%	0.8%	14.3%		
2004 Vukovar	52.0%	27.5%	4.1%	16.4%		
2004 Priština	70.2%	14.7%	0.0%	15.1%		
2004 Belgrade	25.0%	6.7%	65.0%	3.3%		
2005 Belgrade	12.2%	22.0%	58.5%	7.3%		
Jurisdiction for Karadžić & Mladić[a]						
Croats (N=449)	59.0%	24.5%	0.7%	15.8%	460.9***	.587
Bosniaks/Muslims (N=442)	53.2%	35.5%	0.5%	10.9%		
Serbs (N=176)	35.2%	21.0%	39.2%	4.5%		
Albanian + Others (N=273)	70.3%	13.9%	1.5%	14.3%		
Croats (N=449)						
1997 Zagreb	80.2%	6.4%	0.6%	12.8%		
2000 Sarajevo	77.3%	22.7%	0.0%	0.0%		
2003 Sarajevo	33.3%	53.6%	0.0%	13.0%		
2004 Vukovar	47.0%	30.3%	1.1%	21.6%		
Bosniaks/Muslims (N=442)						
1997 Zagreb	85.7%	0.0%	0.0%	14.3%		
2000 Sarajevo	71.2%	22.9%	0.6%	5.3%		
2003 Sarajevo	40.8%	44.7%	0.4%	14.1%		
Serbs (N=204)						
2003 Sarajevo	31.3%	50.0%	6.3%	12.5%		
2004 Vukovar	61.4%	20.5%	18.2%	0.0%		
2004 Belgrade	25.5%	7.3%	63.6%	3.6%		
2005 Belgrade	12.8%	20.5%	61.5%	5.1%		

Continued

TABLE 5.2

Continued

	ICTY	Local courts (BiH)	Local courts (Serbia, RS)	Victims' families	*Chi-Square*	*Phi*
Others (N=276)						
2003 Sarajevo	64.3%	14.3%	0.0%	21.4%		
2004 Vukovar	92.9%	7.1%	0.0%	0.0%		
2004 Priština	70.0%	14.8%	0.0%	15.2%		

*** $p < .001$

[a] The question was worded as follows: "In your opinion, who should try Radovan Karadžić and Ratko Mladić?" The possible answers were: "a) courts in Bosnia and Herzegovina; b) courts in Serbia/Republika Srpska; c) the International Tribunal in The Hague; d) the families of the victims; e) other ______."

TABLE 5.3

Victim Designations of Appropriate Jurisdiction for Blaškić

	ICTY	Local courts (HR)	Local courts (BiH)	Victims' families	*Chi-Square*	*Phi*
Jurisdiction for Blaškić[a]						
1997 Zagreb	74.0%	16.2%	3.5%	6.4%	401.6***	.556
2000 Sarajevo	76.5%	0.5%	20.6%	2.5%		
2003 Sarajevo	43.8%	4.2%	40.9%	11.0%		
2004 Vukovar	27.5%	29.9%	36.3%	6.4%		
2004 Priština	74.2%	6.2%	6.2%	13.3%		
2004 Belgrade	28.8%	40.7%	22.0%	8.5%		
2005 Belgrade	25.5%	39.2%	29.4%	5.9%		
Jurisdiction for Blaškić[a]						
Croats (N=405)	49.1%	20.5%	23.5%	6.9%	183.9***	.378
Bosniaks/Muslims (N=442)	56.6%	2.0%	33.5%	7.9%		
Serbs (N=183)	35.0%	29.0%	29.0%	7.1%		
Albanian + Others (N=259)	72.2%	7.3%	8.1%	12.4%		

TABLE 5.3

Continued

	ICTY	Local courts (BiH)	Local courts (Serbia, RS)	Victims' families	*Chi-Square*	*Phi*
Croats (N=405)						
1997 Zagreb	75.2%	16.4%	3.0%	5.5%		
2000 Sarajevo	77.3%	4.5%	18.2%	0.0%		
2003 Sarajevo	39.1%	8.7%	42.0%	10.1%		
2004 Vukovar	20.9%	32.4%	38.5%	8.1%		
Bosniaks/Muslims (N=442)						
1997 Zagreb	50.0%	16.7%	0.0%	33.3%		
2000 Sarajevo	75.7%	0.0%	21.3%	3.0%		
2003 Sarajevo	44.7%	3.0%	41.7%	10.6%		
Serbs (N=183)						
2003 Sarajevo	30.3%	6.1%	51.5%	12.1%		
2004 Vukovar	48.8%	22.0%	26.8%	2.4%		
2004 Belgrade	29.1%	41.8%	20.0%	9.1%		
2005 Belgrade	26.5%	38.8%	28.6%	6.1%		
Others (N=259)						
2003 Sarajevo	85.7%	0.0%	0.0%	14.3%		
2004 Vukovar	35.7%	28.6%	35.7%	0.0%		
2004 Priština	74.1%	6.3%	6.3%	13.4%		

*** $p < .001$

[a] The question was worded as follows: "In your opinion, who should have tried Tihomir Blaškić?" In the 2003 version we added the explanation: "In your opinion, who should have tried Tihomir Blaškić (the commander of the regional headquarters of the HVO Armed Forces in central Bosnia as of June 1992)?" The possible answers were the same: "a) courts in Croatia; b) courts in Bosnia and Herzegovina; c) the International Tribunal in The Hague; d) the families of the victims; and e) other ______."

with the exception of the 2004 Priština sample, only a *minority* of the respondents in all post-2000 samples evaluated the ICTY as fair.

There are two opposite extremes—respondents from both Belgrade samples (who have a low level of confidence in the ICTY's fairness to begin with) on the one hand and the respondents from Priština, the 1997 Zagreb sample, and the 2000 Sarajevo sample (who have an exceptionally high level of confidence in the ICTY's fairness of both its decisions and procedures) on the other hand. For the respondents from the samples in between these two extremes (i.e., the 2003 Sarajevo sample and the 2004 Vukovar sample), the declining level of trust in the ICTY seems to be more strongly related to their perceptions of outcome fairness (i.e., distributive justice) than of procedural fairness. Specifically, while only one-third of the respondents from both samples (29 percent of the respondents from the 2003 Sarajevo sample and 33 percent of the respondents from the 2004 Vukovar samples) evaluated ICTY decisions as fair, the majority (75 percent of the respondents from the 2003 Sarajevo sample and 51 percent of the respondents from the 2004 Vukovar sample) evaluated the ICTY procedures as fair.

As the number of cases tried by the ICTY increased, we kept adding questions about specific decisions and specific defendants. When we started with the survey in 1997, the first trial was ongoing, but there was no decision yet. It was the trial of Duško Tadić, caught in Germany and tried for his role in the forceful transfer and mistreatment, including murder, of prisoners of non-Serb ethnicity in the concentration camps (ICTY, 2009). He was sentenced to 20 years. The Blaškić case was the next case we included in our questionnaire (ICTY, 2009). Blaškić's sentence was meted out on March 3, 2000, just as we were starting the data collection in Sarajevo (Blaškić's case was one of the five cases related to the Lašva Valley that Stover [2005] discussed in his book). It was a highly relevant case for our purposes because it included a Bosnian Croat in the Croatian Defense Council (HVO) who was convicted based on both individual and command responsibility for inhumane and cruel treatment of Bosnian Muslims/Bosniaks. In 2000, Blaškić was initially sentenced to 45 years, but on appeal, in 2004, the sentence was reduced to 9 years. The next case we added was that of Esad Landžo, a guard in the Čelebići prison camp who was convicted for willful killing and torture of prisoners. His methods were particularly gruesome and resulted in the deaths of a number of detainees. He was convicted and sentenced to 15 years (ICTY, 2009). The last case we included, that of Major General Stanislav Galić, is particularly relevant for the respondents from Sarajevo. Galić was the commander of the Romanija Corps of the Bosnian Serb Army (VRS) that maintained the siege of Sarajevo from 1992 to 1994 (ICTY, 2009). On December 9, 2003, at the time we were starting data collection in Sarajevo, he was convicted for conducting the campaign of sniping and shelling attacks on the city of Sarajevo and sentenced to 20 years. Three years later, on November 30, 2006, the Appeals Chamber changed his sentence to life imprisonment.

The respondents were asked to assess whether they viewed these sentences as fair (Table 5.4), and there was no clear and unanimous view. The respondents from Belgrade—almost exclusively Serbs by ethnicity—tended to evaluate the convictions of non-Serbs (e.g., Blaškić, Landžo) as more fair than the convictions of Serbs. They particularly favored the harsh, 45-year sentence for Blaškić (the majority of the respondents in the 2004 Belgrade sample and close to one-half in the 2005 Belgrade sample evaluated this decision as fair), which was later substantially reduced on appeal. In contrast, the majority of the respondents in the 2000 Sarajevo sample, the only pre-2003 sample that had predominantly Muslim respondents, but also had nontrivial representation of Croat and Serb respondents, did not regard the 45-year conviction of the Croat Blaškić as fair.

TABLE 5.4

Respondents' Views of the ICTY and Its Fairness

	1997 Zagreb	2000 Sarajevo	2003 Sarajevo	2004 Vukovar	2004 Priština	2004 Belgrade	2005 Belgrade	*Chi-Square*	*Phi*
ICTY Fairness[a]									
% Fair	87.6%	85.4%	40.2%	48.1%	86.5%	25.6%	16.9%	345.5***	.500
ICTY Fairness of Decisions[b]									
% Fair	87.1%	86.5%	28.7%	32.9%	93.0%	27.1%	20.3%	499.6***	.604
ICTY Fairness of Procedures[c]									
% Fair	87.6%	92.1%	75.2%	50.6%	94.0%	26.2%	18.6%	351.8***	.504
ICTY Fairness of Decisions: Duško Tadić (Serb)[d]									
% Fair	N/A	82.8%	20.5%	36.9%	37.7%	28.6%	21.1%	231.6***	.458

*** $p < .001$; ** $p < .01$; * $p < .05$; ^z $p < .10$

[a] The question was worded as follows: "Do you think that the decisions/verdicts by the International Tribunal are fair?" The answers ranged on a four-point scale from "very fair" to "very unfair." Categories "very fair" and "fair" were merged, as were categories "unfair" and "very unfair."

[b] The question was worded as follows: "Do you think that the decisions/verdicts by the International Tribunal are fair?" The answers ranged on a four-point scale from "very fair" to "very unfair." Categories "very fair" and "fair" were merged, as were categories "unfair" and "very unfair."

[c] The question was worded as follows: "Do you think that the procedure by the International Tribunal is fair?" The answers ranged on a four-point scale from "very fair" to "very unfair." Categories "very fair" and "fair" were merged, as were categories "unfair" and "very unfair."

[d] The question was worded as follows: "Do you think that the decision by the International Tribunal to sentence Duško Tadić to 20 years of imprisonment is fair?" The 2003 version was worded as: "Do you think that the decision by the International Tribunal to sentence Duško Tadić (a guard at the Omarska concentration camp) to 20 years of imprisonment is fair?" The answers ranged on a four-point scale from "very fair" to "very unfair."

Continued

TABLE 5.4

Continued

	1997 Zagreb	2000 Sarajevo	2003 Sarajevo	2004 Vukovar	2004 Priština	2004 Belgrade	2005 Belgrade	*Chi-Square*	*Phi*
ICTY Fairness of Decisions: Tihomir Blaškić (Croat)[c]									
% Fair	N/A	32.7%	21.8%	7.3%	56.0%	59.5%	44.1%	171.8***	.384
ICTY Fairness of Decisions: Esad Landžo (Muslim)[f]									
% Fair	N/A	82.3%	40.3%	29.3%	37.3%	50.7%	32.8%	133.2***	.362
ICTY Fairness of Decisions: Stanislav Galić (Serb)[g]									
% Fair	N/A	N/A	6.0%	30.0%	30.3%	35.1%	15.3%	85.06***	.312

*** $p < .001$; ** $p < .01$; * $p < .05$; [z] $p < .10$

[c] The question was worded as follows: "Do you think that the decision by the International Tribunal to sentence Esad Landžo to 15 years of imprisonment is fair?" The 2003 version was worded as: "Do you think that the decision by the International Tribunal to sentence Esad Landžo (a guard at the Čelebići concentration camp) to 15 years of imprisonment is fair?" The answers ranged on a four-point scale from "very fair" to "very unfair."

[f] The question was worded as follows: "Do you think that the decision by the International Tribunal to sentence Tihomir Blaškić to 45 years of imprisonment is fair?" The 2003 version was worded as: "Do you think that the decision by the International Tribunal to sentence Tihomir Blaškić (the commander of the regional headquarters of the HVO Armed Forces in central Bosnia as of June 1992) to 45 years of imprisonment is fair?" The answers ranged on a four-point scale from "very fair" to "very unfair."

[g] The question was worded as follows: "Do you think that the decision by the International Tribunal to sentence Stanislav Galić (the major general who lead the Romanija Corps and maintained the siege of Sarajevo from 1992 to 1994) to 20 years of imprisonment is fair?" The answers ranged on a four-point scale from "very fair" to "very unfair."

The evaluations of these ICTY decisions were quite different in the 2003 Sarajevo sample. Like the respondents from the 2004 Vukovar sample, the majority of the respondents in the 2003 Sarajevo sample viewed the ICTY decisions as fair in *none* of the cases (Table 5.4). Finally, our respondents from the 2004 Priština sample thought that only one of these decisions was fair: the majority of the Priština respondents thought that the sentencing of Blaškić to 45 years was fair. Despite the differences across the six samples, the similarities are that, with the exception of the 2000 Sarajevo sample, the majority of the respondents evaluated the sentences of two Serbs, Duško Tadić and Stanislav Galić, as fair. The similarities probably stop here because the Belgrade respondents likely view these sentences as too harsh, while the respondents from other parts of the former Yugoslavia probably view them as too lenient.

VIEWS ABOUT PROCEDURAL RIGHTS

The potential discrepancy between the level of trust in the ICTY's ability to make fair decisions and run trials in a fair manner (which we detected among the respondents who neither completely dismissed the ICTY nor absolutely embraced it) further surfaces in the analysis of the defendants,' victims,' and prosecutors' rights (Tables 5.5. and 5.6). As Table 5.5 shows, respondents were willing to grant a number of procedural rights to the defendants. A series of items on the questionnaire asked respondents to state whether they would grant certain rights to the defendants (Table 5.6), ranging from the right to be silent to the right to be tried by an impartial judge. With the exception of two rights—the right not to be in custody and the right to be silent—the mean scores above five on a scale from one to ten indicate that the respondents would grant these different rights, central to notions of liberal legalism, to defendants tried before the ICTY. In fact, the respondents from the post-2000 samples (2003 Sarajevo sample, 2004 Vukovar sample, 2004 Priština sample, 2004 Belgrade sample, and 2005 Belgrade sample) seem to be more likely to approve of and grant these rights to the defendants (especially the rights to have an attorney, present a defense, propose witnesses, have an impartial judge, and be tried by a jury) than the respondents from the earlier samples were (1997 Zagreb sample and 2000 Sarajevo sample). Two rights were particularly problematic and respondents were unwilling to grant them to the defendants: the right not to be in custody (which is not a right enjoyed by ICTY defendants) and the right to remain silent (which is a right enjoyed by ICTY defendants). This strong disapproval of the potential pretrial release of defendants was probably a reflection of the severity of the charges and the difficulty the ICTY had initially, and still has, in getting NATO troops to make arrests for the ICTY (Hagan, 2003).

In the more recent surveys we added several questions about additional defendants' rights, the prosecutors' rights, and victims' rights. With the exception of the respondents from the 2003 Sarajevo sample, the majority of the respondents in all other samples (Table 5.6) agreed that presumption of innocence should be a starting point in every case.

TABLE 5.5

Respondents' Views of the Defendants' Rights[a]

	1997 Zagreb	2000 Sarajevo	2003 Sarajevo	2004 Vukovar	2004 Priština	2004 Belgrade	2005 Belgrade	*F-test*
To have an attorney	5.66	3.09	8.39	8.55	7.68	8.59	8.53	98.04***
Not to be in custody	2.52	1.91	1.77	4.39	2.45	4.94	6.64	40.96***
To be silent	4.02	2.82	4.78	4.59	3.90	4.36	4.17	6.41***
To present a defense	5.75	3.70	7.46	8.02	7.63	8.49	8.56	70.23***
To propose witnesses	6.31	4.26	7.28	8.28	7.29	8.41	8.68	54.47***
To an impartial judge	5.94	3.28	8.34	8.15	7.56	8.57	8.86	105.93***
To a jury trial	5.57	4.53	4.81	7.96	7.77	8.15	8.61	60.10***
To an appeal	3.90	4.44	5.08	7.80	7.64	8.36	8.68	56.75***

*** $p < .001$

[a] The question was worded as follows: "Which of the rights below should be guaranteed to the defendants tried by the International Tribunal (please circle a number from 1 to 10)." Each item was accompanied by a 10-item scale from 1 "definitely no" to 10 "definitely yes."

The voices from the Belgrade respondents were particularly strong, which is not surprising because the majority of the defendants at the ICTY are Serbs. The right to plea bargain did not receive much approval. In fact, in no sample did the majority of the respondents approve of this right. According to the majority of our respondents from all samples, the right to plea bargain, provided by the ICTY's *Rules of Procedure and Evidence* (2010) since 1994 and used more often recently, should not be provided to the ICTY defendants; as few as 5 percent approved of it in the 2003 Sarajevo sample and at most 40 percent approved of it in the 2004 Belgrade sample (Table 5.6).

The prosecutors' rights about which we inquired (e.g., sealed or secret indictments and their importance) did not resonate similarly in all samples. Although the majority of the respondents in all five samples thought that "non-disclosure of confirmed indictments is [important] for catching the offenders who are at large" (see Table 5.6), only the majority of the respondents in the 2003 Sarajevo and 2004 Vukovar samples actually approved of the prosecutors' right to ask the ICTY for the temporary non-disclosure of confirmed indictments.

TABLE 5.6

Approval of Defendants,' Prosecutors,' and Victims' Rights

	2003 Sarajevo	2004 Vukovar	2004 Priština	2004 Belgrade	2005 Belgrade	χ^2	*Phi*
Defendants' Rights							
Presumption of innocence[a]	47.9%	79.3%	61.8%	88.4%	96.6%	119.0***	.351
Right to plea bargain[b]	5.2%	19.8%	32.6%	40.7%	32.2%	105.3***	.325
Prosecutors' Rights							
Sealed indictments[c]	64.3%	52.2%	32.4%	43.0%	23.7%	76.6***	.280
Importance of sealed indictments[d]	64.0%	75.1%	88.9%	55.3%	50.8%	64.4***	.259
Victims' Rights							
Testifying in closed sessions[e]	58.8%	81.6%	51.6%	52.4%	57.6%	54.7***	.235
Expunging names from records	53.4%	66.1%	35.2%	45.7%	33.9%	51.8***	.230
Testifying through image- or voice-altering devices	59.3%	74.1%	43.0%	51.2%	30.5%	65.0***	.256

*$p < .05$; **$p < .01$; ***$p < .001$

[a] The question was worded as follows: "One of the presumptions of the criminal process is that the defendant is presumed innocent until proven guilty in the court of law. Do you think that the presumption of innocence should be used in every case tried by the International Tribunal?" The answers ranged on a four-point scale from "definitely yes" to "definitely no."

[b] The question was worded as follows: "Do you think that the defendants should be able to plea bargain with the prosecution?" The answers ranged on a four-point scale from "definitely yes" to "definitely no."

[c] The question was worded as follows: "Do you approve of the prosecutor's right to ask the Tribunal for the temporary non-disclosure to the public of the confirmed indictments (i.e., "sealed indictments")?" The answers ranged on a four-point scale from "strongly approve" to "strongly disapprove."

[d] The question was worded as follows: "How important do you think that this non-disclosure of confirmed indictments is for catching the offenders who are at large?" The answers ranged on a four-point scale from "very important" to "not important at all."

[e] The question was worded as follows: "Do you approve of the following victims' and witnesses' protection measures: 1) testifying in closed sessions; 2) expunging their names from official records; 3) giving testimony through image- or voice-altering devices?" For each protection measure, the answers ranged on a four-point scale from "strongly approve" to "strongly disapprove."

Similarly, there was substantial disagreement over the victims' and witnesses' protection measures, such as testifying in closed sessions, expunging their names from official records, and giving testimony through image- or voice-altering devices (Table 5.6). Although the majority of the respondents in all samples agreed with the witnesses' right to testify in closed sessions, the majority of the respondents in only the 2003 Sarajevo and 2004 Vukovar samples approved of the idea of expunging witnesses' names from the court records and giving witnesses the right to testify through image- or voice-altering devices. Respondents from other samples (with the exception of 2004 Belgrade for the image- or voice-altering devices) tended to disapprove of such measures.

The impression emerging from the previous analyses is that the respondents are becoming increasingly more skeptical of the appropriateness and fairness of the ICTY jurisdiction over war crimes and crimes against humanity cases. A better understanding of the relative role of the various correlates of the respondents' assessments of the ICTY's fairness requires a multivariate analysis of the process involved.

MULTIVARIATE MODELS OF THE ICTY'S FAIRNESS

We further explore the issue of ICTY's fairness with logistic regression analyses in which the perception of the ICTY's overall fairness is the dependent variable (Table 5.7).[4] The inclusion of only the respondents' demographic characteristics in the model yields the result that the respondents' ethnicity and education are key variables in explaining their perceptions of fairness. Specifically, compared to Croats, Albanians from Kosovo had a more positive view, while Serbs had a more negative view, of ICTY's fairness (Table 5.7). However, a gradual addition of further explanatory variables into the model (e.g., sample, fairness of decisions, fairness of procedures, political scale) completely mediates the role of the respondents' ethnicity as a strong predictor of their views of the ICTY's fairness (Table 5.7). The story is the same with education: although in the initial model college graduates had a more positive view of the ICTY's fairness than those who were less educated did, the effect of education disappears as mediating variables are added into subsequent models.

Similarly, although belonging to a particular sample was a strong predictor of how the respondents would evaluate the ICTY's fairness, the respondents from all non-Belgrade samples (1997 Zagreb; 2000 Sarajevo; 2003 Sarajevo; 2004 Vukovar; 2004 Priština) showed more positive views of the ICTY's fairness than the respondents from the two

[4] The question was worded as follows: "Do you think that the International Tribunal conducts the trials correctly and fairly and makes just decisions?" Possible answers ranged from "definitely yes" (i.e., very fair) to "definitely no" (i.e., very unfair). Because our primary interest lies in comparing the views held by the respondents who evaluated the ICTY as fair with the views held by the respondents who evaluated the ICTY as unfair, we condensed the four-point Likert scale into a dichotomized scale of "fair" and "unfair."

TABLE 5.7

Logistic Coefficients from the Regression of Perceived Fairness of ICTY on Respondents' Attitudes and Background Characteristics[a]

	Model 1			Model 2			Model 3			Model 4		
	B		s.e.	B		s.e.	B		s.e.	B		s.e.
Ethnicity[b]												
Muslims	−.178		.143	.386		.227	−.088		.324	.214		.396
Serbs	−1.081	***	.175	.650	**	.259	.467		.420	.762		.510
Albanians + Others	.998	***	.185	.650		.349	.319		.636	.338		.764
Gender[c]	.132		.118	.106		.131	.398	*	.195	.385		.235
Education[d]												
Below high school	−.864	***	.210	−.850	***	.244	−.558		.380	−.480		.449
High school	−.466	**	.162	−.296		.184	−.202		.267	−.197		.314
Sample[e]												
1997 Zagreb				4.199	***	.485	1.522	a	.820	1.422		.953
2000 Sarajevo				3.543	***	.475	2.157	**	.744	1.116		.908
2003 Sarajevo				1.418	**	.429	1.438	*	.668	1.016		.821
2004 Vukovar				2.137	***	.428	2.737	***	.691	2.203	**	1.103
2004 Priština				3.495	***	.546	1.845	*	.905	1.942	a	.842
2004 Belgrade				.507		.429	.837		.672	.978		.835

* $p < .05$; ** $p < .01$; *** $p < .001$; [a] $p < .10$;

[a] The question was worded as follows: "Do you think that the International Tribunal conducts the trials correctly and fairly and makes just decisions?" The answers ranged on a four-point scale from "definitely yes" (i.e., very fair) to "definitely no" (i.e., very unfair). The dependent variable is coded as follows: 0 = unfair or very unfair; 1 = fair or very fair.

[b] Ethnicity is dummy coded with Croats as the omitted comparison category.

[c] Gender is coded as follows: 0 = males; 1 = females.

[d] Education is dummy coded with college graduates as the omitted comparison category.

[e] Sample is dummy coded with 2005 Belgrade as the omitted comparison category.

Continued

TABLE 5.7

Continued

	Model 1			Model 2			Model 3			Model 4		
	B		s.e.	B		s.e.	B		s.e.	B		s.e.
Fairness of decisions[f]							2.487	***	.255	1.902	***	.303
Punishment purpose[g]							.497	*	.214	.484	a	.254
Fairness of procedures[h]							1.715	***	.275	1.166	**	.346
Defendants' rights							.011		.007	.011		.008
Political scale[i]										−.713	***	.074
Constant	.859	***	.172	−1.953	***	.462	−4.480	***	.760	3.701	**	1.214
Pseudo R^2	.118			.332			.620			.726		

* $p < .05$; ** $p < .01$; *** $p < .001$; [a] $p < .10$;

[f] Fairness of decisions is coded as follows: 0 = unfair; 1 = fair.

[g] Punishment purpose is coded as follows: 0 = retribution; 1= deterrence (special and general).

[h] Fairness of procedures is coded as follows: 0 = unfair; 1 = fa r.

[i] We created the political scale using the respondents' answers on four questions: "Do you think that the International Tribunal in The Hague resists political pressure" (four-point scale from "definitely does" to "definitely does not"); "Do you think that the independence of the judges of the International Tribunal in The Hague has been achieved?" (four-point scale from "definitely yes" to "definitely no"); "Do you think that the nationality of a judge from the International Tribunal will influence the decision the judge will vote for?" (four-point scale from "definitely yes" to "definitely no"); and "According to your opinion, what role will the polit cs play in the work and the decisions by the International Tribunal?" (four-point scale from "very important" to "not important at all"). The last two questions were recorded in the reverse order to fit the scale. The scale ranged from 4 to 16. Cronbach's Alpha is .612.

Belgrade samples (2004 Belgrade; 2005 Belgrade) did; consequently, the effect of the sample itself started to disappear with the inclusion of the respondents' views about procedural fairness and substantive fairness (Table 5.7). It completely disappeared with the inclusion of the political scale into the model. The only exception is the Vukovar sample, which yielded a more positive opinion of the ICTY than the 2005 Belgrade sample did, even when all the mediating variables were controlled for.

The bottom line is that, in the final model, the respondents' views of the ICTY's fairness are strongly related to how fair the respondents judged the ICTY's decisions and procedures to be, and how politically biased they viewed the ICTY judges to be (see Table 5.7). The odds that the respondents who evaluated the ICTY *decisions* as fair would regard ICTY overall as fair are estimated to be 6.7 times as high as those of the respondents who evaluated the ICTY decisions as unfair, all other covariates being equal.[5] Similarly, the odds that the respondents who evaluated the ICTY *procedures* as fair would regard the ICTY overall as fair are estimated to be 3.2 times as high as those of the respondents who evaluated the ICTY procedures as unfair. Finally, a one-unit increase on the scale of perceived political influence decreased the odds that the respondents would evaluate the ICTY as fair overall by 0.5 times. Thus, the respondents' perceptions of justice at the ICTY are related to the feelings that the ICTY decisions are fair, that the ICTY procedures are fair, and that ICTY judges are not politically biased. None of the remaining variables—including most notably ethnicity—are statistically significant at the .05 level. The effect of ethnicity is mediated by perceptual variables.

As the ICTY's *Rules of Procedure and Evidence* evolved, we added more questions about procedural issues in the later versions of the questionnaire. For example, Rule 62 *ter*, added on December 13, 2001, now addresses basic matters surrounding the plea bargaining agreement. As discussed earlier, when asked whether they approved of the defendant's right to plea bargain—one of the few procedural rights that leads directly into reduced sentence—the majority of the respondents in all five post-2000 samples indicated they disapproved of this right. We also include the scaled version of the defendant's rights (to have an attorney, not to be in custody, to be silent, to present a defense, to propose witnesses, to an impartial judge, to a jury trial, to an appeal) and the victims' rights (including testifying in closed sessions, expunging victims' names from official records, and giving testimony in ways that further conceal identity) in the logistic regression using the five post-2000 samples.

The results of this logistic regression are summarized in Table 5.8. The findings are quite similar to the results of the prior analysis with the full sample (fairness of the decisions, punishment purpose, and political scale all influence the respondents' perceptions of ICTY fairness), with an additional variable—punishment purpose—becoming relevant. The odds that the respondents who emphasized either general or special deterrence

---

[5] The odds effects are obtained by exponentiation of the logistic coefficients.

TABLE 5.8

Logistic Coefficients from the Regression of Perceived Fairness of ICTY on Respondents' Attitudes and Background Characteristics[a]

	Model 1			Model 2			Model 3			Model 4		
	B		s.e.	B		s.e.	B		s.e.	B		s.e.
Ethnicity[b]												
Muslims	.255		.223	.646	*	.267	−.002		.375	.218		.460
Serbs	−.169		.210	.643	*	.272	.451		.475	.683		.573
Albanians + Others	2.423	***	.255	2.152	**	.644	1.561		1.077	2.070		1.288
Gender[c]	−.092		.143	.023		.148	.306		.229	.310		.283
Education[d]												
Below high school	.167		.257	−1.251	**	.383	−.546		.593	−.972		.753
High school	−.148		.226	−.178		.236	.034		.350	.139		.420
Sample[e]												
2003 Sarajevo				1.120	*	.441	1.567	*	.749	1.251		.914
2004 Vukovar				2.991	***	.531	3.205	***	.900	3.338	**	1.155
2004 Priština				2.172	**	.772	.628		1.278	.402		1.522
2004 Belgrade				.557		.435	.944		.738	1.151		.926

Fairness of decisions[f]							2.546	***	.306	2.102	***	.359
Punishment purpose[g]							.850	**	.258	.825	**	.315
Fairness of procedures[h]							1.880	***	.315	1.313	**	.395
Defendants' rights							.004		.009	.002		.011
Plea bargaining[i]							.055		.349	.138		.439
Victim rights							−.105	*	.043	−.091	a	.052
Political scale[j]										−.703	***	.087
Constant	−.446	a	.263	−1.941	***	.487	−4.087	***	.935	3.733	*	1.459
Pseudo R^2	.233			.280			.637			.743		

* $p < .05$; ** $p < .01$; *** $p < .001$; [a] $p < .10$;

[a] The question was worded as follows: "Do you think that the International Tribunal conducts the trials correctly and fairly and makes just decisions?" The answers ranged on a four-point scale from "definitely yes" (i.e., very fair) to "definitely no" (i.e., very unfair). The dependent variable is coded as follows: 0 = unfair or very unfair; 1 = fair or very fair.

[b] Ethnicity is dummy coded with Croats as the omitted comparison category.

[c] Gender is coded as follows: 0 = males; 1 = females.

[d] Education is dummy coded with college graduates as the omitted comparison category.

[e] Sample is dummy coded with 2005 Belgrade as the omitted comparison category.

[f] Fairness of decisions is coded as follows: 0 = unfair; 1 = fair.

[g] Punishment purpose is coded as follows: 0 = retribution; 1= deterrence (special and general).

[h] Fairness of procedures is coded as follows: 0 = unfair; 1 = fair.

[i] Plea bargaining is coded as follows: 0 = no; 1 = yes.

[j] We created the political scale using the respondents' answers on four questions: "Do you think that the International Tribunal in The Hague resists political pressure" (four-point scale from "definitely does" to "definitely does not"); "Do you think that the independence of the judges of the International Tribunal in The Hague has been achieved?" (four-point scale from "definitely yes" to "definitely no"); "Do you think that the nationality of a judge from the International Tribunal will influence the decision the judge will vote for?" (four-point scale from "definitely yes" to "definitely no"); and "According to your opinion, what role will the politics play in the work and the decisions by the International Tribunal?" (four-point scale from "very important" to "not important at all"). The last two questions were recorded in the reverse order to fit the scale. The scale ranged from 4 to 16. Cronbach's Alpha is .612.

would regard the ICTY as fair overall are estimated to be 2.3 times as high as those of the respondents who emphasized retribution as the primary purpose of punishment.

CONCLUSION

The reality for most victims of the wars in the former Yugoslavia is that they will never get an opportunity to testify before the ICTY judges, confront those accused of attacking them, and tell the story of their suffering. Instead, their impressions of the ICTY and judgments about the ICTY's fairness will be based on media accounts of the ICTY's decisions and processes, colored by local politicians' interpretations of these events, and the views of their families and friends.

Over the eight-year period considered in our research, our respondents—people viewing themselves as victims of war crimes and crimes against humanity committed in the territory of the former Yugoslavia—show an increasing level of dissatisfaction with the ICTY. With the passage of time, they are less likely to pick the ICTY as the appropriate decision-maker for trying these crimes and less likely to view it as fair. Simply put, the perceptions of the ICTY's fairness have worsened over time. Whereas the overwhelming majority of the respondents surveyed in the pre-2003 surveys thought that the ICTY was fair, with the exception of the respondents from Priština, less than one-half of the respondents in the post-2000 surveys thought the same. These dramatic changes do not seem to be as affected by their perceptions about the fairness of the procedures, as they are affected by their perceptions about the fairness of the decisions. Doubts about the ICTY's political neutrality (i.e., low scores on neutrality, trust, or impartiality, in the parlance of the procedural justice language) carry more influence with the respondents' overall perceptions of the ICTY's fairness than the respondents' views of procedural fairness do, although views of procedural fairness also affect their views. It really does not matter to the respondents what rights are provided to the defendants because they approved almost all of them and, in fact, their approval of these rights seems to grow stronger over time.

One of the key variables in explaining respondents' views of the ICTY's fairness is how they viewed the purpose of punishment. The ICTY has been in existence since 1993, but the purposes of sentencing are mentioned neither in the *Statute* (2006) nor in the *Rules of Procedure and Evidence* (2010). The ICTY judges discussed the functions and purposes of sentencing for the first time in an early sentencing—that of Dražen Erdemović, who pleaded guilty. Notwithstanding the fact that the ICTY's mission is "to deter further crimes" (ICTY, 2006), its emphasis is on retribution as much or more than deterrence (Bulletin, 1997):

> One of the purposes of punishment for a crime against humanity lies precisely in stigmatising criminal conduct which has infringed a value fundamental not merely to a given society, but to humanity as a whole . . . it would seem that the particulari-

> ties of crimes falling within the jurisdiction of the Tribunal rule out [the rehabilitative function, because] the concern for the above-mentioned function of the punishment must be subordinate to that of any attempt to stigmatise the most serious violations of international humanitarian law, and in particular an attempt to preclude their reoccurrence.

For the respondents who viewed retribution as the key purpose for the ICTY, the appropriate punishment for the people guilty of abusing, torturing, or killings dozens could only be the death penalty or life imprisonment. If that is the case, the fact that the most severe sanction—the death penalty—is taken off the table (i.e., the ICTY is not authorized to impose the death penalty) seriously challenges the prospect that the ICTY will ever be able to provide a full sense of justice to the victims. Consequently, if the victims are seeking retribution and favor the death penalty for this purpose, it is quite likely that they will be generally unhappy with *any* ICTY outcome, regardless of how unbiased they perceive the judges to be or how fair they judge the ICTY procedures to be.

In sum, our results suggest that three issues explain the respondents' growing dissatisfaction with the ICTY: their increased doubts about the ICTY's neutrality, decision fairness, and process fairness. The findings of our study regarding a transnational institution are similar to the results of prior research in the domestic legal environment, in which standing and trust seem to be the most important factors (although standing is not applicable in this context because victims have no standing before the ICTY; see Tyler and Lind, 1992: 150). Ultimately, it seems that constituencies' perceptions of the ICTY and its fairness are multifaceted and complex.

6

RECLAIMING JUSTICE

The Ideal and the Reality

THE WARS IN THE FORMER Yugoslavia were a bloody, horrifying, and degrading human experience; in a period of four years (1991–1995), the wars in Croatia and Bosnia and Herzegovina resulted in more than three million refugees, 200,000–250,000 persons killed, 50,000 victims of torture, 20,000 cases of rape, and a large-scale destruction of public and private property (UNGA, 1994). In the ideal world that seeks to provide justice in the aftermath of such events, the perpetrators of these crimes would receive the deserved punishment and the victims would see justice done. Yet, the reality is different.

In this book we explored the views about justice delivered by the ICTY and the local courts in the countries of the former Yugoslavia. Our respondents—samples of citizens of the countries in the former Yugoslavia—were rather optimistic about the ICTY in the 1990s, but the subsequent, post-2000 surveys, indicate a declining trust in the ICTY. At the same time, the respondents seem to have been leaning increasingly toward advocating for a more substantial role for the local courts. Several themes emerged from our research: (1) the ICTY's legitimacy; (2) the role of ethnicity at the ICTY; (3) issues of collective responsibility and pre-structural conditionality; and (4) the prospect of a justice cascade of international and domestic legal efforts. In this, the final chapter of our book, we provide an overview of our findings and place them in the perspective of reclaiming justice.

THE LEGITIMACY OF THE ICTY

Legitimacy, the judgments citizens make about governmental organizations, provides these governmental organizations with the authority necessary to carry out their tasks. Viewed as both diffuse support ("generalization of support for the institution"; Dennis, 1975: 50) and specific support ("a return for the specific benefits and advantages that members of a system experience as part of their membership [in the system]"; Easton, 1965: 38), justice is measured in terms such as the perceived obligation to obey the law, support for legal authorities (e.g., Tyler, 1990: 45), trust in legal institutions, and so on.

Unlike domestic or local national courts, which can draw from the legitimacy of the state government, international courts and tribunals suffer from a democratic deficit. This democratic deficit is defined by Caldeira and Gibson (1995: 356) as "a shortfall of institutional democracy," and is associated with "[t]he lack of direct electoral connection, the inability to share in the legitimacy of the nation-state,... and the traditionally heavy reliance on legal institutions on the goodwill of ordinary citizens." Thus, the legitimacy of the ICTY does not rest on the legitimacy of a specific state, but the international association that established the court, the United Nations (particularly the UN's Security Council). Caldeira and Gibson (1995: 358) further argue:

> Transnational political institutions cannot rely on the "presumption of legitimacy" associated with national institutions. Since nation-states enjoy a higher level of allegiance from citizens than do transnational polities, the most direct and common source of legitimacy for institutions such as the Court of Justice is either not available or significantly diminished. Moreover, since these institutions are relatively new, tradition cannot sustain them.

Compared to the Court of Justice of the European Union, established almost six decades ago (in 1952; Court of Justice, 2010), the ICTY is a relatively new institution, in existence only since the 1990s. Despite the Court of Justice's considerably longer tenure, "slightly more than a third of the mass public in the EU has virtually no information or opinion about the Court" (Caldeira and Gibson, 1995: 363). In contrast, literally all of our respondents not only have heard about the ICTY, but also have formed an opinion about it and its trials and procedures, regardless of whether they were surveyed in the 1990s or in the 2000s; in Croatia, Bosnia and Herzegovina, Serbia, or Kosovo; whether they were young or old; female or male; highly educated or barely literate.

Thus, compared to the Court of Justice, the ICTY seems to have a much more "attentive public," as did the Nuremberg Tribunal in its day (Karstedt, 1998). The nature of the disputes that the Court of Justice and the ICTY decide is likely related to this striking differential. Although the decisions by the Court of Justice could affect the lives of citizens across the EU, the nature of the citizens' rights violated by the state members (e.g., the right to a paid annual leave, sex equality as it pertains to female police officers not being allowed to carry firearms) typically does not reach the level of severity of the violations that the ICTY is addressing (e.g., war crimes, crimes against humanity). Furthermore, as the level of casualties indicates (e.g., UNGA, 1994), the four-year war in the former Yugoslavia affected directly the lives of almost each and every member of the ICTY constituency. People living in the countries of the former Yugoslavia (e.g., Bosnia and Herzegovina, Croatia, Serbia), be they victims, perpetrators, or observers of the war, have a keen interest in learning what happens at the ICTY and an opportunity to do so, if not by directly observing the trials, then by at least occasionally following the media accounts. The ICTY directly taps into their lives by seeking them as potential offenders, victims, and/or witnesses. Indirectly, the governments in their respective countries are asked to respond to the ICTY requests for cooperation by turning over the defendants, giving access to the documents, or securing cooperation from the victims. They can also debate whether, and how, to respond to the ICTY requests. Governments and leading political parties also provide political interpretation of the ICTY requests and shape public views about the ICTY (see Chapters 2 and 3). In addition, the level of cooperation with the ICTY could be a key factor in determining the country's future membership in the European Union and the extent of international financial support it receives (see Chapter 4).

Prior research on the legitimacy of the ICTY is quite limited (e.g., Artz, 2006; Human Rights Center, 2000; International Institute for Democracy and Electoral Assistance, 2002; Stover, 2005; Stover and Weinstein, 2004). It suggests that the ICTY's legitimacy varies across the former Yugoslavia (see, e.g., International Institute for Democracy and Electoral Assistance survey, 2002). Our results also capture a substantial degree of heterogeneity of the views about the ICTY (see Chapter 2) and, in addition, illustrate the need to go beyond a single survey conducted in a particular year and engage in repeated, long-term assessments of ICTY performance.

We measured the level of support for the ICTY through the respondents' choice of the decision-maker for the war crimes (i.e., selection of the ICTY v. other decision-makers) and the assessments of the ICTY's fairness (i.e., ICTY fairness, fairness of the ICTY decisions, fairness of the ICTY procedures). Our measure of diffuse support—selecting the ICTY among potential decision-makers for war crimes and crimes against humanity—taps into the basic question of whether the ICTY is the most appropriate decision-maker for war crimes and crimes against humanity. This measure is similar in nature to one of the measures of diffuse support used by Caldeira and Gibson's (1995), namely their question asking about dispensing with the Court of Justice if it made many unpopular decisions.

We find that the ICTY enjoyed a very high level of support among the respondents surveyed before 2001 (1997 Zagreb, 2000 Sarajevo) and among the respondents surveyed in Kosovo in 2004—the overwhelming majority in those samples evaluated the ICTY as fair and picked the ICTY as the preferred decision-maker. While the ICTY enjoyed some level of support among the respondents surveyed in Vukovar, Croatia, in 2004 and Sarajevo, Bosnia and Herzegovina (about one-half of the respondents in Vukovar thought that the ICTY is fair and about one-third would pick the ICTY as their preferred decision-maker; about four-tenths of the respondents in Sarajevo evaluated the ICTY as fair and would pick the ICTY as the preferred decision-maker), the level of support among our Belgrade, Serbia respondents (surveyed in 2004 and 2005) seems to have been rather low, with less than one-third of those respondents evaluating the ICTY as fair and picking the ICTY as the preferred decision-maker.

Our findings about the perceptions of ICTY fairness, coupled with those concerning the choice of the primary decision-maker for war crimes, indicate that the level of support for the ICTY is lower in recent years than it was at the time the ICTY began its first trials (the post-2001 samples were much less likely to select the ICTY). Although the nature of our samples is not longitudinal, it nonetheless seems clear that there are large differences between the levels of support in the pre- and post-2001 samples. We argue that these differences may be related to the extent of the ICTY's level of activity in those two time periods. The ICTY was established in 1993; its first trial, that of Duško Tadić, was launched two years later, in April of 1995. By the time of the first surveys (1997–2000), the ICTY had just begun trials, completed only a handful of them, and still had many indictees at large. Over the next five years (2000–2004), the ICTY intensified its activities, captured some of the "big fish" (e.g., Slobodan Milošević was transferred to the ICTY on June 29, 2001), and tried 43 additional defendants.

During the initial, "honeymoon period," the respondents had limited information at their disposal about the outcomes of the ICTY trials, as few trials took place, and about the ICTY procedures, as those have been evolving and were changing in various ways. Quite likely, respondents' assessments were more heavily grounded in their general views about the ICTY and the positive atmosphere surrounding its establishment, the UN, and the court and legal systems in general in the first period than they were in the second period, by which time the ICTY had decided a large number of cases and thus offered the constituencies a more realistic opportunity to assess the fairness of its outcomes and procedures. Indeed, our analysis of the support for the ICTY corresponds with the arguments made by Caldeira and Gibson (1995: 356) that, in the absence of specific information, people assess institutions "based on their general values and preferences." The results of the analysis of the level of support for the Nuremberg Tribunal, a tribunal somewhat similar in its jurisdiction and public attentiveness to the ICTY, suggest that the overall assessments formed at the beginning for both bore some similarity (see Karstedt, 1998: 23).

Although the Nuremberg Tribunal was entrusted with a task similar to that assigned to the ICTY—to try individuals responsible for war crimes and crimes against humanity—the Nuremberg Tribunal rested on the Allied victors' power and resulted in a higher level of legitimacy than the ICTY has been afforded; between 70 and 80 percent of the respondents on the Office of the Military Government of the U.S. (OMGUS) surveys conducted before, during, and at the end of the Nuremberg Trials (October 1945–October 1946) agreed that the Nuremberg Trials were conducted justly (Karstedt, 1998: 24). Compared to the situation in the former Yugoslavia, the situation in Germany before the Nuremberg Trials seemed simple: the Nazis were the perpetrators and others, be they Jews, Germans, or others, were the victims. In fact, almost all of the respondents in the OMGUS survey (more than 90 percent; Karstedt, 1998: 24) regarded themselves as victims of the Nazi regime. Consequently, the Nuremberg trials "contributed to dissolving allegiance toward former authorities, and to establishing a new collective identify as a 'betrayed people'" (Karstedt, 1998: 25) and thus provided a sense of community, which made it easier to blame the past regime for the atrocities.

On the other hand, the ICTY does not face such a simple situation: it is *creating* a war history for the former Yugoslavia (see, e.g., Donia, 2004; Wilson, 2005). A survey of completed cases between 1995 and 2005 reveals that Serbs constitute the majority of the defendants (about two-thirds), Croats constitute about one-quarter of the defendants, and Bosnianks constitute about one-tenth (see Chapter 1). In addition, the governments and leaders of political parties which dominated the countries during the war participated in Dayton peace negotiations, signed the peace accord, remained in power for a few years after the war had ended, and shaped the public view about the ICTY (see Chapters 2 and 3). Consequently, it is not surprising that the level of support for the ICTY is not as uniform as the level of support for the Nuremberg Tribunal was. The level of the ICTY's legitimacy—as determined by the results of our study and a few others (e.g., International Institute for Democracy and Electoral Assistance, 2002)—ranges from non-existent in certain parts of the former Yugoslavia (e.g., Serbia, Republika Srpska) to overwhelming in others (e.g., Kosovo).

PROCEDURAL AND DISTRIBUTIVE JUSTICE

The war in the former Yugoslavia created millions of victims (with varying levels of victimization) and, in principle, each and every one of these victims and their families are entitled to see the perpetrators brought to justice. Although the ICTY "has provided thousands of victims the opportunity to be heard and to speak about their suffering" (ICTY, 2010), the majority of the victims will never get a chance to see the inside of the ICTY courtroom and testify. For most of them, the assessment of the ICTY and its legitimacy is based on the information obtained through the media.

Unlike the procedural justice literature on parties' experiences in domestic courts, the literature on victims in the international tribunals is almost non-existent. Stover (2005: 17), who conducted one of the very few studies, argues that "[l]ittle, if anything, is known about the experiences of victims and witnesses who have testified before international war crimes tribunals." Their testimony is used as evidence in cases and the offices for the protection of victims and witnesses may help them with the emotional and organizational aspects of their experience, but they are rarely, if ever, asked to evaluate their experience before these international tribunals. For most victims, there will be no direct contact with the ICTY and their views of the ICTY will be shaped by their indirect knowledge of the ICTY. The majority of the victims in the former Yugoslavia, then, will assess the ICTY on an abstract level, as did the respondents in opinion polls regarding the Nuremberg Tribunal in the post-WWII Germany (see, e.g., Karstedt, 1998).

Karstedt (1998) reports that most of the respondents evaluated the post-WWII trials as fair and that the majority rated none of the final verdicts as "too harsh" (direct measures of procedural justice were not included). The research on denazification procedures undertaken from 1945 to 1947 suggests the importance of both procedural and distributive justice, with satisfaction regarding procedure declining over time (Karstedt, 1998: 28). Challenges of unequal and inconsistent treatment of higher- and lower-ranked members of the Nazi party became a critical issue for the assessment of distributive justice. On the other hand, Karstedt's research (1998) suggests that a frequent criticism was the concern regarding decision-makers' impartiality, an issue directly related to matters of procedural justice.

Our study of the legitimacy of the ICTY (measured as the selection of the ICTY as the preferred decision-maker for war crimes and crimes against humanity cases over other plausible courts) also indicates that the assessments of the fairness of the decisions and fairness of the procedures are directly related to the respondents' choice of preferred decision-maker, with distributive justice (fairness of decisions) carrying more weight than procedural justice (fairness of procedures). Our analyses include a separate measure of judges' impartiality or neutrality, one of the elements of procedural justice theory (see, e.g., Leventhal, 1976; 1980; Tyler, 1990; 2000). Judges' political neutrality—the assessment of the degree to which the judges remain politically independent—continues to be one of the key explanatory variables in our model of the respondents' choice of the decision-maker (see Table 2.6).

Tyler and Lind's model of procedural justice (Tyler and Lind, 1990: 87) "views group-related variables as especially powerful determinants of procedural justice concerns [and] it predicts that group membership and a sense of community will be crucial variables in justice-related attitudes and behavior." Their model is based on the assumption that the basic propositions or elements of procedural justice are evaluated through group interaction. However, in the context of the former Yugoslavia, there is no single group. In fact, there are three ethnic groups with conflicting interests, with a fourth group composed of the members of the international community (being directly represented through the ICTY). Theory and research that explore the issues of procedural justice between and across groups, as is the case for the former Yugoslavia, is underdeveloped (see, e.g., Karstedt, 1998: 19).

We explored the views of the ICTY and the justice it delivers, as expressed by the respondents who identified themselves as victims of war crimes and crimes against humanity (Chapter 5). Their overall evaluations of the ICTY fairness are primarily influenced by the assessments of outcome fairness, procedural fairness, and judges' political independence. Whereas both issues of procedural and distributive fairness mattered, the latter carried more weight. Our respondents, particularly in the post-2001 surveys—those that tend to be more critical of the ICTY—had no problems approving of many defendants' rights (e.g., right to have an attorney, to present defense, to propose witnesses, to an impartial judge, to a jury trial, to an appeal) and, with the exception of Belgrade respondents, mostly evaluated the procedures as fair. At the same time, with the exception of Priština respondents, respondents in post-2001 surveys mostly viewed ICTY decisions as unfair. In a nutshell, what mattered more for our respondents was whether someone was convicted and whether the punishment was appropriate than whether the procedure used to evaluate someone's guilt was fair. Our findings are in accordance with the existing research suggesting that, compared to intra-group assessments, inter-group assessments indicate greater concern about outcome or distributive justice than about procedural justice (e.g., Tyler, Lind, and Huo, 1995; Huo, Smith, Tyler, and Lind, 1994).

Of the whole range of procedural rights, from the presumption of innocence and the right to have an attorney, to the right to propose witnesses and present a defense, two issues were most critical to respondents: keeping defendants in custody while the trial was proceeding, and allowing them to plea bargain. It is not a surprising finding that respondents rejected defendants' pre-trial rights to be released from custody; according to the ICTY rules (Article 101, *Rules of Procedure and Evidence*, 2010), war crimes and crimes against humanity are punishable with severe punishments (lifetime imprisonment is the maximum penalty) and, as a rule, a judge orders the provisional detention of the defendant if, among other factors, "the Judge considers provisional detention to be a necessary measure to prevent the escape of the suspect, injury to or intimidation of a victim or witness or the destruction of evidence, or to be otherwise necessary for the conduct of the investigation" (Rule 40*bis* BIII, *Rules of Procedure and Evidence*, 2010). Given that a lengthy prison sentence is a severe punishment, and given that the defendants usually do not turn themselves in voluntarily, and instead typically are arrested by state agents and turned over to the ICTY, it is likely the defendants would flee if given a chance. The majority of the defendants are kept locked in the ICTY's prison unit until their trial and, in some cases, until their appellate proceedings are final. The implication is that our respondents agree with the ICTY's actual practice and approve of it as fair.

The second specific procedural right that our respondents were reluctant to grant to defendants tried by the ICTY is the right to plea bargain (see Chapter 5). The right to plea bargain was initially incorporated in the ICTY set of procedural rules as a mitigating possibility (for "substantial cooperation with the Prosecutor before or after conviction;" Article 101, *Rules of Procedure and Evidence,* 2010). Although plea bargaining initially was not a regular practice at the ICTY (see, e.g., Cook, 2005), in the crucial period between 2001 and 2003, during which we began to observe a decline in ICTY support, the ICTY started relying on plea bargaining to clear its docket; about 40 percent of the cases were plea bargained during this period (Scharf, 2004, p 1074).

Because it results in reduced sentences, plea bargaining is a procedural right that directly influences the outcome of the case and thus affects perceptions of distributive justice. For respondents who grew up in continental criminal justice systems, and thus are unaccustomed to common-law approaches, the right to plea bargain directly undermines a sense of both equity and equality of punishment. Victims of the defendant's crimes, once they observe the final outcome of the case, likely conclude that the punishment is substantially more lenient than the punishment that the defendant would be handed by the ICTY in the absence of plea bargaining. Victims may reason that the ICTY is not fair when they compare the sentences meted out to two defendants: a defendant of their own ethnicity, who not only is not viewed as guilty in their eyes but is even celebrated as a hero, who did not plea bargain and, consequently, ended up with a harsher punishment; and a defendant of another ethnicity, who is definitely guilty in their eyes, who plea bargained, and, consequently, received a less severe punishment.

The issue of plea bargaining is a difficult balancing act with no clear-cut or easy answers. There are many complex issues involved which empirical research has not yet explored. One of the implicit underlying assumptions is that the victims as a group uniformly share preferences about sentencing outcomes. Yet, as our research suggests, victims' interests obviously diverge across ethnic lines not only in terms of their outcome preferences, but also in terms of the preferred purposes of punishment and punishment severity.

Furthermore, although public opinion polls indicate that the level of support for courts, be they domestic or international, can change over time, empirical research has not explored the degree to which victims' preferences themselves change over time and the factors associated with these changes. Are some victims more likely to remain determined that plea bargaining should not be allowed while others are more likely to change their views once they realize that time is running out or that convictions are difficult to obtain without the help from co-defendants? As the ICTY is closing its doors, do victims prefer to maximize the chances of obtaining severe punishments at the end of a long trial held for a small number of defendants or to maximize the chances of convicting and labeling a larger number of defendants, even if it means relying on plea bargaining?

The issue of impartiality (Paternoster et al., 1997: 168) or neutrality (Tyler and Lind, 1992; Tyler, 2000), the key procedural issue which we incorporated as a separate variable in the final analysis, proved to be quite significant. Our analyses show that respondents have expressed doubts about the ability of the ICTY to resist political pressure, the independence of the ICTY judges, the influence of the nationality of the judge on the decision, and the influence of politics on the work and decisions by the ICTY. They also doubted that the ICTY would be fair. For the victims, who found that belonging to a particular ethnic group could result in what they perceived to be biased and wrong decisions with horrifying outcomes, neutrality of the judges is one of the key issues. Indeed, the ICTY judges, selected by the UN, are expected to represent different nationalities (Article 12, *Statute,* 2006) to eliminate potential bias or complaints of impartiality. At the same time, it is not difficult to envision a case in which judges' nationalities could be interpreted to have exactly the opposite effect and actually challenge the ICTY's impartiality in the eyes of its constituencies. For example, for the Serb respondents, the inclusion of the judges from any Muslim country, be it Turkey or Senegal, could raise doubts about ICTY neutrality, particularly if they learn about a case in which, hypothetically speaking, a Muslim/Bosniak defendant is put on a trial for a crime against humanity committed on the Serb population and in which a judge from another Muslim country is making the decision. Thus, while the issue of procedural justice in general may not be emphasized as strongly as the issue of distributive justice seems to be, this particular procedural issue—doubts about judges' neutrality—could have far-reaching effects and could affect views about consistency in decision-making (i.e., differential treatment) and honesty, as well as the views about distributive justice, particularly equality.

THE ICTY, LEGITIMACY, AND ETHNICITY

The war in the former Yugoslavia was primarily fought across ethnic lines and the views of the ICTY of post-war justice are colored by perceived treatment along those lines. Unlike the Nuremberg Tribunal, the ICTY does not rest on the shoulders of the winners, and it plays a symbolic role in determining who the "defeated" and "defended" groups in the conflict are. The war ended through negotiations, orchestrated by the international community. Representatives of all three ethnic groups (Muslims/Bosniaks, Croats, and Serbs) participated in those negotiations and signed the Dayton peace accord (see Chapter 2). Accordingly, members of all three ethnic groups, albeit to different degrees, are now viewed by the ICTY as both offenders and victims. Moreover, unlike the situation at the Nuremberg Tribunal with the clear defeat of the old Nazi regime, the regimes that were in power during the war in the former Yugoslavia—the Milošević regime, the Tudjman regime, and the Izetbegović regime—remained strong for several years after the end of the war and shaped the public opinion about the ICTY (see Chapter 2).

Although the ICTY adheres to the model of individual guilt and does not attribute collective guilt to any ethnic group (i.e., it does not label any ethnic group as the "offenders"), the perceptions of the ICTY by its constituencies are probably shaped by the degree to which these ethnic groups think that the ICTY views them as victims and/or offenders. Biro and colleagues (2004: 193) support this view; they conclude that "Croats and Serbs were deeply convinced that the ICTY was biased against them." The idea of collective victimhood, be it victimhood of the war in the 1990s, past wars, or international interference, was created in each country and it shaped public opinion. Consequently, accepting that the same ethnic group could be both offenders and victims is troublesome, as it does not fit the perspective of victimhood.

Whereas we found that ethnicity is related to the respondents' views of the ICTY, with the Albanian respondents most likely to support the ICTY and the Serb respondents least likely to do so, we argue and provide empirical evidence that a more complete understanding of the relation between the support for the ICTY and ethnicity requires the inclusion of an ecological perspective. We advance the term "cognitive landscapes," developed by Sampson and Bartusch (1998), to theorize and demonstrate the influence of the environment on the formation of attitudes toward the ICTY by members of various ethnic groups.

Sampson and Bartusch (1998) originally utilized the term to explain how views about deviance and its control are shaped by the socio-ecological structure of neighborhoods. To differentiate neighborhoods, they used the distinction of Kapsis (1978) between "defeated" and "defended" peoples and communities. We elaborate these theoretical ideas in an international setting, arguing that the cognitive landscapes of national experience determine attitudes toward the ICTY. However, identifying which communities or countries are defeated and which ones are defended is far from obvious. Unlike the post-WWII situation, with the Allied countries clearly emerging as the defended and the Nazis as the defeated, the war in the former Yugoslavia ended with no military victory and, arguably, with no defeated and defended. Instead, the Dayton peace agreement allowed all three ethnic groups to participate as equal partners in the peace negotiations and, thus, further blurred the issue. Also, while the Nuremberg Tribunal focused only on the crimes committed by the Nazis and excluded any discussion of the potential crimes committed by the Allies, the ICTY is entrusted to try *any* individual, regardless of their national or ethnic identity (ICTY, 2010):

> While the most significant number of cases heard at the Tribunal have dealt with alleged crimes committed by Serbs and Bosnian Serbs, the Tribunal has investigated and brought charges against persons from every ethnic background. Convictions have been secured against Croats, as well as both Bosnian Muslims and Kosovo Albanians for crimes committed against Serbs and others. While its judgements demonstrate that all parties in the conflicts committed crimes, the Tribunal regards its fairness and impartiality to be of paramount importance. It takes no side in the conflict and does not attempt to create any artificial balance between different groups.

Thus, the ICTY has constructed, through its actions and inactions, a historical record of the events in the former Yugoslavia, thereby suggesting who the defended and who the defeated groups are. The record of the completed cases in the period from 1995 to 2005 (see Chapter 2) suggests that the ICTY typically views Serbs as the defeated (i.e., the offenders), Muslims/Bosniaks and Albanians as the defended (i.e., the victims), and Croats as both (i.e., offenders and victims). Our results, indicating that the Serbs show the least level of support for the ICTY and that the Muslims/Bosniaks and, particularly, the Albanians show the highest level of support for the ICTY, match closely this identification of defended and defeated groups.

Our results clearly support the idea of defended and defeated groups and the influence these views have on the groups' perceptions of the ICTY. This differentiation of defended and defeated groups can also be applied in domestic settings for dealing with war crimes and crimes against humanity. For example, the study of the public support for the South African Truth and Reconciliation Commission (Theissen, 2009), which investigated violations of humanitarian law in apartheid South Africa, yields further evidence of the same process at work. Theissen (2009: 114) found that the majority of African respondents (from 54 percent in May 1995 to 72 percent in November 1998)—members of the defended communities—supported the Truth and Reconciliation Commission and that their level of support increased over time as the commission commenced its work, wrote the report, and released its contents to the public (from May 1995, before the establishment of the commission, to November 1998, after the publication of the commission report). At the same time, only a minority of White respondents—members of the defeated communities—supported the commission, and the level of support decreased over time, reaching a particularly low level of support after the report had been published (from 36 percent in May 1995 to 15 percent in November 1998).

While ethnicity clearly is a salient explanatory factor in the context of the former Yugoslavia (the war was fought largely along ethnic lines), and is important in our understanding of the respondents' evaluations of the ICTY, we also argue that the influence of ethnicity is more complex. It is not only the respondents' ethnic group, but also their country of residence that influences their views about the ICTY. We expected that when a particular ethnic group is in the majority in a country or part of a country, their attitudes could differ from the attitudes of the members of the same ethnic group when they are in the minority in the country/part of the country. Specifically, we hypothesized that the Serbs who are removed from the localized structural circumstances of defeat in Serbia and are living in either Bosnia and Herzegovina or Croatia would exhibit views of the ICTY that are different from those held by the Serbs living in Serbia.

The limits of our samples (e.g., no Albanians in any sample other than the Priština sample; very few Muslims/Bosniaks in the Belgrade samples) did not allow us to test this proposition across all ethnic groups. Therefore, we focus on the exploration of cognitive landscapes for our Croat and Serb respondents. We consistently find that Croat and Serb views are not homogenous; they vary across the different settings of the cognitive landscapes, regardless of whether the respondents expressed their views about the punishment purpose, preferred punishment, choice of the decision-maker, ICTY fairness, or the ICTY judges' political independence. The case of Serb respondents is particularly poignant, as our samples allow us to compare views across the defended and defeated sites. When asked to select the appropriate decision-maker, the Serb respondents from our two Belgrade samples, the most defeated site, showed the least support for the ICTY and were most vocal in selecting as the appropriate decision-makers local courts in the country of the defendant's origin or the country in whose army the defendant fought. On the other hand, Serb respondents from Sarajevo and Vukovar, two defended sites, showed substantially stronger support for the ICTY and actually picked the ICTY as the preferred decision-maker. The Serbs in Sarajevo, the most defended site in our study, did not feel the pressure that the Serb respondents from Belgrade did to protect their own and advocate for the local courts that, conceivably, might provide more protection than the ICTY judges would. Similarly, the Serbs in Vukovar, who constitute a non-dominant ethnic group in this town in Croatia, did not feel the need to advocate for the local courts.

We did not have the same types of sites for Croat respondents as we did for Serb respondents (i.e., defended v. defeated). Our Croat respondents were located within more or less defended sites (e.g., Sarajevo, Zagreb, Vukovar). The results nevertheless clearly show the effect of the place of residence on their views about the ICTY. Croats' views about the ICTY are quite heterogeneous and often closely correlated with the views held by members of the other ethnic groups from the same site. Specifically, the majority of both Croats and Muslims/Bosniaks from the 2000 Sarajevo sample evaluated the ICTY as fair. On the other hand, the majority of Croats, Muslims/Bosniaks, and Serbs from the 2003 Sarajevo sample evaluated the ICTY as unfair.

Our results suggest that the formation of attitudes about, and support for, the ICTY transcends the boundaries of individual viewpoints and is influenced by group views about the ICTY. Powerful political structures in each country dominate the governing landscape and shape public attitudes about the ICTY, which becomes particularly troublesome if these same political structures, under whose leadership the war was fought and who can potentially become suspects sought by the ICTY, remain in power and shape public views of the ICTY. Views about ICTY political independence and ICTY fairness, shaped at the group level, are critical components in explaining Croat and Serb support for the ICTY (measured as the ICTY being selected as the appropriate decision-maker).

The findings of our study are in accordance with Sampson and Bartusch's (1998) idea of cognitive landscapes; they support the notion that defeated communities generate more negative views about the international tribunal in charge of trying defendants accused of war crimes and crimes against humanity, namely the ICTY, than defended communities do.

COLLECTIVE RESPONSIBILITY AND STRUCTURAL PRE-CONDITIONALITY

The organization of the ICTY does not provide it with opportunities to execute its arrest warrants nor to have direct access to the physical evidence and scenes of crime spread throughout the former Yugoslavia. Rather, the ICTY, a UN institution, has to rely on the international units (e.g., United Nations Protection Force [UNPROFOR], Stabilization Force [SFOR]) or domestic agencies (e.g., Croatian Ministry of the Interior) to make arrests and organize the transfer of the detainees to The Hague. To secure access and collection of evidence (e.g., mass grave exhumations), the ICTY has to seek cooperation from the individual states. These challenges plagued the ICTY from its inception, particularly during the administration of Richard Goldstone, the first ICTY chief prosecutor (see Chapter 1). The situation improved to some extent with the introduction of sealed indictments (under the administration of Louise Arbour, the second ICTY chief prosecutor; see Chapter 1). However, state cooperation with the ICTY is an ongoing source of contention between the ICTY and individual states (e.g., artillery diaries, related to the Operation Storm, for Croatia; the arrest of Ratko Mladić for Serbia).

We have explored how structural pre-conditionality was used to entice Serbia to cooperate with the ICTY. We refer to structural pre-conditionality as the practice by which the USA, the European Union, and other international players are providing financial assistance with the explicit contingency that the individual countries cooperate with the ICTY before the financial aid is received by, for example, making arrests and turning over the most wanted suspects. This situation combines the elements of political economic realism (e.g., when aid or trade benefits are made contingent by international actors) with liberal legalism (e.g., when transfers of defendants follow filings of indictments and the issuance of warrants). The expectation is that the imposed economic conditions will influence the country's politics and lead the country to comply with the requests.

Dobbels (2009) argues that, before 2005, Serbia's financial motivation for the cooperation with the ICTY was primarily driven by U.S. requests. In fact, the USA established an annual mechanism of holding Serbia accountable for its cooperation and, every year before the deadline, Serbia's cooperation seemed to increase (Orentlicher, 2008). In 2003, the activity remained relatively high even after the deadline had passed, quite likely because the European Union intensified its pressure and requested the potential candidate countries to pledge their cooperation with the ICTY (EU-Western Balkans Summit Declaration, 2003). However, until early 2005, when the EU Enlargement Commissioner Olli Rehn explicitly warned Serbia that full cooperation with the ICTY would be the main condition for the European Union to start its negotiations with Serbia, Serbia's cooperation remained more rhetorical than real (e.g., *SETimes*, 2005; Dobbels, 2009). By the end of 2005, Serbia had extradited 14 indictees, notwithstanding earlier indications by the Serbian government that arrests would "enrage public opinion, destabilize the government and encourage Serbia's nationalist opposition" (Wood, 2005a). Carla del Ponte, then ICTY chief prosecutor, gave Serbia a positive evaluation, which encouraged the European Union to open its doors for a Stabilization and Association Agreement (Independent, 2005).

Public opinion about the ICTY in Serbia is far from homogeneous (see Chapter 2); the public opinion poll by the Belgrade Center for Human Rights (2006) indicates that the extent of support for the ICTY is closely related to political party affiliation. The results of our study conducted in Belgrade in 2005 confirm this. The supporters of the Democratic Party (DS) and G17+ tended to choose the ICTY as the preferred decision-maker for war crimes and crimes against humanity, while smaller percentages of supporters of the Serbian Radical Party (SRS), Socialist Party of Serbia (SPS), and Democratic Party of Serbia (DSS) made the same choice. When we asked more specific legitimacy questions, involving ICTY fairness and political bias, our analyses strongly confirmed a relation between views about the ICTY and political affiliation (see Chapter 4), with the pro-Western political party orientation leading toward more supportive views of the ICTY.

For a long time (1987–2000), Serbia was dominated by the Milošević regime which portrayed Serbia as a victimized nation and mobilized resources on a nationalistic platform (see, e.g., Prodger, 2005). The government insisted its actions were politically legitimate and morally right (see, e.g., Dimitrijević, 2008). There was both complete denial of any wrongdoing and refusal to label these actions as violations of international norms. Despite occasional attempts to address the past and cooperate with the ICTY, public opinion favored the pre-emptive claim of victimhood (see, e.g., Dimitrijević, 2008). The surveys by the Belgrade Center for Human Rights (2006) show that Serbs were more likely to report hearing about crimes involving Serbs as victims, more likely to believe that these events actually happened, and more likely to label them as crimes. In fact, the majority of the respondents in the Belgrade Center for Human Rights surveys (2006) failed to label some of the key events during the war—the massacre in Srebrenica, the siege of Sarajevo, and shelling of Dubrovnik, all of which the ICTY condemned in its decisions—as crimes.

Therefore, it is not surprising that, although the majority of the respondents in our survey conducted in Belgrade in August 2005 had heard about the videotape showing the executions of six men (presented as evidence during the Milošević trial two months before), only about one-third believed that Serbs indeed killed 8,000 men in Srebrenica. Once again, whether the respondents believed that the massacre in Srebrenica took place was very closely aligned with their political affiliation, as was their support for the ICTY. The differences in the assessments of the event were huge, with more than two-thirds of the supporters of the DS and G17+, and only one-tenth of the supporters of the SPS and SRS, saying that they believed that the killings in Srebrenica had actually taken place.

Although Nataša Kandić, a human rights activist from Belgrade who turned over the videotape to the prosecutor, expected that it would be a convincing piece of evidence of the Srebrenica killings (see, e.g., Prodger, 2005), our results show that the message has not been received by the supporters of the anti-Western parties. In fact, our analyses further reveal that the supporters of the anti-Western parties mostly disagreed with her decision to turn over the tape to the prosecutor and labeled the ICTY indictments of the Serb top military and political leaders as illegitimate attacks on the Serbs. Thus, while the supporters of the pro-Western parties in our study mostly recognized these indictments as indications of command responsibility, most of the supporters of the anti-Western parties rejected the indictments as reflective of collective Serb responsibility and were swayed by the Serb victimhood image propagated by the Milošević regime.

Political parties shaped not only the level of support for the ICTY among their members, but also influenced how their members viewed the necessity and importance of

Serbia joining the European Union; the supporters of the pro-Western parties expressed much stronger support for the idea that Serbia should join the European Union. Our findings further indicate that the support for European Union membership, support for the DS, and the exposure to the smoking-gun video evidence led toward greater public acceptance of collective command responsibility for Serbian political and military leaders. Although viewing the videotape and believing that it is authentic carried some weight in determining whether the respondents would accept the Serbian leadership's collective command responsibility, and thus be more supportive of the positive responsive to the ICTY requests for cooperation, support for the European Union played an even more salient role.

We find strong effects of the structural pre-conditionality strategy and its operation in conjunction with the political parties. Political party affiliation and support had polarizing effects on the acceptance of the Serbian leadership's accountability in the form of collective command responsibility. SRS support was associated with the rejection of the Serbian leadership's collective command responsibility. However, supporting the DS was associated with a strong positive acceptance of ICTY-imposed Serbian collective command responsibility, particularly in the DS neighborhoods, which enhanced the effect of the videotape on the public acceptance of the Serbian leadership's collective command responsibility. These results provide further evidence for the cognitive landscapes perspective.

THE JUSTICE CASCADE: THE INTERNATIONAL, COORDINATED, AND DOMESTIC EFFORTS

The ICTY will almost certainly be dismantled before completing its work. Miroslav Lajčák, the High Representative in Bosnia, estimated in 2007 that "we would need more than a hundred years to solve all war crime cases. Unless something is changed, the answers will be given by the passage of time and not by justice" (Husejnović, 2007: 3). Even if the ICTY and ICTR were made permanent tribunals, it is quite likely that the defendants, victims, and witnesses would all die of old age before all the trials were completed. Thus, the "justice cascade" (Lutz and Sikkink, 2001; Sikkink and Walling, 2007), the global imposition of accountability and responsibility for human rights violations, must unfold on several different levels. On July 26, 2002, Judge Jorda, then president of the ICTY, proposed a three-tier judicial structure in Bosnia and Herzegovina to the UN Security Council (Jorda, 2002):

> The first tier, the International Tribunal, essentially handles the major political, military, paramilitary, and civilian leaders. Naturally, this first tier is temporary as it must disappear once the International Tribunal's mission has been accomplished. The second tier, the State Court, chiefly handles intermediary-level accused who would be referred by the International Tribunal. From our point of view, the Court is conceived as a national institution accorded a limited and provisional international character

> in order to guarantee its impartiality. The third tier, the local courts, handles low-ranking accused tried in accordance with the Rome Agreement. Within this structure, the International Tribunal would be responsible for overseeing the proper conduct of the second-tier trials and the State Court the third-tier trials.

The results of our research suggest that, as time passed, with the exception of the respondents from Priština, our samples of respondents tended to be less inclined to pick the ICTY as the decision-maker of their choice (see Chapter 2).

At the time the ICTY was established, in 1993, the war was ravaging the former Yugoslavia and most of the local courts in Bosnia and Herzegovina and Croatia were either unable or unwilling to try war crimes and/or crimes against humanity cases, particularly ones committed by the members of their own dominant ethnic group. The UN Security Council Resolution 827 (1993), which established the ICTY, and the ICTY Statute (Rule 9, 2010) determined that, although the ICTY and local courts have concurrent jurisdiction over crimes, the ICTY had the primacy jurisdiction and the local courts had the secondary jurisdiction. Burke-White (2007–2008: 312) argues that this legal setup effectively discouraged the local courts from engaging in domestic investigations and trials:

> Even if national courts chose to initiate proceedings, the ICTY could assert primacy and preempt national action largely at will, as it did in the Tadić case. This potential for intervention, particularly given the lack of any clear standards for when the ICTY would intervene, effectively sanctioned national officials seeking to exercise their own criminal jurisdiction. Given the potential for ICTY intervention in any domestic war crimes prosecution, national prosecutors were often reluctant to invest time and resources in cases that might well be removed to an international forum.

Disincentives continued to grow as the Rules of the Road Agreement (ICTY, 1996), written with the purpose of encouraging the return of refugees and displaced persons and protecting them from arbitrary and biased prosecutions, required local prosecutors to submit domestically generated case files to the ICTY for review and approval. This rule tilted the balance in the relationship between the ICTY and the local courts from the primary jurisdiction of the international court in the direction of absolute international primacy (see, e.g., Burke-White, 2005) and provided an excuse for local prosecutors to shirk their domestic accountability for war crimes and crimes against humanity. Although local prosecutors kept sending cases to the ICTY, the review of the domestically generated cases by the ICTY was slow (e.g., Ellis, 1999) and a large proportion of the cases was never reviewed (see, e.g., OSCE, 2005: 16).

The situation changed with the ICTY's completion strategy, when the balance moved away from the absolute primacy of the ICTY in the direction of a complementary relationship between the ICTY and local courts. The ICTY was required to complete investigations and clear the indictments by the end of 2004 and complete all trials by mid-2012 (with the exception of the Radovan Karadžić trial, expected to be completed by the end of 2012). This shift in the ICTY work, coupled with heavier reliance on plea bargaining and potentially local courts through the transfer of cases, started to occur in 2003–2004, at approximately the same time at which there was a change in the level of support for the ICTY among our respondents.

The revised goal of the ICTY is to try political and military leaders and transfer other cases to national courts (see, e.g., Jorda, 2002). The rules allow the ICTY to transfer cases to local courts (Rule 11*bis*(A), *Rules of Procedure and Evidence,* 2010) if the judges are "satisfied that the accused will receive a fair trial..." (Rule 11*bis*(B), *Rules of Procedure and Evidence*, 2010). Between May 2005 and April 2007, the ICTY approved the transfer of thirteen defendants in eight cases: six cases were transferred to Bosnia and Herzegovina (Court of Bosnia and Herzegovina), one case to Croatia (Zagreb County Court), and one case to Serbia (Belgrade District Court; ICTY, 2010).

As part of the completion strategy, the Rules of the Road were allowed to expire in October 2004 and the ICTY prosecutor handed over responsibility to the Court of Bosnia and Herzegovina prosecutor (OSCE, 2005: 5), which opened the doors for local prosecutors to start developing cases. The Human Rights Watch report (2008: 2) documents a dramatic increase in the number of domestic cases; by 2008, the overall number of cases with verdicts in Bosnia and Herzegovina increased from about 50 to about 150. Although technically a local court, the Court of Bosnia and Herzegovina includes international and domestic judges and international staff within its Registry. It relies heavily on subsidies, in terms of finances, staff, and legal expertise from the international community (the court's original jurisdiction was expanded to include war crimes and crimes against humanity trials).

Trials at the Court of Bosnia and Herzegovina have been carefully monitored by many international players, including the OSCE Mission in Bosnia and Herzegovina (OSCE, 2010). The Court of Bosnia and Herzegovina passed the ICTY muster, as the ICTY did not recall any of the cases transferred to it. In this sense, as Burke-White (2005) argues, the ICTY has had a powerful effect on Bosnia and Herzegovina's domestic governance, particularly on the Court of Bosnia and Herzegovina. But, the Court of Bosnia and Herzegovina will not have the resources to try most of the perpetrators and other local courts are expected to try lower-ranked offenders. Local courts have their own sets of problems, as Ellis (2004: 22) illustrates:

> In general, the investigation and prosecution of war crimes are complicated and problematic. Atrocities are often not recorded. On-site investigations are frequently infeasible, and there are limited options for gathering evidence through requests for mutual assistance. Moreover, governments may have an interest in providing biased information on their own officials. Witnesses must be found and be willing to make

incriminating statements, even though many will be intimidated or threatened with reprisal. And even witnesses who want to testify may be unable to give accurate statements. Further, the lapse of time may have an effect on a person's recollection so that even witnesses who are willing to testify may be unable to give accurate statements.

Yet, the international efforts have been focused on the Court of Bosnia and Herzegovina, and other local courts in Bosnia and Herzegovina did not benefit from these efforts to the same degree. Whereas the Court of Bosnia and Herzegovina has received mostly positive assessments (e.g., Human Rights Watch, 2007), other local courts have experienced serious challenges (Human Rights Watch, 2008), ranging from lack of staff and specialization, to lack of cooperation and resources. The most recent 2010 OSCE report (Djikoli, 2010), covering the trials before Bosnian courts between 2004 and 2009, concludes that the local courts—other than the Court of Bosnia and Herzegovina—do not have adequate capacity to provide support to victims and witnesses.

The situation in Serbia has been problematic too. By 2003, only four war crimes and/or crimes against humanity trials were conducted by local courts (Ellis, 2004: 166). The 2003 OSCE Mission to Serbia study of the Serbian local courts reported that there was no political will to carry out the trials, that "the courts in Serbia did not have the capacity to carry out the larger number of potential war crime trials," and that "Serbia [could not] guarantee that these trials would be conducted consistent with international standards for fair trials" (Ellis, 2004: 168). OSCE and the international community pushed for the establishment of a special War Crimes Court and the enactment of new laws and, after negotiations, the District Court in Belgrade was given exclusive jurisdiction of war crimes and crimes against humanity cases (Article 9, Law on Organization and Jurisdiction of Government Authorities in Prosecuting Perpetrators of War Crimes, 2003). Although not without its problems (see, e.g., Ellis, 2004), the District Court of Belgrade—which relies on financial support from the international community, but does not have international judges or staff members—has been carrying out war crimes and crimes against humanity trials "despite limited funding, inadequate political support, and little public awareness of its work" (Human Rights Watch, 2010).

Similarly, the reports on Croatian courts are far from glowing. Unlike Bosnia and Herzegovina and Serbia, Croatia does not have a specialized court devoted to war crimes and crimes against humanity trials. Unlike Serbia which, before the War Crimes Chamber at the District Court of Belgrade, rarely engaged in war crimes and/or crimes against humanity trials, Croatia has been more active. Although four county courts have special jurisdiction to try war crimes and crimes against humanity, more than three-quarters of county courts have engaged in such trials (OSCE, 2009). In fact, the OSCE Office in Croatia reported that "more than 600 people have been convicted, another 600 have been indicted and several hundreds more are under investigation" (OSCE, 2009). The early trials were held mainly in absentia, primarily against Serb defendants (OSCE, 2009);

the recent trend has been to review the cases involving trials in absentia. The 2004 OSCE report (2004: 14) indicates that "[t]he national origin of defendants and, possibly even more importantly, that of victims continued to affect war-crime proceedings." More recent efforts have started to move forward on proceedings against Croats (OSCE, 2009).

The first tier institution from Judge Jorda's classification will soon close its doors and the burden will primarily remain on the local courts in Bosnia and Herzegovina, Croatia, and Serbia to complete the process. Although the Court of Bosnia and Herzegovina, the second-tier court, has received mostly positive evaluations thus far, questions remain whether the Court of Bosnia and Herzegovina—without international support—and the local courts in Bosnia and Herzegovina, Croatia, and Serbia will be able to provide justice to the victims.

As the example of the former Yugoslavia illustrates, unbiased local trials are probably impossible immediately after the end of hostilities. Emotions run high and justice is contested. At the end of their detailed account of a justice cascade in Latin America, Sikkink and Walling (2007: 443) summarize their findings and conclude that "while trials were considered impossible in many transitional countries immediately after transitions, with the passage of time conditions changed and trials became not just possible but likely." This is the case in the former Yugoslavia as well.

The lesson from the former Yugoslavia is that the combination of international and domestic efforts, with international trials preceding the domestic ones, and then gradually being phased out, may be the preferred approach. Despite the ICTY's far-from-perfect record of convincing the governments in Croatia and Serbia to cooperate, international tribunals may still have a better chance of putting the leaders, both political and military ones, on trial than domestic courts might. Our respondents would agree; those who chose the ICTY as the most appropriate decision-maker for the war crimes and crimes against humanity in the former Yugoslavia did so, among other reasons, because of the certainty of punishment that the ICTY provides (relative to its alternatives).

On the other hand, the reality is that, at some point, local courts have to take over the responsibility from the international tribunal and carry it forward. The question is whether they will have the will and the resources to provide justice. The international community can help support the local courts and can contribute to the success of "the justice cascade." This cascade, in the last analysis, and for all its imperfections, stands out as the most promising path to reclaiming justice.

Bibliography

Akhavan, P. (2001). Beyond impunity: Can international criminal justice prevent future atrocities? *The American Journal of International Law 95*(1), 7–31.

Arendt, H. (1963). Eichman in Jerusalem: A Report on the Banality of Evil. New York: Viking Press.

Arzt, D. (2006). Views on the ground: The local perception of international criminal tribunals in the former Yugoslavia and Sierra Leone. *Annals of the American Academy of Political and Social Science 601*(1), pp. 226–39.

Ashdown, P., & Holbrooke, R. (2008, October 22) A Bosnian powder keg. *The Guardian Newspaper*. Retrieved January 5, 2010, from http://www.guardian.co.uk/commentisfree/2008/oct/22/ashdown-holbrooke-bosnia-balkan-dayton.

Askin, K.D. (1997). War crimes against women: Prosecution in international war crimes tribunals. The Hague: Klewer Law International.

Babb, S. (2007). Embeddedness, inflation, and international regimes: The IMF in the early postwar period. *American Journal of Sociology 113*, pp. 128–64.

Babb, S., & Buira, A. (2005). Mission creep, mission push, and discretion: The case of IMF conditionality. In Buira, Ariel (Ed.), *The IMF and the World Bank at sixty* (pp. 59–84). London, UK: Anthem Press.

Babb, S., & Carruthers, B. (2008). Conditionality: Forms, function, and history. *Annual Review of Law and Social Science 4*, pp. 13–29.

Bandović, I. (2004). Remarks of Igor Bandović. In Ratner, S.R. & Bischoff J.L. (Eds.), *International war crimes trials: Making a difference?* Austin: University of Texas Press.

Bass, G. (2000). *Stay the Hand of Vengeance: The Politics of War Crimes Tribunals*. Princeton: Princeton University Press.

BBC (2001, April 7). *Serbia: Several thousand protest in Belgrade over Milošević's arrest*. FoNet News Agency, Belgrade, in Serbo-Croat. Retrieved January 7, 2010, from LexisNexis Academic database.

BBC News (2005, December 11). *Massive rally for Croatian suspect*.

BBC (2001, July 11). *Social Liberals surprised by Chairman's resignation*. HINA New Agency, Zagreb, in English. Retrieved January 8, 2010, from LexisNexis Academic database.

BBC (1999, October 23). *Croatian Minister disappointed with ICTY Report*. BBC Summary of World Broadcasts.

Belgrade Center for Human Rights (2006). Public opinion in Serbia: Views on domestic war crimes judicial authorities and The Hague tribunal. OSCE. Retrieved January 8, 2010, from http:www.osce.org/documents/srb/2007/03/23518_en.pdf.

Beograd. (2010). Population. Available at http://www.beograd.rs/cms/view.php?id=201201 visited July 29, 2010.

Bell-Fialkoff, A. (1993). A brief history of ethnic cleansing. *Foreign Affairs 72*, p. 110.

Benford, R.D. and Snow, D.A. (2000). Framing processes and social movements: An overview and assessment. *Annual Review of Sociology 26*, pp. 611–39.

Bilefsky, D. (2008, December 13). Fears of new ethnic conflict in Bosnia. *New York Times*, p. A6.

Biro, M., Ajduković, D., Čorkalo, D., Dijpa, D., Milin, P., & Weinstein, H.M. (2004). Attitudes towards justice and social reconstruction in Bosnia and Herzegovina and Croatia. In Stover, E. and Weinstein, H.M. (Eds.), *My neighbor, my enemy: justice and community after mass atrocity* (pp. 183–205). Cambridge: Cambridge University Press.

Black, I. (2001, June 30). *Milošević extradited: Donations: pounds 1 billion aid rewards Serbia: relieved West stumps up cash to rebuild economy*. The Guardian Newspaper. Retrieved January 8, 2010, from LexisNexis Academic database.

Boyle, E., & Meyer J.W. (2002). Modern law as a secularized and global model: Implications for the sociology of law. In Dezalay, Y., & Garth, B. (Eds.), *Global Prescriptions*. Ann Arbor: University of Michigan Press.

Burke-White, W. W. (2007–2008). The domestic influence of international criminal tribunals: The International Criminal Tribunal for the Former Yugoslavia and the creation of the State Court of Bosnia & Herzegovina. *Columbia Journal of International Law, 46*, pp. 278–350.

Buzawa, E.S., & Hotaling, G.T. (2006). Victim satisfaction with the criminal justice system. *NIJ Journal 253*, pp.16–18. Retrieved January 9, 2010, from http://www.cjrs.gov/pdffiles1/jr000253.pdf.

Caldeira, G. (1986). Neither the purse nor the sword: Dynamics of public confidence in the Supreme Court. *American Political Science Review 80*, pp. 1209–26.

Caldeira, G.A., & Gibson, J.L. (1995). The legitimacy of the Court of Justice in the European Union: Models of institutional support. *American Political Science Review 89*, pp. 356–76.

Canton Sarajevo. (2004). *Population*. Available at http://www.ks.gov.ba/eng. Visited on June 28, 2004.

Casey, G. (1974). The Supreme Court and myth: An empirical investigation. *Law and Society Review 8*, pp. 385–419.

Chamblis, W., & Seidman, R., (1982). Law, order and power. Reading, Massachusetts: Addison Wesley.

Clark, R.S. (2003). Justice without borders: The international criminal court (panel discussion). *Temple International & Comparative Law Journal 17*, pp. 85–96.

Clark, R.S., & Sann, M., (1996). *The Prosecution of International Crimes: A Critical Study of the International Tribunal for the Former Yugoslavia*. New Brunswick, NJ: Transaction Publishers.

Cook, J. (2005). Plea bargaining at The Hague. *Yale Journal of International Law 30*, 473.

Čorkalo, D., Ajduković, D., Weinstein, Harvey M., Stover, E., Djipa, D., & Biro, M. (2004). Neighbors again? Intercommunity relations after ethnic cleansing. In Stover, E. and Weinstein, H. M. (Eds.), *My neighbor, my enemy: justice and community after mass atrocity* (pp. 143–61). Cambridge: Cambridge University Press.

Cousens, E., & Doyle, M. (1995, December 26). Dayton Accord's dangerous dueling missions. *The Christian Science Monitor*.

Court of BiH. (2010). Najčešća pitanja o sudu. Retrieved May 10, 2010 from http://www.sudbih.gov.ba/?opcija=sadrzaj&kat=7&id=15&jezik=b.

Court of Justice. (2010). Curia-General presentation. Retrieved May 15, 2010 from http://curia.europa.eu/jcms/jcms/J02_6999/.

Daily Mail (2008, July 30). *Bosnia beast rioters battle with the police*. Retrieved January 7, 2010, from LexisNexis Academic database.

Daily Telegraph (2001). *Milošević would have killed me if I'd failed*. Retrieved January 8, 2010, from http://www.telegraph.co.uk/news/1358693/Milosevic-would-have-killed-me-if-Id-failed.html.

Dembour, M.B., & Haslam, E. Silencing hearings? Victim-witnesses at war crimes trials. *EJIL 1*, pp. 151–77.

Deutsch, M. (1975). Equity, equality, and need: What determines which value will be used as the basis of distributive justice? *Journal of Social Issues 31* (3), pp. 137–50.

Dezalay, Y., & Garth, B.G. (2006). From the cold war to Kosovo: The rise and renewal of international human rights law as a socio-legal field. *Annual Review of Law and Social Science 2*, p. 231.

Dimitrijević, N. (2008). Serbia after the criminal past: What went wrong and what should be done. *International Journal of Transitional Justice 2* (1), pp. 5–22.

Djikoli, J. (2010). OSCE: Success of War Crimes Processing Endangered. *BIRN*. Retrieved June 30, 2010, from www.bim.ba/en/1/80/284727/?tpl=30.

Dobbels, M. (2009). Serbia and the ICTY: How effective is EU conditionality? College of Europe's EU Diplomacy Papers 6, pp. 1–35. Retrieved January 5, 2010, from http://aei.pitt.edu/11556/01/EDP_6_2009_Dobbels.pdf.

Donia, R. (2004). Encountering the past: History at the Yugoslav War Crimes Tribunal. *Journal of the International Institute 11*, (*2–3*).

Ellis, M.S. (1999). Bringing justice to an embattled region—Creating and implementing the "Rules of the Road" for Bosnia-Herzegovina. *Berkeley Journal of International Law, 17*, pp. 1–25.

Erez, E., & Bienkowska, E. (1993). Victim participation in proceedings and satisfaction with justice in the Continental systems: the case of Poland. *Journal of Criminal Justice 21*, pp. 47–60.

EU-Western Balkans Summit Declaration (2003). Thessaloniki, Greece. Retrieved January 7, 2010, from http://www.stabilitypact.org/reg-conf/030621-thessaloniki/declaration.asp.

Fabris Peruničić, V. (2001). Jugoslavenska vlada prihvatila zakon o suradnji s Haagom. *Vjesnik Petak 15*, p. 8. Retrieved January 5, 2010, from http://www.vjesnik.hr/pdf/2001/06/15/08A8.pdf.

Fletcher, L.E., & Weinstein, H.M. (2002). Violence and Social Repair: Rethinking the Contribution to Justice to Reconciliation. *Human Rights Quarterly 24*(3), pp. 573–639.

Gibson, J., & Caldeira, G. (1995). The legitimacy of transnational legal institutions: compliance, support, and the European Court of Justice. *American Journal of Political Science 39*, pp. 459–89.

Gibson, J., & Caldeira, G. (1998). Changes in the legitimacy of the European Court of Justice: A post-Maastricht analysis. *British Journal of Political Science 28*, pp. 63–91.

Goldstone, R.J. (2000). *For humanity: reflections of a war crimes investigator*. New Haven: Yale University Press.

Grad Vukovar. (2010). Stanovništvo Grada Vukovara. Available at http://www.vukovar.hr/index.php/informacije-mainmenu-89/stanovnistvo.html Visited July 29, 2010.

Hagan, J. (2003). *Justice in the Balkans: Prosecuting war crimes at The Hague Tribunal*. Chicago: University of Chicago Press.

Hagan, J. (1989). Micro- and macro-structures of delinquency causation and a Power-Control Theory of Delinquency. In Liska, A., Krohn, M., & Messner, S. (Eds.), *Theoretical Integration in the Study of Deviance and Crime: Problems and Prospects*. Albany: State University of New York at Albany Press.

Hagan, J., & Alboneti, C. (1982). Race, class, and perception of the criminal injustice in America. American *Journal of Sociology 28*(2), pp. 329–55.

Hagan, J., & Levi, R. (2004). Social skill, the Milošević indictment, and the rebirth of international criminal justice. *European Journal of Criminology* 1(4), pp. 445–75.

Hazan, P. (2004). *Justice in a time of war: The true story behind the international criminal tribunal for the Former Yugoslavia* (Snyder, J., trans.). College Station: Texas A&M University Press.

Heinz, A.M., & Kertetter, W.G. (1979). Pre-trial settlement conference: Evaluation of reform plea bargaining. *Law and Society Review 13*, pp. 349–66.

Houldon, P. (1980). The impact of procedural modifications on evaluations of plea bargaining. *Law and Society Review 15*, pp. 267–92.

Human Rights Center and the International Human Rights Law Clinic (2000). Report: Justice accountability and social reconstruction: An interview study of Bosnian judges and prosecutors. *Berkeley Journal of International Law 18*, pp. 102–64.

Human Rights Watch (1999). Croatia's democracy deficit: A pre-electoral assessment. Human *Rights Watch Report 11* (16). Retrieved January 5, 2010, from http://www.hrw.org/legacy/reports/1999/croatia2.

Human Rights Watch (2004). *Justice at risk: War crime trials in Croatia, Bosnia and Herzegovina, and Serbia and Montenegro*. Retrieved January 5, 2010, from http://www.hrw.org/en/reports/2004/10/13/justice-risk.

Human Rights Watch (2007). *Bosnia: Local Trials Key as Hague Tribunal Winds Down*. Retrieved May 10, 2010 from www.hrw.org/en/news/2007/01/11/bosnia-local-trials-key-hague-tribunal-winds-down.

Human Rights Watch (2008). *Bosnia and Herzegovina: Local Courts Face Obstacles in War Crimes Trials*. Retrieved May 10, 2010 from http://www.hrw.org/en/news/2008/07/09/bosnia-and-herzegovina-local-courts-face-obstacles-war-crimes-trials.

Human Rights Watch (2010). *World Report 2010: Serbia*. Retrieved June 30, 2010, from www.hrw.org/en/world-report-2010/serbia-1?print.

Humanitarian Law Centre (2006). *Transitional Justice Report: Serbia, Montenegro and Kosovo, 1999–2005*.

Huo, Y.J., Lind E.A., Smith, H.J., & Tyler, T.R. (1994). Superordinate identification, subgroup identification, and justice concerns: Is separatism the problem; Is assimilation the answer? ABF, Working Paper No. 9410. Chicago: American Bar Foundation.

Husejnović, M. (2007). BIRN: Waiting for a Strategy. BIRN. Retrieved May 10, 2010 from http://www.bim.ba/en/95/10/7165/?tpl=30.

ICTY (1997). *ICTY Bulletin 17*, 22-IV-1997, pp. 1–2.

ICTY (2005). *ICTY at a glance*. Retrieved June 13, 2005, from http://www.un.org/icty/glance-e/index.htm.

ICTY (2006, May 31). Letter dated May 29, 2006 from the President of the International Tribunal for the Prosecution of Persons Responsible for Serious Violations of International Humanitarian Law Committed in the Territory of the Former Yugoslavia since 1991, addressed to the President of the Security Council. United Nations S/2006/353.

ICTY (2006). Rules of the Road Agreement. Retrieved May 10, 2010, from http://www.icty.org/sid/96.

ICTY (2009). Voice of the Victims. Retrieved January 8, 2010, from http://www.icty. org/sections/Outreach/VoiceoftheVictims.

ICTY (2009). *Cases*. Retrieved January 5, 2010, from http://www.icty.org/action/cases/4.

ICTY (2009). *Mandate and jurisdiction*. Retrieved January 5, 2010, from http://www. icty.org/sid/320.

ICTY (2010). About the ICTY. Retrieved May 10, 2010, from http://www.icty.org/sections/AbouttheICTY.

ICTY (2010). Achievements. Retrieved May 10, 2010, from http://www.icty.org/sid/324.

ICTY (2010). Rules of Procedure and Evidence. Retrieved May 10, 2010, from http://www.icty.org/sections/LegalLibrary/RulesofProcedureandEvidence.

ICTY (2010). Status of Transferred Cases. Retrieved May 10, 2010, from http://www.icty.org/sid/8934.

Ignatieff, M. (2000). *Virtual war: Kosovo and beyond*. New York: Metropolitan Books.

Independent (2005, September 30) *Hague Tribunal Praises Serbia*. Retrieved February 11, 2010, from LexisNexis Academic database.

Ikenberry, G.J. (2001) *After victory: Institutions, strategic restraint, and the rebuilding of order after major wars*. Princeton N.J.: Princeton University Press.

International Institute for Democracy and Electoral Assistance (2002). *South East Europe (SEE) Public Agenda Survey*. Stockholm, Sweden. Retrieved January 5, 2010, from http://www.idea.int/europe_cis/balkans/see_survey.cfm.

International Crisis Group. (1998). *Too little too late: Implementation of the Sarajevo Declaration*. Available at http://www.crisisgroup.org/~/media/Files/europe/balkans/bosnia-herzegovina/Bosnia%2020.ashx visited July 29, 2010.

International Crisis Group (1999). *Is Dayton failing? Bosnia four years after the peace Agreement*. Retrieved January 5, 2010, from http://www.crisisgroup.org/home/index.cfm?id=1524.

International Crisis Group (2002). *Policing the police in Bosnia: A further reform agenda*. Retrieved January 5, 2010, from http://www.crisisgroup.org/home/index.cfm?id=1242&l=1.

International Crisis Group (2000). *War criminals in Bosnia's Republika Srpska: Who are the people in your neighborhood?* Retrieved January 5, 2010, from http://www.crisisgroup.org/home/index.cfm?id=1518&l=1.

Jorda, C. (2002). Address by his excellency, Judge Claude Jorda, President of the International Criminal Tribunal for the former Yugoslavia, to the United Nations Security Council. Retrieved May 10, 2010, from www.icty.org/sid/8080.

Jorda, C. (2004) The major hurdles and accomplishments of the ICTY, what the ICC can learn from them. *Journal of International Criminal Justice 2* (2), pp. 572–84.

Jutarnji List (2000, August 19). Survey shows "Anti-Hague atmosphere" increasing in Croatia. FBIS Doc. EUP20000823000244 (trans. of Jutarnji List (Zagreb)).

Kampschror, B. (2005, June 15). Serbs divided over grim video. Christian Science Monitor.

Kapsis, R.E. (1978). Black Ghetto Diversity and Anomie: A Sociopolitical View. American *Journal of Sociology 83* (5), pp. 1132–53. Retrieved January 8, 2010, from LexisNexis Academic database.

Kapur, D., & Naim, M. (2005). The IMF and global governance. *Journal of Democracy 16(1)*, pp. 89–102.

Karstedt, S. (1998). Coming to terms with the past in Germany after 1945 and 1989: Public judgments of procedures and justice. *Law & Policy, 20*, pp. 15–56.

Kelly, D.P. (1984). Victims' perceptions of criminal justice. *Pepperdine Law Review 11*, pp. 15–22.

Kelly, D.P. (1984) Delivery legal services to victims: An evaluation and prescription. *Justice System Journal 9*, pp. 62–86.

Kerr, R. (2004). *The International Criminal Tribunal for the Former Yugoslavia: An Exercise in Law, Politics, and Diplomacy*. Oxford: Oxford University Press.

Kitzmann, K.M., & Emery, R.E. (1993)). Procedural justice and parents satisfaction in a field of study of child custody dispute resolution. *Law and Human Behavior 17* (5), pp. 553–67.

Klarin, M. (2004). The tribunal's four battles. *Journal of International Criminal Justice 2*(2), pp. 546–57.

Kutnjak Ivković, Sanja (2001). Justice by the International Criminal Tribunal for the Former Yugoslavia. *Stanford J. of International Law, 37*, pp. 255–346.

Kutnjak Ivković S., & Hagan, J. (2006). The politics of punishment and the siege of Sarajevo: Toward a conflict theory of perceived international (in) justice. *Law and Society Review, 40* (2), pp. 369–410.

Lakatos, A.C. (1995). Evaluating the rules of procedure and evidence for the International Tribunal in the Former Yugoslavia: Balancing witnesses' needs against defendants' rights. *Hastings Law Journal 46*, p. 909.

Law on Organization and Jurisdiction of Government Authorities in Prosecuting Perpetrators of War Crimes (2003). Retrieved May 10, 2010, from http://www.osce.org/documents/fry/2003/07/446_en.pdf.

Leigh, M. (1996). The Yugoslav Tribunal: Use of unnamed witnesses against accused. *The American Journal of International Law 90*, pp. 235–38.

Leventhal, G.S. (1976). The distribution of rewards and resources in groups and organizations. In Berkowitz, L., & Walker, E. (Eds.) *Advances in experimental social psychology (vol. 9)*. New York: Academic Press.

Leventhal, G.S. (1980). What should be done with equity theory? New approaches to the study of fairness in social relationships. In Gergen, K.J., Greenbers, M.S., & Willis R.H. (Eds.), *Social Exchange: Advances in Theory and Research* (pp. 27–53). New York: Plenum.

Lind, E., & Lissak, R. (1985). Apparent impropriety and procedural fairness judgments. *Journal of Experimental Social Psychology* 21, pp. 19–29.

Los Angeles Times (2003, December 30). *Milosevic Due Seat in Serb Parliament*. Retrieved May 10, 2010, from http://articles.latimes.com/2003/dec/30/world/fg-serb30.

Lutz, E., & Sikkink, K. (2001). The justice cascade; The evolution and impact of foreign human rights trials in Latin America. *Chicago Journal of International Law, 2*, pp. 1–33.

MacCoun, R.J., & Kerr, N.L. (1988). Asymmetric influence in mock jury deliveration: Jurors' bias for leniency. *Journal of Personality and Social Psychology 54*, pp. 21–33.

Mallaby, S. (2004). *The World's Banker*. New York: Penguin Press.

Matić, V. (2004). *Serbia at the crossroads again: Can the country firmly embark on the reform path with President Boris Tadić?*. Washington D.C.: United States Institute of Peace.

Mazower, M. (2000). *The Balkans, A Short History*. London: Wiedenfield and Nicolson.

McDonald, G. K. (2004). Assessing the impact of the International Criminal Tribunal for the Former Yugoslavia. In Ratner, J.R. & Bischoff, J.L. (Eds.), *International war crimes trials: Making a difference?* Austin: University of Texas Press.

McDonald, G.K. (2000). In May, R., Tolbert, D., & Hocking, J. (Eds.), *Essays on ICTY procedure and evidence in honour of Gabrielle Kirk McDonald (International Humanitarian Law Series, V. 3)*. The Hague: Kluwer Law International.

McLean, R. & Simons, M. (2005, December 8). Croatian War Crimes Suspect is Arrested in Spain. *New York Times*.

McMahon, P., & Miller, J. (2009, April 2). *On a wing and a prayer: The effect of the ICTY on the Balkans*. Paper presented at the annual meeting of the Midwest Political Association 67th Annual National Conference, The Palmer House Hilton, Chicago, IL.

Meyer, J.W., & Rowan B. (2002). Institutional organizations: Formal structure as myth and ceremony. *American Journal of Sociology 83* (*2*), pp. 340–63.

Meyer, J.W., Thomas, G., Ramierez, F., & Boli, J. (1987). *Institutional structure: Constituting state, society, and the Individual*. Beverly Hills: Sage.

Meyer, J.W., Frank, D., Hironaka, E., Schofer, E., & Tuma, N. (1997). The structure of a world environmental regime, 1870–1990. *International Organizations 51* (*4*), pp. 623–51.

Momeni, M. (1997). Balancing the procedural rights of the accused against a mandate to protect victims and witnesses: An examination of the anonymity rules of the International Criminal Tribunal for the Former Yugoslavia. *Howard Law Journal 41*, p. 155.

Morris, V., & Scharf, M. (1996). *An insider's guide to the International Criminal Tribunal for the Former Yugoslavia: A documentary history and analysis*. New York: Transnational.

Orentlicher, D. (2008). *Shrinking the space for denial: The impact of the ICTY in Serbia*. Washington, D.C.: Open Society Institute. Retrieved January 5, 2010, from http://www.impunitywatch.com/special_features/files/Yugoslavia.pdf.

OSCE (2004). Status Report No. 14. Retrieved May 10, 2010, from http://www.osce.org/documents/mc/2004/07/3291_en.pdf.

OSCE. (2005). War Crime Trials Before the Domestic Courts of Bosnia-Herzegovina—Progress and Obstacles. Retrieved May 10, 2010, from http://www.oscebih.org/documents/1407-eng.pdf.

OSCE. (2008). Pristina. Available at http://www.osce.org/documents/mik/2008/04/1199_en.pdf visited July 29, 2010..

OSCE (2009). Prosecution of War Crimes. Retrieved May 10, 2010, from http://www.osce.org/zagreb/29857.html.

OSCE Mission to BiH. (2010). Domestic war crime prosecutions. Retrieved May 10, 2010 from www.oscebih.org/human_rights/monitoring.asp?d=1.

Parenti, M. (2000). *To kill a nation: The attack on Yugoslavia*. London and New York: Verso.

Paternoster, R., Brame, R., Bachman, R., & Sherman, L.W. (1997). Do fair procedures matter: The effect of procedural justice on spousal assault. *Law and Society Review 31*, pp. 163–204.

Prodger, M. (2005). Serbia holds "death squad" trial. BBC. Retrieved January 8, 2010, from http://news.bbc.co.uk/2/hi/europe/4543072.stm.

Prosecutor of the Tribunal v. Babić (2003). Retrieved January 5, 2010, from http://www.icty.org/x/cases/babic/cis/en/cis_babic_en.pdf.

Prosecutor of the Tribunal v. Blaškić (1996). Retrieved January 5, 2010, from http://www.icty.org/x/cases/blaskic/cis/en/cis_blaskic.pdf.

Prosecutor of the Tribunal v. Dokmanović (1997). Retrieved January 5, 2010, from http://www.icty.org/x/cases/dokmanovic/cis/en/cis_dokmanovic.pdf.

Prosecutor of the Tribunal v. Galić (2003). Retrieved January 5, 2010, from http://www.icty.org/x/cases/galic/ind/en/gal-ii990326e.pdf.

Prosecutor of the Tribunal v. Karadžić and Mladić (1995). Retrieved January 5, 2010, from http://www.un.org/icty/indictment/english/kar-ii950724e.htm.

Prosecutor of the Tribunal v. Karadžić (2009). Retrieved January 5, 2010, from http://www.icty.org/case/karadzic/4.

Prosecutor of the Tribunal v. Krajišnik, (2000). Retrieved January 5, 2010, from http://www.icty.org/case/krajisnik/4.

Prosecutor of the Tribunal v. Limaj et al. (2003). Retrieved January 5, 2010, from http://www.icty.org/x/cases/limaj/cis/en/cis_limaj_al_en.pdf.

Prosecutor of the Tribunal v, Milošević (2001). Retrieved January 5, 2010, from http://www.icty.org/case/slobodan_milosevic/4.

Prosecutor of the Tribunal v. Milošević et al. (1999). Retrieved January 5, 2010, from http://www.icty.org/case/slobodan_milosevic/4.

Prosecutor of the Tribunal v. Milutinović et al. (2006). Retrieved January 5, 2010, from http://www.icty.org/cases/party/740/4.

Prosecutor of the Tribunal v. Mrkšić, et al. (1997). Retrieved January 5, 2010, from http://www.icty.org/x/cases/mrksic/cis/en/cis_mrksic_al_en.pdf.

Prosecutor of the Tribunal v. Mucić, et. al. (1996). Retrieved January 9, 2010, from http://www.icty.org/cases/party/677/4.

Prosecutor of the Tribunal v. Plavšić (2002). Retrieved January 5, 2010, from http://www.icty.org/x/cases/plavsic/cis/en/cis_plavsic_en.pdf.

Prosecutor of the Tribunal v. Simić, et. al (2000). *Order on the request for provisional release by Milan Simić*. Retrieved January 8, 2010, from http://www.icty.org/x/cases/simic/tord/en/00516PR512844.htm.

Prosecutor of the Tribunal v. Stanišić and Simatović (2003). Retrieved January 5, 2010, from http://www.icty.org/cases/party/783/4.

Prosecutor of the Tribunal v. Tadić (1995). Retrieved January 8, 2010, from http://www.icty.org/cases/party/787/4.

Raudenbush, S., & Bryk, A. (2002). Hierarchical Linear Models: Applications and data analysis methods (2nd Edition). Thousand Oaks, CA: Sage.

Reichel, P. (2008). *Comparative criminal justice systems: A topical approach*. Englewood Cliffs, NJ: Prentice Hall.

Republic of Croatia. (2006). *2001 Census*. Available at http://www.dzs.hr/default_e.htm, visited July 29, 2010.

Reuters (1988, November 13). *Concerns grow over instability in Bosnia*.

Robertson, G. (1999). *Crimes against humanity: The struggle for global justice*. London: Penguin.

Sampson, R.J., & Bartusch, D. J. (1998). Legal cynicism and subcultural tolerance of deviance: The neighborhood context of racial differences. *Law and Society Review 32*, pp. 777–804.

Šaponja-Hadžić, Milanka (2003). Serbia after Djindjić: The maelstrom of its own crimes. *World Press Review 50 (6)*, p. 32.

Schabas, W. (2006). *The UN International Criminal Tribunals: The Former Yugoslavia, Rwanda and Sierra Leone*. Cambridge: Cambridge University Press.

Scharf, M.P. (1997). *Balkan Justice: The story behind the first international war crimes trial since Nuremberg*. Durham, NC: Carolina Academic Press.

Scharf, M.P. (2004). Trading justice for efficiency: Plea-bargaining and international tribunals. *Journal of International Criminal Justice 2*(4), pp. 1079–81.

Silber, L., & Little, A. (1995). *The Death of Yugoslavia*. London, England: Penguin Books, Ltd.

Simpson, D. (2003, March 13). Serbs' Premier is assassinated: Led in reforms. *New York Times*. Retrieved January 8, 2010, from http://www.nytimes.com/2003/03/13/international/europe/13SERB.html?scp=1&sq=simpson%20djindjic%20warrant%202003&st=cse.

SETimes (2005, January 2). *Rehn: Feasibility Study of Serbia-Montenegro Depends on Co-operation with ICTY*. Retrieved January 7, 2010, from http://www.setimes.com/cocoon/setimes/xhtml/en_GB/features/setimes/newsbriefs/2005/02/01/nb-02.

Shapiro, D.L., & Brett, J. (1993). Comparing three processes underlying judgments of procedural justice: A field study of mediation and arbitration. *Journal of Personality and Social Psychology 65* (6), pp. 1167–77.

Simons, M. (2005, December 12). War crimes case revives passions in a divided Croatia. *New York Times*.

Sikkink, K., & Walling, C.B. (2007). The impact of human rights trials in Latin America. *Journal of Peace Research*, *44*, pp. 427–445.

Slaughter, A. (2004). *A new world order*. Princeton, NJ: Princeton University Press.

Smith, H.J., Tyler, T.R., Huo, Y.J., Ortiz, D.J., & Lind, E.A. (1998). The self-relevant implications of the group-value model: Group membership, self-worth, and procedural justice. *Journal of Experimental Social Psychology*, *34*, pp. 470–93.

Sommer, T., Tindemans, L., Cutler, L., Geremek, B., Roper, J., Veil, S., & Anderson, D. (1997) *Unfinished Peace: Report of the International Commission on the Balkans (Carnegie Endowment for International Peace)*. Washington D.C.: Brookings Institution Press.

Statistical Office of the Republic of Serbia (2002). Population by national or ethic groups, gender and age groups in the Republic of Serbia, by municipalities. *Communication 295*. Retrieved February 10, 2010, from http://webrzs.stat.gov.rs/axd/en/popis.htm.

Statistical Office of the Republic of Serbia (2003) Population Book 4: Educational attainment and literacy, by municipalities. Retrieved February 10, 2010, from http://webrzs.stat.gov.rs/axd/en/popis.htm.

Stiglitz, J. (1998, October 19). *Towards a new paradigm for development: Strategies, policies, and processes*. Prebisch Lecture presented at the United Nations Conference on Trade and Development, Geneva.

Stover, Eric (2005). *The witnesses war crimes and the promise of justice in The Hague*. Philadelphia: University of Pennsylvania Press.

Stover, Eric, & Weinstein, Harvey M. (2004). *My neighbor, my enemy: Justice and community in the aftermath of mass atrocity*. Cambridge: Cambridge University Press.

Theissen, G. (2009). Common Past, Divided Truth: The Truth and Reconciliation Commission in South African Public Opinion. S. Karstedt (Ed.), *Legal Institutions and Collective Memories*. Oxford: Hart Publishing.

Tyler, T.R. (1990). *Why people obey the law*. New Haven: Yale University Press.

Tyler, T.R. (2000). Social justice: Outcome and procedure. *International Journal of Psychology 35*, 117–25.

Tyler, T.R., & Huo, Y.J. (2002) *Trust in the Law: Encouraging public cooperation with the police and courts*. New York: Russell Sage Foundation.

Tyler, T.R., Smith, H.J., Huo, Y.J., Ortiz, D.J., & Lind, E.A. (1998). The self-relevant implications of the group-value model: Group membership, self-worth, and procedural justice. *Journal of Experimental Social Psychology 34*, pp. 470–93.

Tyler, T.R., & Blader, S.L. (2000). *Cooperation in groups: Procedural justice, social identity and behavioral engagement*. Philadelphia: Psychology Press.

Tyler, T.R., & Lind, E.A. (1992). A relational model of authority in groups. *Advances in Experimental Social Psychology 25*, pp. 115–91.

Tyler, T.R., Lind, E.A., & Huo Y.H. (1995). The relational model of authority: Social categorization and social orientation effects on the psychology of legitimacy. ABF, Working Paper No. 9504. Chicago: American Bar Foundation.

United Nations General Assembly (1994, May 27). *Final Report of the Commission of Experts Established Pursuant to Security Council Resolution 780 (1992), Chair, Commission of Experts, Cherif Bassiouni*. General Document S/1994/674.

United Nations General Assembly (1992, December 18). *The situation in Bosnia and Herzegovina: Resolution* adopted by the General Assembly, A/RES/47/121.

UN Security Council Resolution 827, S/RES/827, (1993). *Annual persons responsible for serious violations of international humanitarian law committed in the territory of former Yugoslavia since 1991*, no. 12, UN, A/59/215-S/2004/627.

USIP Peace Watch (2001, June 6). Perceptions in Serbia. *USIP Peace Watch 7*, 6.

Vjesnik (2009, January 14). *Ljajić: Mladićevo izručenje za Srbiju bi bilo veći dobitak od nagrade in Croatian Daily Vjesnik*.

Voice of America (2004, January 2). *Serbian parliamentarian elections highlight difficulties in country*. Retrieved January 10, 2010, from http://www1.voanews.com/english/news/a-13-a-2004-01-02-31-1-67479842.html?moddate=2004-01-02.

Williams, D. (2005, June 25). Srebrenica video vindicates long pursuit by Serb activist. Washington Post. Retrieved January 8, 2010, from http://www.lexisnexis.com.proxy2.cl.msu.edu/us/lnacademic/search/homesubmitForm.do.

Wilson, R. (2005). Judging history: The historical record of the international criminal tribunal for the former Yugoslavia. *Human Rights Quarterly 27* (3), 908–42.

Wood, N. (2005, April 3). Serbia moves a step closer to the European Union. *New York Times*. Retrieved January 8, 2010, from http://query.nytimes.com/gst/fullpage.html?res=9405E2D6123EF930A25757C0A9639C8B63&scp=1&sq=wood%20enrage%20public%20opinion%20serbia&st=cse.

Wood, N. (2005, June 12). *Videotape of Serbian police killing 6 Muslims from Srebrenica grips Balkans. New York Times*. Retrieved January 8, 2010, from http://www.nytimes.com/2005/06/12/international/europe/12serbia.html.

Table of Cases

Index

Note: Page numbers followed by "*f*" and "*t*" denote figures and tables, respectively.

www.ingramcontent.com/pod-product-compliance
Ingram Content Group UK Ltd.
Pitfield, Milton Keynes, MK11 3LW, UK
UKHW020923170926
475595UK00031B/38

9 780195 340327